TRAVELING THE
UNDERGROUND RAILROAD

This is one of the few photos of an underground leader at home. Thomas Gray harbored hundreds of runaways in this home in Deavertown, Ohio. (Courtesy of the Ohio Historical Society)

TRAVELING THE UNDERGROUND RAILROAD

*A Visitor's Guide to
More Than 300 Sites*

BRUCE CHADWICK

A CITADEL PRESS BOOK
Published by Carol Publishing Group

A Citadel Press Book
Published by Carol Publishing Group
Citadel Press is a registered trademark of Carol Communications, Inc.

Editorial, sales and distribution, rights and permissions inquiries should be addressed to Carol Publishing Group, 120 Enterprise Avenue, Secaucus, NJ 07094.

In Canada: Canadian Manda Group, One Atlantic Avenue, Suite 105, Toronto, Ontario M6K 3E7.

Carol Publishing books may be purchased in bulk at special discounts for sales promotion, fund-raising, or educational purposes. Special editions can be created to specifications. For details, contact Special Sales Department, Carol Publishing Group, 120 Enterprise Avenue, Secaucus, NJ 07094.

Manufactured in the United States of America
10 9 8 7 6 5 4 3 2 1

Library of Congress Cataloging-in-Publication Data

Chadwick, Bruce.
    Traveling the underground railroad : a visitor's guide to more
than 300 sites / Bruce Chadwick.
        p.   cm.
    Includes bibliographical references (p.   ) and index.
    ISBN 0–8065–2093–0 (pbk.)
    1. Underground railroad—Guidebooks.   2. Historic sites—East
(U.S.)—Guidebooks.   3. Historic sites—Canada, Eastern—Guidebooks.
4. Fugitive slaves—United States—History.   5. East (U.S.)—
Guidebooks.   6. Canada, Eastern—Guidebooks.   I. Title.
E450.C46   1999
973.7′115—dc21   98–53474
                                                        CIP

973.7
115
Chad

For Margie and Rory

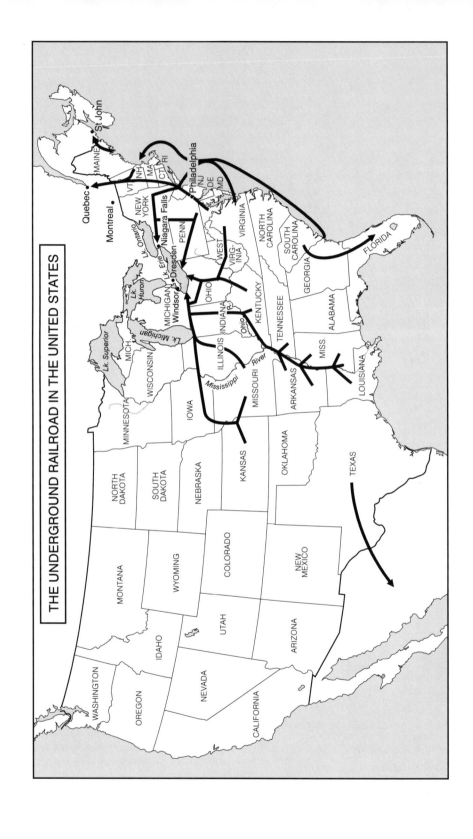

THE UNDERGROUND RAILROAD IN THE UNITED STATES

CONTENTS

This Connecticut hideaway beneath the parlor of artist Robin Hay's home in Farmington was typical. A trap door, hidden by furniture or rugs, led to a secret basement room where runaways hid if slavehunters were in town. (Photo by Author)

ACKNOWLEDGMENTS

I went on a journey, too, in chronicling the travels of the runaways slaves before the Civil War, although it was a safe one. My journey was to dozens of existing Underground Railroad sites in several states and through the bookshelves of many libraries. Like the runaways, I, too, found friends along the way who extended a helping hand.

I am yet another writer who relied on the painstaking research on the underground completed by Dr. Wilbur Siebert of Ohio State University in the 1890s. I pored through dozens of boxes of his papers, which included hundreds of letters from actual underground leaders and their friends and neighbors at the Ohio Historical Center, in Columbus. I received much help there from Ann Frazier, Duryea Kemp, Gary Arnold, and Louella Jones. In trips to Oberlin, Elyria, Lorain, and Cleveland, I was aided by Erin Smith of the Lorain County Tourism Office and a number of local historians and tour guides, such as Gerald Johnson, Charlotte Norris, Ruth Schwaegerle, and Sue Brewer.

In Connecticut, considerable assistance was provided by Ron Bernard and Peg Young of the Farmington Historical Society, and David White, chairman of the Connecticut Historical Commission. Other Connecticut help was provided by Cathy Bermon of the Harriet Beecher Stowe Center, Richard Koch of the Mark Twain Home, Bill Foakes of North Stonington, and the members of the New Haven Colonial Historical Society. Lorna Condon, of the Society for the Preservation of New England Antiquity, and Frank Middleton, of the National Park Service in Massachusetts, helped me in Boston. Brian Higgins, of Maine, provided a wonderful history of underground preservation problems.

In Canada I was assisted by Francine Chick and Sandra Bradt of the Windsor, Essex County, and Pelee Island Visitors and Convention Bureau and Gary Hardy of the Greater Niagara Tourism Office. Help in Delaware came from Ellen Rendell, of the Delaware State Museum. Help in New York arrived from Kevin Cottrell, of Niagara's Schoellkopf Museum. Aid in Washington, D.C. was from Cathy Ingram of the Frederick Douglass Center.

And on the national level, I received much encouragement and assistance from Vince DeForest at the National Park Service, Iantha Ganntwright of the National Parks and Conservation Association, and Diane Hennes and the officials of the newly formed National Underground Railroad Freedom Center in Cincinnati.

I would also like to thank Liv Henson of the Cincinnati Art Museum, Betty Louis of New York's William Seward House, Brent LaLonde of the Columbus, Ohio, Convention Center, Marci Gauder of the Green County (Ohio) Visitors and Convention Bureau, and Janice McGuire of the Levi Coffin House, in Fountain City, Indiana. Also, Georgeanne Royter of Kelton House, in Columbus, Joel Frey of the Memphis Convention and Visitors Bureau, and Elaine Turner of Heritage Tours in Memphis.

I would also like to thank my agent, Carolyn Krupp, of IMG Literary, for having faith in me on this and other books and my editor at Birch Lane Press, Hillel Black, who understands that the key to the future is the past. I could never have written this book without the new insights into American history and race relations I obtained by going back to school to earn my doctorate at Rutgers University. Many thanks to all the history professors there, particularly Dr. Jackson Lears.

My travel and research on this project was funded by a generous grant from my university, New Jersey City University, whose administrators continue to give me support and encouragement in my historical endeavors.

IMPORTANT DATES
IN THE HISTORY OF SLAVERY
AND THE
EVOLUTION OF THE UNDERGROUND RAILROAD

1619   The first Africans arrive in the United States at Jamestown, Virginia, as indentured servants and slaves; all are soon enslaved.

1642   Virginia passes a law penalizing anyone who shelters runaway slaves.

1672   Virginia approves a bounty for the capture of "maroons," or mulattos, hiding in Carolina swamps.

1676   Hundreds of white laborers in Virginia, unhappy with unfair extensions of their indentured worker contracts, low pay, and limited opportunities, riot in Bacon's Rebellion; Virginia's tobacco plantation owners decide they are better off with docile black slaves working for them instead of angry whites.

1688   Pennsylvania Quakers draft the first anti-slavery resolution.

1690   Several slaves flee New England owners, but are apprehended.

1705   A slave in Albany, New York, flees and makes it to Canada.

1712   Rebellious slaves in New York City burn down a building and kill whites trying to put out the fire; twenty-one slaves are executed.

1714   South Carolina authorizes the death penalty for runaway slaves.

1720   Slaves flee the Carolinas and emigrate to St. Augustine, Florida, where they are protected by Spaniards.

1721   Freed blacks barred from voting in North Carolina.

1723   The murder of a slave in Virginia ruled legal; Virginia law permits the cutting off of runaway slaves' ears as punishment.

1736   Slaves revolt on the Caribbean island of Antigua.

1740   On several plantations near the Stono River, in South Carolina, armed blacks kill ten whites and burn down several homes; in pitched battle, forty slaves and twenty whites are killed.

1741   Slaves unfairly accused of arson in New York City; eleven are executed and fifty deported to the West Indies as punishment.

1775   Pennsylvania Quakers form the first anti-slavery society.

1776   Following heated debate, language for the elimination of slavery is deleted from the Declaration of Independence.

1776–1781   The British Government frees over 25,000 slaves in southern counties occupied by British Army in the Revolutionary War.

1777   North Carolina forbids free status for any slaves.

1780   Pennsylvania passes a gradual emancipation law that permits slaves there to become freemen when they reach the age of 28.

1784   Connecticut and Rhode Island pass gradual emancipation laws; the Pennsylvania Abolitionist Society is formed.

1786   Runaways from George Washington's plantation find shelter in a freed black community in Philadelphia.

1787   Congress outlaws slavery in the Northwest Territory (now the Midwest); the U.S. Constitution is written and counts each slave as three-fifths of a man for apportioning representatives in Congress.

1788   Connecticut, New York, and Pennsylvania outlaw the slave trade.

1793   Congress passes the first Fugitive Slave Act, permitting owners to retrieve runaway slaves in free states and territories; Eli Whitney invents the cotton gin, which starts a boom in the cotton export business and begins an every-growing demand for slaves to work cotton fields; Canada ends slavery.

1802   Slave revolt in Haiti.

1807   Congress officially ends the African slave trade, effective January 1808, but does not prohibit the buying and selling of slaves within the United States; England also bans African slave trade effective March 1808.

1816   Hundreds of runaway slaves find refuge within the borders of the Seminole Nation, in Florida, following the Seminole War.

1820   The Missouri Compromise is passed, admitting Missouri as a slave state.

1822   The Denmark Vesey slave revolt, an uprising intended to turn thousands of slaves into an army, takes place in Charleston, S.C., and fails; thirty-six slaves are hanged.

1831   The Nat Turner slave revolt occurs in Virginia; sixty whites are murdered by a gang of slaves in a planned uprising led by Turner. Twenty slaves are executed.

1832 The New England (later American) Anti-Slavery Society is formed in Boston.

1837 Abolitionist Elijah Lovejoy is murdered by a pro-slavery mob in Alton, Illinois.

1838 Frederick Douglass escapes from slavery in Baltimore, Maryland and, disguised as a sailor, travels by train to New York.

1839 Kidnapped slaves seize the schooner Amistad, killing two of its crew, and are arrested; after two years of imprisonment and trials, the U.S. Supreme Court acquits them in 1841.

1842 In Prigg vs. Pennsylvania, the U.S. Supreme Court rules that states are not required to return runaways to their owners.

1848 Henry Brown escapes slavery by having himself nailed inside a large wooden box and formally mailed via cargo schooner from Richmond, Virginia, to Philadelphia.

1849 Harriet Tubman escapes from her plantation on the Choptank River, in Maryland.

1850 A second Fugitive Slave Act is passed by Congress as part of the Compromise of 1850; it permits slaveowners to go North to retrieve runaways and forbids state governments to prevent their capture. As a result, many black freedmen are kidnapped and returned to slavery.

1851 In a battle between slave catchers and white Underground Railroad operators over a runaway slave in Christiana, Pennsylvania, a white slaveholder is killed and his son wounded.

1852 Publication of Uncle Tom's Cabin, by Harriet Beecher Stowe, provokes a worldwide sensation.

1854 Congress passes the Kansas-Nebraska Act, giving residents of those territories the right to decide if they will permit slavery.

1856 Abraham Lincoln returns to politics and joins the new Republican Party; pro-slavery riders sack Lawrence, Kansas, as the battles over proposed freedom for slaves in that state intensify.

1857 The U.S. Supreme Court rules in the case of Dred Scott, a slave who lived for four years in a free state and was then returned to slavery, that slaves are property, not people, and must be returned to their owners even if they were transported to a free state.

1859 John Brown and his men seize a federal arsenal at Harpers Ferry, Virginia.

1860 Abraham Lincoln is elected president of the United States.

1861 The Civil War begins.

1863 The Emancipation Proclamation goes into effect, freeing slaves in those states in rebellion, but not border states such as Kentucky, Maryland, and Missouri.

1865   The Thirteenth Amendment to the U.S. Constitution abolishes slavery in the United States.

A TICKET ON THE UNDERGROUND RAILROAD

"Medina Sept 6 1858
Prof. Monroe and Peck
    Gents, here are five Slaves from the House of Bondage, which I
need not say to you that you will see to them—they can tell their
own story

                                        Yours etc
                                        H. G. Blake"

This is one of the few existing notes sent between underground leaders. This one, sent to James Monroe of Oberlin, ignored the usual code word for runaways, "packages," and simply called them "slaves." (Courtesy of the Ohio Historical Society)

Opposite   Several homes used by the Underground Railroad were connected to nearby woods or rivers by underground tunnels, such as this one in Ohio. (Courtesy of the Ohio Historical Society)

PART I: THE HISTORY

INTRODUCTION

The story of the Underground Railroad is one of the most powerful in American history. The Underground Railroad was the network of hundreds of safe houses, churches, and farms throughout the North and South that served as way stations on the road to freedom for tens of thousands of runaway slaves in the nineteenth century. It is the story of enormous courage exhibited by fugitive slaves, alone or with spouses and, in some cases, their entire families, who risked their lives in a long, hazardous journey, often on foot, that frequently stretched more than one thousand miles. It is the tale, too, of perseverance, bravery, and humanity in which thousands of whites risked social scorn, business setbacks, arrests, fines, prison, and even death to lend the fugitives a helping hand.

Slavery was a controversial institution in the United States until 1865, when the Thirteenth Amendment to the Constitution eliminated it. From 1619, just after the first settlement was established at Jamestown, Virginia, until the end of the Civil War, millions of African Americans—men, women, and children—were held in bondage in southern and midwestern states such as Missouri. There were over four million slaves, 13 percent of the population of the United States, at the outbreak of the Civil War. Slaves labored hard on small farms and large plantations for years to create successful tobacco, cotton, rice, and sugar industries for their owners. In return, they had no freedom, were sometimes whipped and beaten, and worked long, exhausting hours with no hope that their bondage would end.

Africans were enslaved in the United States for so long that slavery became an accepted part of the American landscape. Slavery, which started as a means for planters to make money on the rich tobacco crops of the southern colonies, became an institution in the southern states, a powerful

3

economic and political institution which prevailed for almost 250 years. It was protected by wealthy merchants, ministers, influential politicians, and newspaper editors.

African Americans never saw themselves as the mere "property" owners claimed they were. Most could not or would not attempt to escape, afraid of leaving families behind or of the harsh penalties, including death, inflicted upon them by their owners or the law upon capture. Yet thousands of others, men, women, and entire families, risked their lives to escape from slave plantations and along the way had to outrun and outwit slavecatchers in a long, dangerous flight to freedom. At first, slaves tried to escape on their own, without guides or hideaways, traveling by night and sleeping during the day in dank caves and rock-strewn ravines, ever fearful of apprehension. Some had maps and some did not, but all looked heavenward as they fled. They searched the night skies for God's protection, to be sure, but they also looked for the North Star. They knew that if they followed that star they would make it to freedom.

Throughout the 1700s, runaway slaves believed they might find a place to spend a night in northern cities and towns on their long trip to Canada, and carefully sought out friendly farmers or ministers who might help them. They looked for someone who might provide food and shelter for a day or two so that, sustained, they might make the final sprint to Canada. It was, at first, a chancy race for liberty.

All of that changed in the early 1800s. The Great Awakenings, the evangelical religious movements of the eighteenth and nineteenth centuries, gave birth to the abolitionist movement that was supported at first by Quakers and later by thousands of whites and black freedmen opposed to slavery. The movement grew large enough so that by the beginning of the nineteenth century it gave birth to a network of safe houses for runaway slaves. This freedom chain of residences, barns, stores, ship's holds, warehouses, and churches stretched from the Potomac River in Washington, D.C. to the cities and towns of Canada and included every major northern seaport. Everyone in the chain offering protection to slaves risked prosecution, jail, injury, and death from slavecatchers, so it became an underground movement—one in which slaves and their families were hustled to freedom from one home to another on a direct or winding trail. By 1800, this "underground railroad", as it gradually came to be called, was intact and operational.

Since the Underground Railroad was illegal and dangerous, few kept records of all the people working on it as "conductors," or protectors, or a list of the "depots," or safehouses. No one really knew how extensive it was. The Underground Railroad quickly became legendary when the war ended and newspapers and magazines competed with each other in extolling its virtues and success. Some postwar abolitionists claimed that over one million slaves escaped to freedom on the Underground Railroad network of safehouses while some historians later claimed the number was about 40,000. It seems probable, though, that somewhere between 40,000 and 100,000 African Americans traveled its lines and, in the end, found freedom.

The real story of the railroad is not historical or political, but personal. Runaways risked everything. Mothers urged their sons to flee, never to see them again. Parents sent their children off with friends, knowing it was the last time they would embrace. Entire families traveled North together. The lives of the runaways were always filled with fear and panic. They traveled mainly at night, stumbling through rock-filled creeks, trying to navigate their way through meadows, thickets, and forests, hiding every time they heard the sound of horses' hooves or carriage wheels on darkened roads. They slept little as they moved from home to home, barn to barn, church to church.

The northerners who assisted them devised inventive hideaways for the fugitives. One homeowner in Gettysburg, Pennsylvania, built secret rooms with sliding wooden doors connected to hall closets. A man in Connecticut built a false basement under his barn where slaves lived until it was safe to move to the next stop. A man in Pennsylvania added seven sets of back stairs, inside his home and behind it, so that if slavecatchers arrived fugitives could flee down a nearby staircase from whatever room they were in and make a quick getaway. One abolitionist whose home was built near a river dug an underground tunnel from the basement of the house to the riverbank so that slaves could flee unobserved if slavecatchers arrived. A man in Ohio built an oversized fireplace in his home and, inside it, constructed a hand-operated elevator to take runaways downstairs to a secret apartment. Another Ohio man built a dumbwaiter into what appeared to be a fireplace, and slaves used it to pull themselves up into a hidden room. A Connecticut woman built a secret room beneath her kitchen, connected by a trap door that was hidden under rugs and furniture. Sea captains constructed secret compartments in the cargo holds of their ships to hide runaways as their vessels sailed up the coast to New York or Boston.

The Underground Railroad eventually had over five hundred safe houses and several thousand people worked at any one time as conductors. Many were prominent citizens, such as businessman Levi Coffin, whose Indiana and Ohio homes served as railroad stops for over two thousand runaways over the years. Ministers, such as John Rankin of Ohio, often worked on the railroad, harboring fugitives or placing them in a parishioner's house. Some of the safe houses belonged to the homes of very prominent Americans, including Allen Pinkerton, who later became Abraham Lincoln's bodyguard and then established the fabled Pinkerton Detective Agency, Lincoln's Secretary of State William Seward, poet John Greenleaf Whittier, and several congressmen.

But average northerners worked on the railroad, too. Poor farmers in Pennsylvania hid fugitives in barns and haylofts and ordinary sailors on ships wedged them in between oversized wooden cargo crates. Teenagers and small children helped parents hide slaves. Sometimes entire towns served as a stop. Xenia, Oberlin, and Ripley, Ohio, and Farmington, Connecticut, each had more than a dozen homes where slaves were hidden. Cities, too, such as New York, Boston, Philadelphia, Detroit, Chicago, and Cleveland were frequently used as resting places. Their enemies feared the protectors, but their friends admired them. "They were the boldest and most self-sacrificing men for the cause of freedom," said Phillip Chatterton—one of the leaders of the underground—of his friends in Ohio.

The story of the railroad was filled with drama. The heroine of the novel *Uncle Tom's Cabin*, Eliza, was based on a real woman who, chased by slave-catchers, jumped onto a chunk of free floating ice in the Ohio river and leaped from one chunk to another until she finally reached safety. Several slaves had themselves nailed into wooden boxes and "mailed" themselves on trains and ships to the North; the boxes were addressed to abolitionists who freed them. Several months after the passage of the second Fugitive Slave Act, in 1850, more than thirty armed farmers and townspeople in Christiana, Pennsylvania, came to the aid of a runaway at a safe house there and, in a bloody encounter, killed one slaveowner and wounded another. Thaddeus Stevens, later head of the Radical Republicans during Reconstruction, defended them in a trial where all were acquitted.

Runaways adapted creative disguises to make it to the North. Many slaves dressed as women in order to escape a manhunt; several women dressed as men. One inventive light-skinned runaway couple dressed as a wealthy white couple and traveled first class on boats and trains out of the South and to freedom. One woman talked an unwitting young white boy into driving her wagon, pretending she was his slave, into another state. Several hid inside boxes, chests, and barrels. One spent several days in a ship's boiler room and another sailed from Charleston to Philadelphia wedged between two smokestacks.

They took great risks. Some were shot and killed and others wounded when slavecatchers caught up with them. Some drowned at sea during escapes and others died of frostbite while escaping during winter storms.

That combination of danger, humanity, and the long secretive trip filled with peril—with white Americans helping black Americans at great risk— made the Underground Railroad a great American saga. The story faded over the decades, but during the last few years historical, ethnic, and civic organizations, often aided by state, county, and local agencies, under the helpful umbrella of the National Park Service, have given it new life. Many homes from the Underground Railroad have been restored and turned into national landmarks and communities have refurbished other homes and sites as educational showcases. Today Americans can travel as individuals or with special groups to hundreds of the original sites, or sites with historical ties to the railroad. Many are open to the public and some can be reached with tour groups, as a new generation of people are heartened by the triumphant story of blacks and whites who worked together for freedom so long ago.

This book is an effort to tell that story. Part I explains the history of the Underground Railroad and its participants, white and black. Part II describes the sites readers can visit, with historical anecdotes concerning many of them. These sections also contain some vivid accounts of the dangers faced by runaways and those who aided them. Readers will be able to trace the history of the Underground Railroad, its travelers and conductors, in Part I and rediscover it in modern America by using Part II as a guide to visiting the Underground Railroad sites. The story of the frightened runaways on the Underground Railroad fleeing to freedom is inspiring. It is the story of Americans helping Americans during their darkest days.

1

ON THE UNDERGROUND RAILROAD

The complicated, hazardous escape had been planned for months. Seventeen slaves from different plantations twenty miles south of the Ohio River, in Kentucky, carefully selected other slaves—men and women who were reliable—to participate in a mass escape they hoped would lead them through forests and fields of neighboring plantations, across the Ohio River and into Indiana and then to Canada and safety. The slaves saved all the money they could, profits from selling their own produce, and pooled it, knowing from stories they had heard that they would need it for food and clothing, for bribes to pay boatmen for passage and farmers for protection. They met in a wide clearing near midnight, waiting an extra hour until the final traveler, an anxious young man's fiancée, arrived from her plantation. They all dressed lightly and carried their clothes and worldly possessions in neatly tied bundles attached to sticks that they slung over their shoulders. Moving in a large group was unusual and dangerous, too noticeable, but they risked it anyway.

The seventeen runaways moved across the countryside, walking as quickly as they could in the darkened fields, and close to 4 A.M. arrived at a small house on the bank of the Ohio River. Here one of the organizers of the escape paid the farmer who met them to take them across the Ohio in two trips in his boat. They landed on the heavily wooded north bank, unseen, just before dawn, a few miles from Madison, Indiana. Under a rapidly lightening morning sky, they ran as fast as they could away from the wide open river bank into nearby fields, where they slept all day. The next night, under the cover of darkness, they traveled through several corn-fields, all sloping up from the riverbank, avoiding the main roads, but halted abruptly when they heard the distant sound of horses' hooves pounding on the hard dirt road nearby.

Several riders, part of a slavecatching posse, saw the outlines of the fugitives amid the rows of thick green cornstalks and yelled out for them to stop. "Halt or we'll shoot you down!" yelled one man, whose voice a fugitive recognized as his master's. The men, trapped, shouted to the others to scatter and run. As soon as they began to move, there was a burst of gunfire and shots from the slavecatchers ripped through the air, cutting in half several cornstalks near the runaways.

Fortunately, the cornfield was protected by a high wooden fence and by the time their pursuers dismounted and climbed over the fence the runaways had enough time to reach the end of the field and hide in a ravine. Half the men and women were in the ravine, but the other half were missing, split up the previous night. The runaways in the ravine slept all day and traveled again the next night. They had escaped detection, but their friends did not. The other half of the group ran into a second, separate group of slavecatchers and were ambushed. One slave was shot in the right rib cage by a single musket ball and a second was shot in the back with buckshot. Clasping hands over their wounds and assisted by their comrades, they fled before the men could fire again.

One group of runaways was spotted by a black freedman cutting wood and the second group, carrying their wounded, by a white abolitionist who lived nearby. They were all led to the farm of the Hicklin family, operators of the local underground railroad, where they hid for a day. That night, Hicklin hid the seventeen runaways under canvases carefully tied over two wooden farm wagons and drove them to a second railroad depot. The following night they were driven under the stars to a third house, and then a fourth and fifth. They finally reached the home of Levi Coffin, in Newport, Indiana, one of the most active stops on the underground network of safe houses, where they were warmly greeted. They told their tale in great detail to Coffin, who later included it in his autobiography.

The town of Newport was a stop in itself, full of fiery abolitionists who did everything they could for runaways. Several abolitionists brought clothing, two local doctors tended to the wounds of the men who were shot, and the Coffins provided sleeping facilities and food. Two days later, the seventeen runaways were again hidden in a pair of wagons and driven late at night over bumpy roads to the home of John Bond in a nearby Quaker village twenty-five miles away. In a rural area with little traffic, they were then moved by daylight and taken toward another Quaker settlement in Grant County, in northeast Indiana.

Back at Newport, danger struck. A rider, his horse breathing heavily, appeared at Coffin's home to tell him fifteen Kentucky slavecatchers, including the owners of the runaways, were headed his way. Coffin sent word to Bond, who jumped onto his horse and rode across a field to the dirt lane and then raced as hard as he could after the slaves' wagons. He found the wagons rambling slowly down the road, the drivers' eyes scanning the countryside for trouble. As was often the case, the underground railroad men had a backup plan for emergencies. This time they separated the slaves into several groups and took each to a different home in the countryside, far from each other, and hid them the best they could.

The Kentuckians rode all over the area for nearly two weeks, questioning everyone they found about the large group of fugitive slaves. No one seemed to remember seeing them. Finally, away too long from their plantations, they gave up and returned home. As soon as spies saw them leave the area, Coffin sent word to Bond, who rode to the safe houses and herded the runaways together again as a single group, procured two more wagons and fresh teams of horses, and sent them toward Adrian, Michigan, in an effort to get them away quickly before any more slavecatchers could pursue them.

Once again, the fugitives were off on their journey, lying on their backs in the wagons as they rolled across country roads filled with holes and rocks, the hard wooden wagon beds pounding against their bodies, the darkness under the canvas frightening them a bit. The Underground Railroad took them to a tiny Quaker settlement in Adrian, closer to Canada, where the fugitives stayed overnight. The group took an afternoon off from their journey in Adrian, however, so that the young man and his fiancée— still fearful of capture—could be married. Then they moved on to Detroit, where they were hidden in the homes of several underground railroad conductors. Their hosts kept them fed, provided them with more clothes, and told them to wait. Finally, one quiet night, when few people were on the street or near the waterfront, the seventeen runaways from the plantations of Kentucky crossed the Detroit River and made it out of the United States and into Canada, the final depot on the Underground Railroad, a journey of more than three hundred miles, where they found safety.

The first big slave ships, carrying human cargo captured in Africa and the Caribbean, began arriving in the newly established seaport towns of the southern American colonies in 1619. A Dutch sea captain was the first, unloading a cargo of twenty slaves at the Jamestown settlement, in Virginia. Almost all were slaves, although a few were indentured black servants who were soon enslaved. In the years that followed hundreds of large slave ships, their holds jammed with shackled slaves, sailed from African countries and some Caribbean islands to the American colonies.

By 1660 most slaves arriving in the colonies were from Africa. Those who arrived in the Chesapeake bay area, later to be carved into the states of Maryland and Virginia, and those who arrived in the Carolinas, came in chains. They lived in small huts and worked long hours in stifling heat and driving rain on the new tobacco and rice plantations, which promised to become profitable.

The mix of black and white laborers who worked the broad, swampy coastal lands growing tobacco or rice did not last long. The white indentured workers, whom the owners counted on for the success of the growing plantations, were often unreliable. They were young, single, headstrong men and women with no skills who had either failed at work in English cities, or could not find work and headed to the American colonies to seek a new life. Some were criminals. Some were arriving in Virginia and the Carolinas to escape unremitting poverty in London. Those who survived the long, rough passage across the Atlantic (over 25 percent of whites and blacks died on the early voyages) contracted diseases and never recovered. Many from England had difficulty adjusting to work in the warm, humid climate of the American South.

These white indentured servants were an angry group. They had agreed to work for several years in return for land and jobs but resented their servitude. They complained of unfair rules, such as one that forced women who became pregnant to work in servitude two extra years. These indentured whites experienced poor living conditions, suffered from malaria, and saw a limited future. They exchanged one form of poverty for another: When their contracts were up, they were given small farms that produced little tobacco or rice. They also resented the wealth and political power of the large plantation owners, were jealous of their fine clothes, well groomed horses, and social influence. Their animosities reached the boiling point in 1676, when Nathaniel Bacon led hundreds of angry white laborers and black slaves in a rebellion against the landowners in the Williamsburg area. The rebellion failed, but the landowners and local politicians immediately understood that they could not permit blacks and whites to work together and that the anger of white laborers would only grow unless changes were made.

In 1680, just three years after Bacon's Rebellion was put down, Virginia's government ordered the execution of any runaway black slave and made it a crime for any slave or black indentured servant to strike a white Christian. By 1690 all free blacks were ordered out of the colony, all indentured blacks were turned into slaves, and almost all white indentured workers were removed from the fields where slaves worked. The Virginia gentry class, which ruled the colony, rapidly convinced the white laborers that they had a future—including the right to own property, to vote, and a role in legislative politics—if they allied themselves with the landowners to keep the blacks enslaved. At the same time, they believed that docile black slaves, with no political influence, would never threaten them as Bacon and his rebels had. There was also a virulent racism by the whites in the southern colonies toward blacks. They could always enslave blacks, regardless of their numbers, because the white population saw African blacks as inferior and, being black, different. Their color made it easy for whites to make them outcasts and acceptable victims. This racism was bolstered by their interpretation of passages from the Bible in which the sons of Ham, who were black, were enslaved. It was also done out of racial fears that black men would assault white women and fears that blacks would take jobs away from the angry white workers the planters needed for their success. Black slavery had been firmly established in the southern colonies by 1700 (Georgia originally outlawed slavery but later permitted it).

The river regions of the Chesapeake area were eagerly sought out by planters, and black slaves hastily recruited, because of the European sweet tooth. Europeans had booming economies in the early 1700s and, for the first time, the large middle class finally had extra income to spend on leisure items—the two most popular being tobacco, for smoking, and sugar. The best place in the British Empire to grow tobacco was along the American southern coast and the best place for sugar cane was the West Indies. Unable to lure or control poor white workers, the tobacco and sugar barons imported gangs of African slaves to work their land and help them earn large profits.

A unique capitalism drove the slave economy of the southern colonies. A normal capitalistic market thrives on supply and demand in which the supply is determined by production and labor costs, but the American tobacco and sugar markets—and later the cotton market—did not. European middle class buyers of tobacco, sugar, and cotton represented a widespread demand and American planters could provide a seemingly endless supply because, using thousands of slaves, they did not have to worry about paid labor.

Slavery was not unique to the South. There were slaves in the Middle Atlantic and New England colonies, too, but far fewer, never exceeding 2 percent of the population in the northern colonies. Since the colder climates there were not conducive to growing tobacco, rice, or cotton, there was no market and no urgent need for slaves. The slaves in the northern colonies worked as domestics or in seaports for merchants. The northern colonies were also populated by large families who had no need for slaves to work their farms because they used their children. Strong religious sects in the North that detested slavery, such as the Puritans in New England and the Quakers in the Middle Atlantic States, helped curb the number of slaves. Some businessmen in the North made money from the slave trade, however, by selling goods to slaveowners and some northern shipowners profited by trafficking in the slave trade.

Profits were so steady in southern crops that by the eve of the American Revolution there were 350,000 African slaves in the colonies, over 22 percent of the population, and slaves represented over 40 percent of the total population of the southern colonies (in some South Carolina counties they represented 85 percent). Thousands of slaves were imported each year from Africa, South America, and the Caribbean. Women slaves were urged to have as many children as they could and the slave population grew steadily. The slave economy changed from 1619 to 1770. By the middle of the century most white indentured workers had earned freedom and started to grow tobacco or rice nearby on their own land or moved away from the large coastal plantations to start farms in the interior. Many of them saved earnings to buy their own slaves, but could only afford a few. Others decided not to buy slaves and found it easy to live as farmers by only growing enough crops to support their family. The large plantations on the coast remained, but by the 1770s the interiors of the southern colonies had been populated with thousands of tiny farms worked by a farmer with few or no slaves. The huge plantations with over 100 slaves had become a minority and the small farm with less than ten slaves a majority in the growing slave empire of the South. Over three-quarters of the farmers in the South, however, did work without slaves.

The tobacco business was profitable, but it was only profitable because of slave labor and the succession of laws that were passed in the southern colonies to maintain the slave system. South Carolina authorized the death penalty for runaways in 1714. Virginia officials, in 1723, ruled that owners could murder slaves without prosecution and added that runaways would have parts of their ears cut off. Some counties permitted male runaways to be castrated. The few freed blacks were barred from voting. Indentured white women who were impregnated by black slaves had seven years of labor added to their contracts. Most towns and counties imposed 8 P.M. curfews for slaves. Any slaves traveling outside the plantation, to visit relatives or lovers on nearby plantations or on errands for their owners, had to carry signed passes and militias patrolled southern colonies to check passes to prevent runaways. Families were told that husbands, wives, and children would be sold and the families separated forever if anyone talked of escape or became lazy.

By the time the first shots of the American Revolution were fired, the southern slaveholders had shrewdly made allies of the small subsistence white farmers who had no slaves, which represented most of the white population. They convinced them that as long as there were slaves they would all prosper. They also convinced them that as long as whites stood together to hold the black slaves down they would live in an untainted social order and their white women, whether the wealthy socialites of Williamsburg or the hard scrabble farm women of the hills, would not be raped by the black heathens. They persuaded them, too, that the white race was superior and that poor whites could always mingle with rich whites at political and social barbeques, church services, and sporting events and, in socializing, raise themselves to the levels of the wealthy. That could never be done, they constantly reminded them, if there were no slaves, and those poor whites would be doing the work of the slaves and taking the slaves' place at the bottom of the social ladder. This carefully organized coalition of poor, middle class, and wealthy slaveowners, along with the great mass of non-slaveholding white farmers, proved to be a powerful force. There were a few men and women throughout the South who had deep moral doubt about slavery and some of them were quite prominent. James Wood, one of the colonial governors of Virginia, also served as the vice president of the state's abolitionist society. Thomas Jefferson, another prominent Virginian, had deep moral doubts about slavery. In 1774 Jefferson wrote that "the abolition of domestic slavery is the great object of desire" in the American colonies and then, in his draft of the Declaration of Independence, he attacked England for its role in the slave trade and, in a roundabout way, condemned it in the colonies. The section was eliminated, however, under pressure from pro-slavery forces.

Later, in 1787, the anti-slavery forces were again thwarted when they tried to have slavery eliminated in the United States Constitution. Luther Martin, who left the Constitutional Convention in disgust after efforts to eliminate slavery were halted, told those who remained that they risked eternal damnation for the actions. He said, "The continuance of the slave trade, and thus giving it a national sanction and encouragement, ought to be considered as justly exposing us to the displeasure and vengeance of Him . . . who views with equal eye the poor African slave and his American master."

Slaveholders not only stopped the small group of anti-slavery delegates, but won the right to count each of their slaves as three-fifths of a white person in any tabulation of voters to determine the number of Congressional seats apportioned to southern states, thus giving white slaveowners considerable political power. The Constitution also guaranteed that the new federal government would not free slaves within any states and would uphold a slaveowner's right to retrieve runaways.

The single concession the anti-slavery forces were awarded was a promise that in twenty years, in 1807, Congress would eliminate the importation of slaves from other countries. The pro-slavery forces left the Philadelphia convention certain that there would be no further efforts to abolish slavery. Governor Edmund Randolph, of Virginia, assured southern slaveholders they had little to fear. He told them, "There was not a member of the Virginia delegation who had the smallest suspicion of the abolition of slavery." Charles Pinckney, a South Carolina delegate, was equally satisfied with the arrangement he and his colleagues made with the northern representative to the convention. He told friends, "We have made the best terms for the security of this species of property it was in our power to make."

Their confidence was rewarded just a year later, in 1788, when the United States government sent a sharp letter to Spain demanding the return of fugitive slaves who fled their American plantations and escaped to Spanish possessions in Florida and in the Caribbean. It was the start of unimpeded federal support of slavery, despite numerous challenges from mostly Northern politicians and ministers. Southerners enjoyed even more power in the early years of the Republic as men from slave states were elected President and others, through seniority, quickly won and kept chairmanships of key Congressional committees. The slaveowners were able to control Congress and protect their slave empire for generations.

The lives of the slaves in the southern states, whose number grew to more than four million by 1861, was often harsh. Most slaves were awakened at dawn and began work in the fields just after the sun peeked over the horizon. With only a few breaks for rest, food, and water, they usually worked long days, until darkness, and then returned to their crude cabins, often two or three families living in a ten-foot by twenty-foot structure, slept and then rose the next morning for more work. The work they did was monotonous and difficult. They picked, stacked, and dried large piles of tobacco leaves in Virginia, constructed and worked levees and water sluice gates for the rice fields of South Carolina, often catching colds and pneumonia from hours spent wading in water, hacked sugar cane in Louisiana, and, in later years, spent tedious hours picking cotton under a hot sun in lower Southern states. When there was an off season, or if winter prevented some chores, owners found other work for slaves. Overseers, some black and some white, usually drove slave gangs to work as hard as they could. Women often had to work in the fields alongside men, and boys and girls joined them when they reached the age of twelve or thirteen.

Slaves who did not work hard enough, or offended overseers or owners, were severely punished. Some were dunked repeatedly in ponds. Some were tied to stakes and left in hot, open fields all day where insects could bite them. Many were whipped. Some were whipped for running away, stealing, or failing to work hard, but others were whipped for minor infractions of plantation rules or simply on a whim.

One slave, Gus Smith, of Rich Fountain, Missouri, complained in a slave narrative that an owner he knew was merciless in his beatings. Said Smith, "He whipped them all the time. I've seen their clothes sticking to their backs, from blood and scabs, being cut up with the cowhide. He just whipped them because he could. He used to say he always gave his niggers 'a breakfast spell' every morning. That is, he whipped them every morning."

Cruelty sometimes accompanied whippings. Ferebe Rogers, a slave who grew up in Baldwin County, Georgia, said of her oveseers, "When they got ready to beat you, they'd strip you stark naked and say, 'Come here to me, God damn you! Come to me clean! Walk up to dat tree, and, damn you, hug dat tree!' Then they'd tie your hands round de tree, then tie your feet; then they'd lay the rawhide on you and cut your buttocks open. Sometimes they'd rub turpentine and salt in the raw places and then beat you some more."

There was considerable psychological and emotional damage as wives or husbands were sold, leaving their families forever. Some slaves were even murdered by irrational owners, sometimes out of rage or sometimes through neglect.

Slaves who managed to win easier assignments, such as servants in the homes of planters, still worked long days and felt humiliated by their station of servitude. These slaves, like those in the fields, turned to sarcasm and comedy about their owners in evening slave-quarter reveille to ease their pain. Black women often had to fend off sexual advances from white owners and their sons or submit and raise mulatto children scorned by the owner and his wife. Slaves felt bad for beautiful black women because they were not only easy prey for owners, but had little chance of earning decent jobs on the plantation because the owner's wife, fearful of a husband's roving eye, kept them far from the house.

And so the slaves began to run away.

The first recorded runaways were slaves from Connecticut and Massachusetts who fled their masters in 1690, only to be apprehended a few days later. The first recorded runaway slave to flee the country was a man in Albany, New York, who, sick of slavery, fled to Canada in 1705, where he found refuge. Many slaves in North and South Carolina fled from their plantations during the 1720s and, after surviving a long and dangerous journey through swamps and forests of Georgia and Florida, found protection in the Spanish town of St. Augustine on the eastern coast of Florida. Others fled westward and either settled alone or in small groups in the mountains or continued westward and then south into Mexico. Thousands fled. By 1760 there were more than 900 ads in southern newspapers each year concerning runaway slaves. Over 25,000 slaves ran away during the American Revolution and earned freedom under the protection of the British Army. Hundreds of slaves joined the colonists' Continental Army or local militias and fought in return for promised freedom at the end of the war.

There were so many runaways that the legislatures of the Carolinas passed harsh laws to curb runaways and added a number of statutes to punish any whites who aided fugitives. Over the years, it became extremely dangerous for slaves to flee and dangerous for anyone who aided them or harbored them in any of the southern states. Some laws imposed a fine on whites who hid slaves and some compounded the penalty, fining the pro-

Five Pounds Reward.

RAN away, on the 24th of this inflant, from the fubfcriber, a Negro Man named DICK; he calls himjef RICHARD GOOBY; he is about 26 years of age, and about 5 feet 9 inches high; he is a middling black fmooth faced fellow, flim legged, and knock-knee'd; he has a big mouth, thick lips, and flat nofe; he was brought from Guinea when fmall, fo that he talks as plain as a country born; he is fmart and fenfible in his difcourfe; to defcribe him more plainly, he has on his right hand one or two crooked fingers, and has a long, lazy, lubberly walk; he has formerly follwed the water, and I do fuppofe he will endeavour to get on board of fome veffel as foon as poffible. The clothes he carried with him were, one fearnought over jacket, one new pair of tow trowfers and fhirt, and fundry other clothe, fuch as nankeen, ftriped calico, and ftriped cotton and check trowfers, and white fhirt and trowfers, fo that it is uncertain which of thefe he may have on. Whoever takes up the faid runaway, and fecures him in any gaol, fo that the owner gets him again, fhall have the above reward; and if brought home, all reafanable charges, paid by

John Valiant.

Talbot County, April 26, 1790.

N. B. It is expected the above Negro has a forged pafs.   6w.

This advertisement in the *Delaware Gazette and Advertiser* on May 8, 1790, indicates that runaways were common in the years after the American Revolution. (Courtesy of the Historical Society of Delaware)

tectors on a per-day basis. Slaveowners warned whites in the backwoods areas of the southern colonies that they would be shot and killed if they impeded the hunt for runaways.

Captured runaways were brutally punished to prevent them from escaping again and as a warning to others. Some planters had a routine whereby any runaways would be flogged at a specific time each day for two weeks, in front of the other slaves. Other captured runaways had to do the work of three or four slaves for a month. Some slavecatchers had orders to turn their dogs on runaways when captured and dogs often bit off ears and fingers. The runaway, missing body parts, was then paraded before other slaves as an example.

Henry Cheatam, a slave in Clay County, Mississippi, provided a gruesome narrative: "When the slaves would try to run away, the overseers would put chains on their legs with big long spikes between their feet, so they couldn't run away. Then I seen great bunches of slaves [runaways] put up on the block and sold just like they was cows."

Slaves hoping for freedom after the American Revolution and the Declaration of Independence, which they assumed would cover them, were disappointed. They not only didn't win liberty, but their owners, and the politicians who ran their states, were even stricter in discipline in order to make up for the loss of the 25,000 slaves to the British occupation. Patrols were increased, more slavery laws passed, and owners and overseers were more vigilant about permitting travel by slaves between plantations. Slaveowners interpreted their newly won freedom to mean that governments could not interfere with local politics and slave policies. They saw the contemporary human rights political philosophies of John Locke and others, which supported the freedom of all men to enjoy liberty and property, to mean that no one could take away their property—their slaves.

Evangelical religious movements such as the Great Awakening swept through both northern and southern colonies in the eighteenth century, but slaves who believed that the Great Awakening would make owners abandon slavery were wrong. The Great Awakening, whose evangelical ministers asked their flocks to be kind to their fellow man and to look within themselves to find God and not depend on the established churches, did nothing to curb slavery. Slaveowners, still driven by profit and an increasing belief that slaves gave them political and social prominence in the white community, did not interpret the Great Awakening to mean they should release their slaves, but merely that they should treat them better.

Slave conditions did improve. Owners permitted slaves more freedom to grow their own crops and sell them to earn money to buy things. They gave them more freedom to carry guns and hunt on the plantation. More medical care was provided to keep them in good health. More of an effort was made to keep families together. Slaves were permitted to worship in their own churches and even to attend the white churches, seated in the rear or in the balcony.

Slightly better lives for people in bondage coincided with the invention of the cotton gin in 1793, which permitted the quick separation of cotton from seeds. Thus began the cotton textile industry, which rapidly became highly profitable in the southern states where warm climates were perfect for its growing. The cotton demand in Europe and America was enormous and arrived just as the demand for rice and tobacco started to decline. Thanks to the cotton gin and the growing numbers of slaves, southern plantations were soon producing hundreds of thousands of bales of cotton for export to the northern states and Europe and by the 1850s were exporting over four million bales a year. Southern slaveowners soon realized that if they permitted better living conditions for their workers, whether for political or religious reasons, they would have a more productive work force to earn even higher profits.

Southern slaveowners, who began to come under increasing criticism by northerners opposed to bondage, lived in the middle of a world of slavery. Most of the nations of South America, particularly Venezuela and Brazil, permitted slavery, as did most of the islands in the Caribbean, such as Haiti, Antigua, and Cuba. Planters shrugged off all attacks on slavery by reminding their critics that people opposed to slavery were in the minority in the western hemisphere. They sarcastically reminded northerners, too, that many of their shipowners and merchants were making fortunes from the slave trade.

By the end of the eighteenth century, slaves were convinced that they would spend their lives in bondage, as would their children and grandchildren. Most tried to get along with their owners, marrying and raising families and developing a satisfactory slave culture within the borders of the plantations. Others, however, chafed at their bondage and wanted desperately to escape. They bolted from their plantations at the first opportunity and raced to freedom wherever they could find it.

The yearning to be free grew as the century ended and freedom was no longer limited to brash young men and women. By 1800, men and women in their 40s and 50s, as well as entire families, were running away from their plantations. One study of newspaper ads about runaways by historian Edmund Morgan showed a twelve percent increase in the number of entire families fleeing southern plantations. The fugitives ran from small farms in the Carolinas where they were the only slaves. They fled from the large plantations of the Virginia tidewater, where they hoped they would not be immediately missed amid the one hundred or more slaves working the fields. The slaves of the famous planters raced through swamps alongside the slaves of the unknown planters. In 1786, an irate George Washington had to run ads in northern newspapers seeking the return of two of his slaves, who fled his Mount Vernon plantation and were believed to be hiding in Philadelphia.

Runaways were such a problem that southern politicians used all of their influence to pass the country's first law to capture runaways in 1793. The first Fugitive Slave Act authorized slaveowners to retrieve runaways wherever they found them. It was aimed at what appeared to them to be unknown, clandestine protectors, whites and freed blacks, who were routinely hiding fugitives in their homes or on their farms in the north.

Fugitives fleeing plantations, especially those racing to freedom after passage of the 1793 Act, were bold and ingenious. They managed to hide in swamps and forests—and sometimes in barns at neighboring plantations—and travel at night. They moved slowly, struggling to find roads, rivers, and other landmarks, in a tentative trip north, or south to Florida, with little help from maps. They constantly feared detection and apprehension. Runaways traveled on their own, thin shadows on the landscape, with no assistance.

The same year the U.S. Congress passed the Fugitive Slave Act, eliminating any safe haven for runaways headed north, the government of Upper Canada (now Ontario), under intense pressure from Quakers there, passed a law that eliminated slavery. Quebec Province ended slavery in court rulings in 1800. Slavery was outlawed in the rest of Canada in 1833. Now American runaways had a home beyond the northern states where they could be completely free.

In the 1700s, those who made it to Canada or to the large, protective freed black communities in northern cities, such as Philadelphia and New York, did it mostly on their own, hoping they might hide out at single homes in the north when they escaped from Virginia or Maryland and headed toward Canada, some 300 miles away. To do it, they needed friends . . . lots of them.

Those friends were there. What became known as the abolitionist movement, a product of the Great Awakening, can be traced to the Revolutionary era and the decision of many Quaker organizations in the northern colonies to work for the elimination of slavery. The evangelical ministers of the Great Awakening, led by Jonathan Edwards, traveled throughout the country in the middle of the eighteenth century explaining to large, boisterous outdoor rallies, often gathered in meadows lit by hundreds of fiery torches, that God was within everyone and that people could find God without the help of the established church. Part of this new creed was that regardless of any formal religious doctrine, all men and women were humanitarians who had to help each other and that when *any* people were persecuted, all people were persecuted. Edwards and other ministers skewered slavery. Edwards told crowds that, "To hold a man in a state of slavery who has a right to his liberty is to be every day guilty of robbing him of his liberty, or of manstealing, and is a greater sin in the sight of God than concubinage or fornication."

The Quakers were a powerful force on both sides of the Atlantic. The original Quakers lobbied against slavery in England for generations and, since many Quakers were respected and very successful British businessmen, they had enough political influence to force Parliament to constantly reassess England's support of slavery in the British Empire and, in 1832, to finally end it. On the western side of the Atlantic, Quakers, in 1775, began to formally work for the elimination of slavery in America with the creation of the first anti-slavery society, and never stopped.

The abolitionist movement, however, remained a secretive, underground activity for many years because the number of anti-slavery Quakers remained small. It also remained in the shadows because public sentiment in the North was ambivalent about slavery. Over several generations northern politicians made little effort to curb slavery beyond halting the slave trade in 1807. As the nineteenth century progressed, the abolitionists found that they had no political power and could do little to either free the slaves or punish their owners. Daily, they faced what they saw as an immoral monster in their country and yet did not have the means to combat it. What could they do?

Bold, determined men and women decided to take the law into their own hands. They might not be able to do anything publicly, but they could do much secretly. There might not have been enough anti-slavery advocates to change laws, but there were enough abolitionists in large cities such as New York, Philadelphia, and Boston and in smaller cities and tiny rural villages as well, to start a small but surprisingly efficient ad hoc network of safe houses—whether residential homes or barns—where runaway slaves might hide. Many abolitionists were educators, ministers, and businessmen. They knew people in their area as well as in nearby towns and cities on routes to Canada and were able to establish a loose chain of protectors who might help fugitives—an underground railroad with many stops on the line.

2

THE DREAM FLOURISHES

Edward Magill was a schoolteacher in Langhorne, Pennsylvania, in the spring of 1845 and, unknown to all but his closest friends, a worker on the Underground Railroad. He was not surprised when one summer afternoon another man casually walked over to the schoolhouse, called him aside and talked to him quietly, as one man would talk to another about the weather. The other man was the head of the Underground Railroad chapter in Langhorne. He had a dangerous assignment for the young teacher, one which Magill accepted immediately.

Six runaway slaves from Maryland had traveled up the Delaware River, hidden on the boat of a friendly captain. The boatman took them to a safe house in Langhorne, whose owner had been informed by a coded letter that the fugitives were on their way. The local Underground Railroad leader was also contacted. He coordinated the arrival of the boat, the overnight stay, and Magill's assignment the next night—an assignment, like all in the underground, that might cost the young teacher a fine of several thousand dollars, a prison sentence and, if trapped in a shootout with slavecatchers, injury or even death.

Magill had access to a wagon and team of horses, and when the six fugitives arrived, he played the role of a farmer taking produce to a market across the Delaware from Langhorne to Trenton, New Jersey, thirty miles away. With the runaways carefully hidden under canvas in the rear, he crossed the river on a ferry and drove them to a farm near Trenton owned by another member of the railroad. He was told to pull into a barn, but before the slaves could scramble out of the wagon, Magill was warned that there were slavecatchers riding throughout Trenton that day. The farmer did not feel anyone was safe in the area and gave Magill the name of another farmer, in Princeton, fifteen miles away, who could offer safety. Magill thanked him, turned his team of horses around, drove out of the barn and slowly, like any farmer on the way to market, guided his wagon toward Princeton.

Princeton was safe that night and the six fugitives slept there, free for the moment, as the young schoolteacher drove his now empty wagon back to Langhorne in the dark. The following morning, as Magiil returned to his classroom, no one in town was aware of his night ride. The six fugitives he transported were now in someone else's wagon, on their way to another stop on the Underground Railroad where, eventually, they made it safely to Canada.

It is difficult to determine precisely when the Underground Railroad first became an organized network. Throughout the 1790s, individuals opposed to slavery living in a few northern cities and towns, such as Philadelphia, harbored runaway slaves, and some ships' captains or officers knowingly carried slaves north to freedom, but there did not appear to be a formal network. Some historians claim the railroad was informally organized by 1804 when a revolutionary war hero, General Thomas Boudes, of Columbia, Pennsylvania, harbored a fugitive and, when discovered, refused to return him to his owner. Ohioans contended that a secret anti-slavery organization existed in their state as early as 1810 and claimed five hundred members. But beyond a few isolated incidents, there was no substantial network of safe houses until the 1820s. The Underground Railroad flourished during that decade and became a vast network throughout the northern and midwestern states by the middle of the 1830s. It was such a recognized, even though secretive, institution by then that when one southerner lost a slave through an escape aided by abolitionists in Ohio, he knowingly told friends that he had lost him on "the underground road."

Slavery became a volatile political issue in 1807, when Congress, as was discussed when the Constitution was ratified, ended the African slave trade. This spurred southern slaveowners to increase their efforts to promote births by their slaves to make up for the loss of slaves imported from Africa. The slave owners also worked much harder to prevent runaways. The 1807 law to ban the slave trade once again underlined the strength of the slave system in the south and the growing animosity toward it among northerners. The law was passed just five years after Haiti eliminated slavery following the decade-long slave insurrection there led by Toussaint-Louverture, a rebellion that seriously shook British confidence in their slave system and frightened American slaveowners, who feared similar rebellions on their plantations.

The Underground Railroad thrived in the 1820s and 1830s as the number of dedicated abolitionists and anti-slavery forces grew dramatically as a series of political and cultural events unfolded. In 1820, after much spirited debate, Congress passed the Missouri Compromise. Under the Compromise, Missouri was admitted to the Union as a slave state and Maine became a free state, carved out of the northeastern reaches of Massachusetts, thus creating a perfect political balance with twelve free states and twelve slave states. This pleased the South, which gained another slave state, but troubled the North because it was a loud signal that slavery, a gentleman's agreement in the South for generations, now threatened to spread into the western territories.

The late 1820s and early 1830s were a time when numerous social, economic, and political tides converged to make the Underground Railroad not only possible, but successful. Although it might have developed and prospered without some of these movements, their presence and existence gave the railroad the legitimacy necessary for its success.

- The collapse of worldwide slavery. Southerners had used the existence of slavery throughout the western hemisphere as a political shield for over one hundred years, but beginning in 1802, with the end of slavery in Haiti, the Caribbean and South American slave empire began to crumble. Slavery was banned in Venezuela in 1810, in Chile in 1823, and in Paraguay, Columbia, and Argentina in 1850. Most importantly, England banned the slave trade in 1807 and by 1832 had eliminated slavery throughout the British empire. The United States soon found itself as the last great nation on earth with slavery.
- There was a nationwide lull in anti-slavery feelings, even among Quakers, after the American Revolution because of a depression in the tobacco and sugar markets. Anti-slavery advocates were certain that slavery, created for economic reasons, would disappear because it would no longer prove economically viable. The development of a booming cotton market in the early 1800s, made possible by the new cotton gin, replaced

the stagnant tobacco and sugar markets in many southern states and created a need for even more slaves. Anti-slavery advocates realized that King Cotton meant permanent slavery unless someone ended it.

- The Second Great Awakening, an even more powerful evangelical religious movement than the Great Awakening of the mid-eighteenth century, swept the nation in the 1830s. The new movement, whose fiery ministers preached against slavery, not only solidified opposition to slavery in most Christian homes, but moved many Christians to see slavery as a political, and not just a religious, issue. This coincided with a growing humanitarian movement whose advocates believed that capitalism and the rapid development of the United States required that people had to take moral responsibility for themselves, their fellow man, and their country, and that included ending slavery.

- By the mid-1830s, the northern states had entered the first stages of the Industrial Revolution and a thriving market economy brought about the end of indentured servants (1816), the creation of labor unions, and the rise of a strong workers' movement. The leaders and members of this Free Labor movement began to see slavery as wrong because hard driving factory bosses, they believed, could treat free white workers as "wage slaves" as long as slavery existed anywhere. Slavery provided the ideological framework for such exploitation of free labor.

- There were two slave insurrections. In 1822, Denmark Vesey led an abortive slave revolt in Charleston, South Carolina, after which 36 slaves were hanged. Later, in 1831, a planned rebellion led by Nat Turner in Southampton County, South Carolina, was quashed before it began and seventeen slaves were executed. Although the rebellions did not liberate anybody, they symbolized a new determination of slaves to be free, ending the much encouraged idea that all slaves were docile and satisfied with their condition. This also spurred the development of large, formal anti-slavery organizations in each northern state, making slavery a very public and often debated issue.

- Finally, technological innovations in the printing industry and increased literacy caused an explosion of newspapers and magazines in the early 1830s. Anti-slavery champions began to print their own newspapers in 1831—for example, William Lloyd Garrison's *The Liberator*—and by the end of the decade there were dozens of abolitionist newspapers that collectively enjoyed a large circulation. The newspapers gave the abolitionist movement a legitimate national status and enabled anti-slavery advocates to reach hundreds of thousands of Americans each week in their columns.

The convergence of all these movements and political changes by the mid-1830s brought thousands of people into the anti-slavery, or abolitionist, movement and induced hundreds of them to open up their homes to runaway slaves and turn this loose network into the Underground Railroad. The abolitionist movement was more than a religious or political experience for many; it became a moral crusade that gave the people in it, particularly the conductors on the "railroad," a boldness and courage to resist the law, defy authorities, and run the risk of prison or physical harm. They found courage within themselves that helped them fulfill this new moral responsibility.

The Underground Railroad was not a national institution, but was national in scope and surprisingly well organized for a secretive association. It was never intended to exist for very long, yet by the time the Civil War began the railroad had been running for nearly sixty years. It had no elected officers, yet everyone knew its leaders. It had no departments or offices, and yet it was, at times, run more efficiently than most state or city governments.

The railroad was, in simplest terms, a network of safe houses run by anti-slavery advocates who provided food, clothing, and shelter for runaway slaves for varied periods of time. They were strung out in carefully designed routes leading to Canada and freedom or, in some cases, large northern cities such as New York, Chicago, Detroit, and Boston that had large freed black populations and offered some safety. The "conductors" who sheltered the slaves were abolitionists with strong convictions who took risks for so long that by the Civil War some young conductors were the grandchildren of the first conductors in their family.

There was no national headquarters for the shadow organization. Each state or metropolitan area had its own network of safe houses, or "railroad" to protect runaways and each network was supervised by one or two highly motivated and well organized men or women or, in large cities, extensive committees of men and women. Slaves moved from one network of railroad homes to another and, eventually, to Canada. They did not follow an organized or established national route. A family of slaves might flee Maryland and find shelter in a home in Chester, on the Pennsylvania Underground Railroad, and then move along to Philadelphia and up through Williamsport to Syracuse, New York, then Rochester, and finally over a long suspension bridge at Niagara Falls into Canada.

The abolitionists who ran these "depots" had to remain secretive because their activities were illegal and dangerous. The 1793 Fugitive Slave Act was a federal law and anyone in violation of it was subject to substantial fines and prison terms. Underground leaders, unpopular for years, were often fined by harsh judges and unsympathetic juries. A group of ten underground workers who prevented a slavecatcher from bringing back a runaway and his family from Michigan to Kentucky were assessed $1,926 in damages to be paid to the slavecatcher who sued them in federal court. Thomas Garrett and John Hunn, the leaders of the underground in Connecticut, went to the aid of another fugitive family fleeing through Delaware, spiriting them into Pennsylvania, and were each fined $5,400. The fine ruined Garrett, as he was forced to sell his home and farm. Hunn, who had more resources, was able to pay the fine, but it drained most of his finances. Other underground leaders were assessed smaller fines, but for men and women of modest means it meant ruin.

Others were imprisoned. William Chaplin, a newspaper correspondent who worked for the underground, spent five months in jail in 1850 for liberating slaves belonging to Senator Robert Toombs and Congressmen Alexander Stephens of Georgia before abolitionist friends could raise enough money to pay his bail. A sea captain, Jonathan Walker, was caught in the Gulf of Mexico with a dozen runaways on a ship he was sailing to the Bahamas. He spent three years in a Florida prison before friends paid his fines, but they could not prevent prison authorities from branding the letters SS into his right hand ("slave stealer"). Charles Torrey, another newspaperman sent to jail for his work on the underground, died after four years in a Virginia prison. Charles Dillingham, caught kidnapping three slaves from Tennessee, was sent to prison for three years and died at the end of the second year when a cholera epidemic swept through the prison population.

Until the eve of the Civil War, the underground workers, who all knew the dangers they faced, remained a rather small group, unrepresentative of their county or towns, except in rare cases, such as Ripley, Ohio, or Farmington, Connecticut. Everything they did had to be carefully guarded and their travels carried out under the cloak of darkness. They could not use public telegraph lines or the mails to send letters or requests concerning runaways, nor could they hold public meetings or write books or newspaper articles about their enterprise. All of the anti-slavery societies supported the railroad, but none could publicly champion it.

Yet the leaders of the railroad enjoyed a sophisticated communication system, a transportation network of ships, horses, wagons, and public trains and even had access to the country's best lawyers if arrested. For an under-financed, understaffed, unpaid, and secretive group, it was an impressive and efficient organization.

All of the messages sent by workers on the railroad, or letters from people to railroad operators, were coded. A lawyer who was harboring fugitives in a small town in Pennsylvania would write a letter to William Still, head of the vigilance committee in Philadelphia, who ran the railroad in that city, and inform him that the lawyer had mailed him "four packages" which should be arriving on Tuesday. Still then knew that four runaways would be at his home on Tuesday night. He would then write back to the lawyer, thanking him for his "packages" or "gifts" and letting him know that they had arrived in good condition.

Other letters between members of the underground would describe the number and condition of "packages" so the receiver of the letter would know if medical aid was needed or if a new set of clothing was required for the runaway. A letter writer would write a second underground worker to let him know that the "packages" he would receive on Tuesday had to be shipped right away to a particular person in Albany, or Cleveland, who would be other workers on the railroad. The letter codes, often attached as a postscript or tucked into the middle of a short note, were so nondescript and casual that they looked like any ordinary correspondence.

Transportation was surprisingly easy for the underground workers. Abolitionists who harbored fugitives at their farms always had a wagon to transport them to another safe house several miles away. Underground workers in a town or city without wagons could call on abolitionist friends in a nearby farm area to borrow transportation. It was also always easy to get horses for runaways. Bold abolitionists, particularly in the late 1840s and 1850s, even sent runaways from one city to another on public railroads, sometimes in freight cars and sometimes in passenger cars, providing them with bogus papers establishing them as freedmen or women. They believed that it was sometimes easier to hide people in plain sight, moving them on public railroads, meeting them at large train stations in the middle of crowds, than it was to do so in secret.

The underground railroad routes were established by the mid-1830s and devised so that railroad workers would not have to transport runaways more than fifteen or twenty miles before they found a safe house. Fugitives making their way between destinations on the railroad were given descriptions of the homes they sought and told to look for single candles their new hosts would keep lit in particular windows as a sign. They were also told to meet some conductors, particularly those in cities, at their place of business, where their arrival would appear to be that of just another black freedman seeking work or purchasing goods.

The Underground Railroad routes followed major roads or rivers and were designed to give travelers reasonably direct lines to Canada or large northern cities. Slaves seemed to know from word of mouth communication where underground railroad depots were located. Slaves fleeing Missouri, as an example, would cross the Mississippi River into Illinois at either Quincy or Alton and seek out underground operators in those communities. They would wait a day or two and then start a trek designed to lead them across the state to Chicago and its large free black community, where they would blend in and gain safety.

Slaves fleeing Maryland would find protection at a railroad home in the Gettysburg area and then, alone or with conductors, head west and north, taking the railroad through western Pennsylvania toward Canada. Others might head east, traveling the railroad line into Philadelphia. There, the vigilance committee would put them on a second trunk line of the railroad that would bring them into northern Pennsylvania on a track that went to Elmira and Syracuse in New York State and then to Canada. Or, the vigilance committee might put them on a trunk line that would take them through New Jersey and then into New York City. There, the New York underground workers would send them into New England.

Fugitives who arrived in New England from New York or by boat found safety in the well-organized railroad in Connecticut and Massachusetts. Travelers in Connecticut might arrive at New Haven and then move north to Farmington, where more than a dozen abolitionists sheltered runaways in their homes, then to Hartford and up into western Massachusetts and Vermont and toward Canada. Runaways arriving in Boston, often by boat, put themselves in the hands of underground workers there who sent them west on a journey that took them to Springfield and into Vermont. Another route took them through the northern part of Massachusetts—at Lynn, Salem, Andover, and Amesbury (poet John Greenleaf Whittier's home)— and then into Vermont.

The busiest railroad line of all started at the shore of the Ohio River in Ohio. Slaves from Virginia (the area that is now West Virginia) and Kentucky would cross the Ohio and at first seek shelter in the Cincinnati area, often in Xenia or Ripley, where dozens of abolitionists resided, and then head through the state and find shelter in homes on a route through Oberlin to either Detroit or Lake Erie ports, such as Cleveland, or travel on to Niagara Falls.

Underground leaders were mostly white men and women such as Levi Coffin in Indiana, John Rankin in Ohio, Laura Haviland in Michigan, the Brown family in Rhode Island, and Thomas Garrett in Wilmington, Delaware, but there were many freed blacks and former slaves, such as William Still and Lucretia Mott in Philadelphia, John Parker in Ohio, David Ruggles in New York, and Josiah Henson of Canada who helped run the railroad. White abolitionists all along the railroad aided runaways, but so did freed blacks and former slaves. The railroad was never a white line; it was always a black and white track. Each major city or region had one or two people who were leaders and organizers and dozens of others who assisted in any way they could, whether sewing clothes, driving wagons, or providing food.

Much has been written about the white abolitionists who helped or harbored fugitives, taking great risks to do so, whether it was the story of John Quincy Adams defending the *Amistad* slaves, white ministers such as Rev. Rankin of Ohio, white sailors hiding runways in ships' holds, or whites who opened up their homes to runaways for months at a time, such as Indiana's Coffin. Lost in the many books about the Underground Railroad was the resolute bravery of the runaways themselves.

There was little help for runaways until they reached the northern states or the safety of ships moving out of the harbors of slave states. Runaways had to first sneak away by themselves and avoid trouble along the way, beginning with the departure from their plantation to navigating their way north in the darkness, over strange, hilly, and often treacherous terrain, to the final, often dangerous step across a river or into a city or town where few abolitionists lived and where they could be captured and turned over to police at any moment.

The journey to freedom was often long and filled with danger. Slaves who left plantations in Maryland, Kentucky, and Missouri had only ten or twenty miles to travel to reach Underground Railroad stops in Pennsylvania, Indiana, Illinois, or Ohio, but others, in deeper southern communities, had to travel hundreds of miles, often in bad weather, usually without maps and frequently without provisions. They were always frightened and to be safe spent days, even months, hiding in caves, woods, or swamps, risking

NEGROES

AT SHERIFF'S SALE!

Pursuant to sundry orders of the Court of General Sessions of the Peace and Jail Delivery, of the State of Delaware, made at the November Term, A. D., 1860, of said Court, held at New Castle, in and for New Castle County, will be sold at Public Sale, at the Public Jail of said County,

On Saturday, 15th day of December

inst., at 11 o'clock, A. M., to the highest and best bidder or bidders, residing within the State, the following

NAMED NEGROES,

TO WIT:

Noah Manlove,	James Vining,
Bemjamin Simmons,	John Guy,
Serena Henry,	Mary A. Simmons,
and Sarah A. Brown,	

for such term as shall be necessary in order to raise the Restitution Money, Fines and Costs, with which they respectively stand charged; provided that such term shall not exceed seven years, within the State.

LEVI B. MOORE, Sheriff.

Sheriff's Office, New Castle, Dec. 6, A. D., 1860.

Diamond State and Record—County Printing Office—New Castle, Del

A typical broadside announcing the sale of African Americans; this one was nailed to a tree in 1860. (Courtesy of the Historical Society of Delaware)

malaria and other diseases, living off the land or relying on slaves from nearby plantations to bring them small baskets of food, constantly fearful of detection or betrayal. They traveled by night, using the North Star to navigate and avoided roads and bridges, sometimes wading through rivers and streams and sleeping under the stars as temperatures plunged at night. Many became ill on the journey and some expired, such as Romulus Hall, who fled his Benedict, Maryland, plantation in 1857 and soon died of frostbite. Another slave, Tom, walked and ran ninety-six miles through the northern counties of Kentucky in the middle of winter, as ice formed on the Ohio River, hiding out for days. Constantly exposed to rain, sleet, and cold, he contracted pneumonia and died within weeks of his safe arrival in Ohio.

Slaves were often pursued. By the 1840s, slaves were valued at between $300 (children) and $800 each, and some as much as $1,500 each (about $40,000 in today's money). Slavecatching became a small industry and rough white laborers hired themselves out to chase runaways, making far more money in rewards than they could as dockworkers or farmers. They were sometimes joined by the fugitives' angry owners, who were deter-

mined to catch and punish them. The gangs of pursuers often brought a
dozen or more highly trained bloodhounds to sniff out runaways and corner
them. Although few slaves were killed or wounded by the dogs (as por-
trayed in many legendary stories), many were trapped and held until the
slavecatcher posse arrived. The best dogs were often purchased for $300;
they were of more value than the dollar value of some human slaves.

Pursuers were armed and although they did not want to kill their slaves,
their valuable property, they sometimes did so in pitched battles. James
Connor, a Louisiana slave who escaped and remained at large for two days,
was pursued by a posse of overseers and, when spotted, was shot down by
men wielding shotguns. Connor was hit by buckshot in four different
places, fell, and was captured. Wesley Harris, of Virginia, fled with three
other slaves and made it safely into the northern counties of the state when
they were betrayed by a farmer who promised to hide them. Their pursuers arrived the next day, with dogs, and the four slaves pulled revolvers
from their waistbands and began firing at them. The horde of pursuers,
who greatly outnumbered the slaves, dismounted and began a fierce
gun battle. Two of the slaves were badly wounded and the other two
surrendered. All four were taken back to their plantation. They later
escaped again.

One of the sadder chapters in the history of the underground was the
story of a group of slaves traveling through eastern Pennsylvania, hotly pursued by slavehunters. Lost between underground safe houses and without
protection, they were rumored to have been massacred somewhere in a
valley and later buried in a Cheneyville, Pennsylvania, cemetery. A number
of slaves drowned trying to cross both the Delaware Bay and the Ohio river
in small boats in winter. Over a dozen slaves hidden on a steamer on Lake
Michigan drowned when the boat sank.

Several enterprising slaves escaped by climbing onto the roofs of train
cars as they slowly chugged out of stations, lying flat against them, and
leaped off when the trains approached a distant town closer to a northern
border. Some slaves escaped on foot. Others escaped on horseback. Six
slaves in Maryland stole two horses from their owners' stables and, three to
a horse, disappeared into the night. Henry Brown had himself nailed inside
a large box in Richmond and shipped to Philadelphia, where underground
railroad workers, expecting the "shipment," retrieved the box and, with a
crowd of abolitionists gathered inside a home, opened it with crowbars,
and applauded loudly as a delighted Brown emerged, a bit hungry but in

good health (Brown's 1848 escape prompted several other such escapes over the years).

Many traveled north as stowaways on ships. James Mercer, who did not trust anyone, sneaked on board a ship and hid himself inside the ship's boiler room, nearly passing out several times from the intense heat as the ship sailed north to Philadelphia. John Jackson, who escaped the plantation of Robert English, 100 miles from Charleston, South Carolina, in the 1850s, hid himself in the hold of a cargo ship bound for Boston that sailed out of Charleston. He did not realize how long the voyage would take and after a week, exhausted and without food, signaled to a ship hand that he needed help. The captain, opposed to slavery, fed him, let him stay on the deck with the rest of the men, and quietly released him when they reached Boston. Many slaves hid themselves in cargo holds. Most slaves on ships, however, were able to stow away because they either knew an anti-slavery seaman who hid them or simply bribed someone ($50 was the established bribery rate in the 1830s and 1840s).

Some slaves escaping plantations did so on impulse, without money or plans. Many fled after a beating or humiliation, or when they learned their master planned to sell them or separate their families. They bundled up a few clothes, stuffed some corn into their pockets, and ran under the cover of darkness. They did not know any safe routes to follow out of their states, knew nothing of underground railroad homes, and did not know which white people they encountered were friends or foes. Dozens of runaways wound up living in swamps or woods for weeks or months before they could plan a route north. One, Anthony Blow, who had been shot during a previous, failed escape lived in huts and forests for ten months before finally escaping north on a steamer. Others, familiar with their home counties, hid out in caves for up to a year.

Still others, whether alone or with their wives or families, sometimes in groups of up to two dozen, had distinct plans. They knew, through rumor, of certain whites and freed blacks who would shelter them on their way north. They were aware that they needed money to pay for food, shelter or, at the end, passage across a river on a skiff. They also knew, from rumor, where Underground Railroad homes were in certain towns.

3

MASTERS OF DISGUISE

In the early 1850s, twenty-eight fugitives crossed the Ohio River just outside of Cincinnati, Ohio, in the morning. Too late to run unseen to an area safehouse, they cowered in a large field near the bank of the river where they lay prone, hidden from view, while underground leaders discussed how to move them. They could not leave them in the field all day and rescue them at night because they might be seen by riders on a nearby road or passengers on boats sailing on the river. They certainly could not abandon them. They could not attempt a typical rescue by driving wagons to the field and trying to load that many runaways and bring them into the city. Such a rescue attempt would probably fail. It could also result in the arrest of underground leaders and perhaps blow the cover of the complex Cincinnati underground operation.

Shortly after 9 A.M., a large funeral procession approached the meadow where the slaves hid beneath tall shrubs. The procession was led by two funeral hearses, with drivers, and included a dozen carriages and large buggies driven by somber-looking men and women dressed in traditional mourning clothes. The hearses and carriages had been borrowed from two white German livery stable owners who were members of the anti-slavery movement. There were no coffins behind the dark hearse drapes. The buggies were owned by underground families who usually used them for Sunday drives. All were driven by men and women of the Cincinnati underground, dressed for the funeral of a beloved family member or friend.

The procession stopped next to the meadow and, on cue, the twenty-eight runaways quickly slipped into the hearse, carriages, and buggies, put on black mourning clothes and became part of the most sorrowful funeral Cincinnati had seen in years. The mourners, crowded into their carriages and buggies, weeping and shuddering in grief, accompanied the funeral procession to the cemetery of the Methodist Episcopal Church, in the suburb of Cumminsville. The slow-moving procession stopped long enough to bury someone as the grieving mourners prayed, and then proceeded to College Hill, a section where freedmen lived. There, the runaways rid themselves of their mourning clothes and slept overnight, safely hidden in several homes, and went on to Canada the next morning, their grief apparently over.

Many runaways carried out elaborate ruses to trick their owners, slave-catchers, and anyone else they might meet on their journey. They not only adopted disguises, but new identities. They believed, correctly, that the effort that went into planning an elaborate escape was just as important as the physical effort that went into the journey itself.

Many dressed as members of the opposite sex. Clarissa Davis probably became one of the handsomest men the dockworkers of Richmond, Virginia, ever saw. Clarissa, of Portsmouth, Virginia, failed in her summer 1854 escape and had to remain in hiding in a chicken coop for two months. A friend finally made arrangements to have her hidden aboard a steamship, the City of Richmond, which was due to sail the next day. Her captain was a member of the underground. The twenty-two-year-old runaway was an extremely attractive, brown-skinned slave woman with large, wide eyes and richly textured skin. Everyone who knew her thought she was one of the most beautiful women in Portsmouth. Fearful of capture because of her looks (there was a $1,000 reward out for her), Clarissa dressed as a man, tying a belt into knots to keep her oversized trousers from falling down and bundling up her hair under a large farmer's hat. She quickly walked to the dock under the cover of a driving rainstorm and boarded the ship undetected.

The most comical woman's disguise belonged to Jackson, a barber. Jackson was married to a free creole woman who lived in New Orleans. She spirited him out of the Crescent City by clothing him in fine, rich dresses and drenching him in perfume. She then passed him off as her loyal female servant when they bought passage on a riverboat headed north. The boat took them up the Mississippi and the Ohio. Jackson bitterly complained all the way about the tight dresses he had to wear and his bonnets, which never fit properly. They finally found freedom in Cincinnati.

The most imaginative disguises were those of William and Ellen Craft, a married slave couple from outside Savannah, Georgia, who, like many others, discussed means of escape for months. They did not think they could sneak out on ships departing from Savannah and were not physically prepared for a journey to Florida through swamps and forests. They envied the rich white planters they knew who, whenever they went north, traveled in style. The planters dressed immaculately, slept over in fancy hotels, dined in the most expensive restaurants, had the best seats on the railroads and steamships, and were treated with great respect by everyone they met. So the Crafts decided to travel as rich white people in their 1835 escape.

Ellen was very light skinned and was often mistaken for a white woman, so she became a young white male planter. She wore polished black boots with lifts built into them to add several inches to her height, purchased an expensive black suit, tailored a silk vest and cravat to fit her, making it tight across her chest to hold in her breasts, and topped off everything with a jet black cape. Ellen became William and looked like she was going to the opera. William, who was darkskinned, played himself—a loyal servant who would do anything for his loving master.

Their ruse was that of a very ill, rich white planter who was traveling to Philadelphia, the only city in the United States with specialists to treat him. Ellen's face was roughed up with dirt and rouge to give her a sickly appearance. She tucked cotton balls into her jaw to make her face look swollen. William, her servant, tended to her every need.

The couple traveled in style, living in the very best hotels in the capitals of southern states as they headed north. Like all runaways, they had saved what little money they made selling extra produce or craftwork sanctioned by their owners and borrowed money from friends on their plantation. They had two close brushes with detection. The first came on a steamship trip between Savannah and Charleston. The ship's captain, who liked to mingle with the rich, sat next to them, uninvited, for dinner and carried on an hour-long conversation with the wealthy, ailing young planter and never suspected anything. Later, in Baltimore, their plans almost came undone when they were told that the servant, William, needed a bond in order to buy a ticket on the railroad that would take them to Philadelphia. The master had to provide some proof that William was his slave.

The Crafts, who knew nothing of this common practice, were shaken. William immediately insisted that as a loyal retainer, he had to transport his master north immediately, and could not wait a day or two for a bond because his owner was very ill and he did not want him to die. The fervent plea, and the loyalty of the slave, convinced the broker, who sold them the tickets. Several hours later, they arrived in Philadelphia, Ellen's health was remarkably restored by the train ride. At last they were free.

Slaves and their protectors always tried to think like slavecatchers in inventing their ruses and disguises. One Cincinnati woman, protecting a young slave girl sought by slavehunters in their neighborhood, put on her own finest clothes and found another dress and straw bonnet for the girl, adding a colorful parasol for effect. The white woman raced to her closet and took out a bundle of rags, folded them up and shoved them inside a bright blue baby blanket. She shaped the rags to make a head and covered the head with a lace bonnet, careful to pull it so that it covered the face of the "baby." A few moments later, as the slavecatchers rode down their street, the two women emerged, a wealthy woman and her nurse, caring for the woman's baby, out for a midday stroll. Smiling at everyone, even the slavecatchers, they made it to the far edge of town to the home of an abolitionist who put the girl on the back of his horse and rode with her, "baby" and all, to another town and safety.

One farmer in Newport, Indiana, harboring two small runaways girls, did not know how to save them when a rider told him slavecatchers were within a hundred yards of his cabin, followed by nearly two hundred protesting townspeople. He walked out of the farmhouse and confronted the slavecatchers, demanding that they show a legal writ to retrieve the slavegirls. They had one, which they handed to the farmer, and insisted that the girls were inside the house. Many of the townspeople began to jeer the slavecatchers but the men, who were armed, said they were determined to bring the girls home and had a legal writ to do it. The farmer went back in the house, he said, to consult his wife, and reemerged. He engaged the slavecatchers in a long debate about slavery as several freed black men and women walked in and out of the house, carefully eyed by the slave catchers. The farmer's wife dressed the two girls as young boys and gave them slouch hats to pull down over their hair, which they rolled up and stuffed under the wide hats, and told them to walk and move like the boys they knew on their plantations.

A moment later, several freedmen and two young boys emerged from the farmhouse. The slavecatchers looked directly at the men, then at the boys, and returned to their debate with the farmer. The two "boys" slipped behind the crowd, were put on horses and, with others, slowly rode away.

Later, the farmer finally let the slavers into his home, just to prove to them that, as he said, there were no runaway girls inside.

Charlotte Giles and Harriet Eglin, two Maryland slaves, completed a carefully planned ruse in 1856. The two women were fearful of capture and considered a number of escape routes, finally deciding that they would flee Maryland from its busiest city, Baltimore, in the most public means of travel, the railroad. They arrived at the Baltimore train station with a friend, who bought them tickets. The women were dressed as grieving mourners, black veils hiding their faces and white gloves covering their hands. They sat in a car reserved for freed blacks and slaves traveling with masters and told a porter they were free women on their way to a funeral in Philadelphia. Then, as the train slowly pulled out of the station, they began to fake quiet weeping and from moment to moment consoled each other. Several people walked past them but were deceived by their disguise. Suddenly, as they began another round of weeping, one of their owners entered the car on a frantic search for his runaways. The startled women bowed their heads as close to their chests as they could and lowered their veils.

The owner, who was looking for two runaway field hands dressed in rags, did not recognize either woman but, by chance, stopped to talk to them.

"Who are you?" he asked Charlotte.

"Sir, I am Mary," she said, sniffling and looking at the floor of the car.

"And who are you?" he said to Harriet.

"Lizzie," she said quietly, staring at his shoes.

The slaveowner wasted no time in further talk and moved on to the next car, eager to find the women who ran away from him.

Several runaway slaves not only found themselves in a funeral procession, but traveled in it as the corpse. Henrietta Bowers Duterte became the first black woman undertaker in Philadelphia in the 1850s and hid fugitives inside empty caskets and then conducted elaborate funeral processions that took the casket, followed by mourners in on the ruse, to the cemetery and, after fake services, down the road to a local safehouse and, eventually, to freedom.

The dead lived well in the midwest, too. One Kentucky slave, well known in the area, failed to return to his plantation from Cincinnati, where he had been sent with a basket of eggs to sell at the market. His owner sent men to find him the following day. The slave, Louis, was too well known to travel the streets and the owner lived so close that he feared he would be sought day after day until captured. An underground railroad conductor agreed with him and decided the only way the hunt for Louis would end was if the slave was dead—and so they "killed" him.

They hid him in a house and sent a man with Louis' coat and his familiar large, wide-brimmed hat, plus a new basket of eggs exactly the size as the one he took that morning, to the Ohio River. The man waited in hiding fifty yards upriver from the ferry dock. An hour or so later, the ferry pulled in and picked up a group of people. As soon as it began its trip back to Kentucky, the abolitionist set the basket, coat, and hat adrift, aiming them toward the path of the ferry. The ferry captain saw the objects floating in the water and retrieved them. The following day, after a short investigation and examination of the familiar clothing, the police sadly informed his owner that poor Louis had drowned in the Ohio.

Exaggerated disguises helped save a slave trapped on a schooner in Boston. A railroad conductor could not devise a way to get him off the ship, bound for a southern state. He certainly could not force the captain to do anything at gunpoint because there was a full crew of men on board. Finally, after much thought, he sailed a skiff to the side of the ship late at night, when it was difficult to see very far. He spent much of the night fastening a dozen poles to the side of his boat and carefully arranging hats and coats on the poles to give the appearance of a gang of men. Then, as he pulled up closer to the side of the ship, he pulled a gun and demanded that the captain and crew turn over the slave or his "men" would open fire. The captain, seeing the dozen "men" in the boat, knew he was outnumbered and had the slave brought to the side of the ship and lowered into the waiting skiff.

One slave named Aunt Betsey, who lived fifteen miles south of Covington, Kentucky, intent on rescuing her entire family who lived on another plantation, knew that she could not get across the Ohio, into Cincinnati and freedom, unless a white person accompanied her.

Betsey knew that a young white boy who lived in a nearby town was eager to go to the big city, but his parents would not let him. She told him that he could travel in and out of Cincinnati with her when she went to market, at no expense, as long as he was willing to get up at dawn and promise not to tell anyone about the trip so that Betsey would avoid getting into trouble with her master. The boy agreed. He was happy he could leave his village to visit Cincinnati. Betsey even let him drive the wagon, which gave the child immense pleasure. They had to pick up more produce, she said, and gave him a meaningless errand when they stopped at another plantation. While he was gone, her husband and eight children sneaked out of a barn and climbed into the wagon, where they were covered with hundreds of vegetables and canvases before the boy returned. A few hours later the wagon approached the bridge into Cincinnati, where guards let it pass because, by law, a white person was driving it. A short time later, the wagon pulled into the marketplace and Betsey's family sneaked out the back when she gave the boy another errand. A few minutes later the unsuspecting boy found himself with a wagon full of vegetables, and all alone, in Cincinnati.

Some escapes were heartbreaking. Many men and women ran away when they discovered that their husband or wife, living on another plantation, had been or was about to be sold. Some raced north when they learned they would be purchased by another slave owner, never to see their wives or children again. Willis Reddick, of Virginia, had only been married five months when his owner told him he would be sold. The crushed newlywed ran away the next day. Emeline Chapman was told by her owner that she was up for sale, while her husband and two children would remain on the plantation. The heartbroken mother ran away the next night. She, too, would never see her family again.

Women were just as bold and brave as men. Ann Maria Jackson, from Delaware, had nine children and a loving husband. Her master sold off her oldest children in 1856 when they reached the age they could work in the fields. The loss of the children so demoralized her husband that he went insane and was confined to a local madhouse, where he died in 1858. A few months later, the owner, an alcoholic, told Ann Maria he was going to sell her next oldest four children as soon as he was able to get a good price for them. The woman carefully planned an escape in which she traveled the entire length of Delaware in a carriage, moving only when dark, while her youngsters bundled up inside. They finally reached an underground railroad stop in Chester, Pennsylvania, where they were spirited to Ohio and then Canada.

A woman named Armstrong escaped to Canada with her husband and baby in the mid-1850s but couldn't bring out her other seven children. Unable to sleep, she returned to Kentucky without her husband, who thought the trip too risky. She managed to slip five of her seven children off their plantation at midnight. Dressed as a man and moving at night, she brought the children to the Ohio River, where they paid a boatman to take them across, eventually returning to her husband in Canada.

A Kentucky woman known as Aunt Rachel lost her husband in the early 1850s when he was sold to a planter in the Deep South. Two years later, her children were bought by a planter in Lexington, Kentucky. She in turn was purchased by a slavetrader who then sold her to a cotton planter in Mississippi. Desperate to see her children, she escaped and managed to make her way back to Kentucky, existing on berries she picked in the woods and some meals offered by slaves who hid her at various plantations. She was captured by her master, whipped, and manacled with handcuffs and a ball and chain, which were fastened so tightly around her ankles that they continually cut her skin as she walked. Aunt Rachel and others he purchased were put in a wagon and the group headed south. When they stopped, she climbed out of the wagon and, holding the ball in her hands, disappeared into the woods. She was able to break open her handcuffs with rocks, but could not unfasten the ball and chain, which she had to carry as she moved through the dimly lit forests.

Sleeping during the day and moving at night, she found shelter at the home of a black freedman who lived near the Ohio River. He managed to cut open her ankle chains with a file and ferried her across the Ohio. Still fearful of capture by her original Kentucky master or her second owner who was still looking for her, members of the underground moved her by wagons to Indiana and, after working there six months, on to St. Catharine's, a settlement in Canada where many former slaves lived.

All kinds of men and women protected the Aunt Rachels and other runaways as they traveled the Underground Railroad from the 1820s until the outbreak of the Civil War. Most were white and most of the legends that later developed surrounded them, but there were many black protectors, too. The white protectors were men, women, and children who were the latest generation in a long line of northerners, stretching back to the Massachusetts Puritans and Pennsylvania Quakers, who were appalled by slavery. Many developed their anti-slavery feelings during the Second Great Awakening. Some became abolitionists because their husbands or wives had strong anti-slavery beliefs. They were from different social and economic backgrounds. Some, like the Brown family of Providence, Rhode Island (they established Brown University), were wealthy. Most were middle-class whites such as ministers, newspaper editors, small businessmen, merchants, and farmers. Many were working-class people: seamen, dockworkers, construction workers, and livery stable owners. Some of the early underground

Perhaps the most famous painting of the Underground Railroad is this 1893 canvas by Charles Webber, which hangs in the Cincinnati Art Museum, showing members of a white family bringing runaways into their home in a snowstorm. (Courtesy of the Cincinnati Art Museum)

leaders were veterans of the American Revolution, such as Dr. Walter Harris, of New Hampshire, who had fought for freedom once and was willing to do it again. "Those to whom liberty may cost nothing do not know how to price it," he told a New Hampshire anti-slavery group in 1841.

Some of the Underground Railroad workers shunned heavy involvement; their work was infrequent and usually consisted of providing a horse or wagon for transportation of runaways or shelter in a barn for a single night. Many worked on the Underground Railroad without participating in any organized way, such as seamen on ships who hid runaways while their vessel was at sea and perhaps brought them a few meals, or railroad ticketbrokers or conductors who believed someone traveling as a freedman or freedwoman was a runaway but did not turn them in. Some police in northern cities, particularly those around the docks or railroad stations, often stood by and did nothing when frightened fugitives passed in front of them as they embarked from a train or ship.

Others were not only heavily involved in running the Underground Railroad, but also considered it their true life's work, devoting as much time to it as they did to their business. These men and women began to aid fugitives when they were teenagers and continued to do so throughout their lives. Some legitimately claimed they had harbored more than a thousand runaways over a forty-year period. The slaves they hid became part of their family for the days or weeks they were in their homes. The profits from their businesses went into horses, wagons, food, and clothes for the railroad and its travelers. They spent large sums renovating their homes, turning stairwells into secret hideaways, building false closets, turning attics into safe rooms, cellars into bunkers, and often building rooms or shelters in their barns. Some built underground tunnels connecting their homes to nearby rivers, meadows, woods, or roadways. They not only sacrificed considerable amounts of money to the cause, but completely changed the way they lived—and the lifestyle of their families—to serve generations of strangers they had never seen before and would never see again.

One of the first successful white leaders of the underground was Isaac Hopper, a Quaker, who began to loathe slavery when he listened to an old black man explain to him how he was captured in Africa. He recalled how his hands were cut by thorns as he tried to grasp the bushes as slavers drove him down a road. Hopper moved to Philadelphia in 1787 at the age of sixteen to become an apprentice to his uncle, a tailor (he made a few jackets for George Washington and Benjamin Franklin). As soon as he reached the largest city in the colonies he began to work with African Americans already in the city by acting as a tutor for black children and, later, their parents. He also joined the Pennsylvania Abolition Society. He began his activities for what would later become the Underground Railroad in 1804, when he rescued a small black child who had been kidnapped and put on a schooner headed south. Throughout his life, Hopper rescued many slave adults and children captured by slavecatchers in Philadelphia, which had a substantial black community constantly at risk. He made so many rescues, was physically beaten several times, and was so outspoken in his anti-slavery views that he was expelled from a mainstream Quaker church, the Society of Friends, because members of that particular church feared reprisals.

One of the most successful Underground Railroad leaders was businessman Levi Coffin, who ran small factories and stores. He began to assist runaways when he was fourteen years old and living in North Carolina, a slave state. He decided to make it his life's occupation when he moved to Newport, Indiana, in 1826 and opened a successful general store. The personable Coffin made many southern friends in the part of Indiana where he settled due to his own upbringing in North Carolina. He also made many northern friends who liked his public anti-slavery philosophy. Coffin built a large home and farm outside of Newport and began to shelter runaways in the late 1820s. Later, he moved his business to Cincinnati, Ohio, where he lived in another large house and harbored even more runaways. He estimated that he assisted over two thousand runaway slaves during his thirty-four years as the midwest leader of the Underground Railroad.

Another major leader was John Rankin, a Presbyterian minister who was born in 1793 in Tennessee and served for thirty-three years as a pastor in Ripley, Ohio, whose townspeople, like those of Xenia, Ohio, were committed to the anti-slavery cause and the Underground Railroad. Rankin was the leader of the Ripley railroad depot. He lived in a large home on top of a 300-foot-high hill that was clearly visible from the Ohio side of the river and even more visible from the slave side, in Kentucky. Every night lights could be seen in his windows as a guide for escaping slaves. His most vivid memory of an escaping fugitive was a woman named Eliza Harris, whom he watched leap from ice flow to ice flow with her baby clutched in her arms as she crossed the Ohio River toward his home in the late 1840s. He later told the story to writer Harriet Beecher Stowe, who lived in Cincinnati. She made that scene the centerpiece of her novel, *Uncle Tom's Cabin*.

Thomas Garrett was born in Philadelphia and moved to Wilmington, Delaware, in 1822. During the next forty years he aided slaves fleeing from nearby Maryland, hiding them in his home or in the homes of friends as he arranged their passage north to Philadelphia or New Jersey. He told friends that if he ever made any money he would use it to build another floor in his home to hide more fugitives. He was a bold man and never denied that he worked for the railroad, even though several southerners threatened to kill him.

He once met a slaveowning southerner who berated him for his activities and told him that if he was "ever in my neck of the woods" he would be tarred and feathered. A year later, Garrett found himself in the man's town on business and boldly drove to his home to see what would happen. The man opened the door, recognized the abolitionist, and was startled.

"I was in your neck of the woods and decided to visit," he said, his eyes staring directly at the slaveowner.

"Go away Garrett, go away . . ." he muttered, closed the door, and did nothing as the Underground Railroad leader slowly rode away.

Some Underground Railroad workers were famous men who could travel throughout the South on business without suspicion. One of the most unusual was Dr. Alexander Ross. He was a Canadian physician and also one of the world's leading ornithologists. His work on birds was often described in American and European books and journals. He visited many southern states ostensibly to study the lives of birds unique to each of them. The well-known doctor often stayed as a guest at some of the largest and most prosperous slave plantations in the South, and was the star of numerous dinner parties.

He quietly talked to thousands of slaves in his travels. He was never detected as an abolitionist as he trudged through cotton fields and tobacco acreage looking for birds with his looking glass and notebook. He offered them advice on escape, told them where safe houses were located, and gave them small sums of money for their trip. Planters always mentioned to friends that slave escapes from their counties often came a few weeks after the ornithologist's visits but never connected the two events.

Some, like John Fairfield, were not content to harbor runaway slaves, but insisted on kidnapping them out of slavery and bringing them north to freedom. Fairfield worked for freed black families, usually in Canada but sometimes in freed black communities in northern cities, who asked him to rescue the loved ones they left behind on their former plantations. He saw "Negro stealing," as southerners called it, as his profession and charged for his services. Families supplied him with descriptions of their husbands, wives, children, family, and friends and carefully explained to him what the surrounding terrain was like.

Fairfield, originally a Virginian, was able to travel freely in the South because of his drawl, knowledge of southern politics, Virginia culture, and southern sophistication. He not only socialized with planters whose slaves he planned on stealing, but often slept in their homes as an honored guest and regaled them with stories of old Virginia. The next day, or a few days later, Fairfield was gone—along with several of the planter's slaves. The enigmatic Fairfield was not afraid to shoot his way to safety and took inordinate risks. He claimed to have rescued over one thousand slaves in his career. He was reportedly shot and killed during a slave insurrection he instigated in western Tennessee.

Some of the most powerful people in the Underground Railroad were not workers at all, but the men who funded it. Although many middle-class people could hide and feed slaves, most could not afford to buy wagons and clothes and provide money for travel, transportation, and bribes. Several wealthy white businessmen, unable to find time to hide or aid slaves, contributed to the anti-slavery cause with their wallets. Two of the most effective were the Tappan Brothers, Arthur and Lewis. In the 1820s and 1830s they became successful businessmen in New York, operating dry goods stores. They gave as much money as they could to the varied anti-slavery organizations in the New York area and Underground Railroad operators and helped subsidize abolitionist newspapers. Lewis Tappan was the chief fund-raiser to the legal defense of the *Amistad* captives at their trials from 1839 through 1841. Another underground financial backer was wealthy New York businessman Gerrit Smith.

Some abolitionists never worked directly for the Underground Railroad, but won it new members through their work. The Rev. Theodore Weld was a fire-breathing dragon of the anti-slavery movement who traveled from city to city delivering fierce anti-slavery lectures. He was often pelted with eggs, rocks, and wads of paper hurled by his audiences. There were many threats on his life and on numerous occasions he had to be led out side doors of lecture halls and hurriedly put into a buggy and whisked out of town for his safety. In his wake he left hundreds of brand-new abolitionists who did what they could for the cause, and for many that was work, however small, for the Underground Railroad. Another minister, Rev. Theodore Parker, of Boston, was one of the leaders of the New England Underground Railroad and told parishioners, pro- or anti-slavery, that when he wrote his sermons he kept a Bible on the left side of his desk and his rifle on the right. Other leading abolitionists in New England were Dr. Samuel Howe and his wife, Julia Ward Howe, Wendell Phillips, Henry Ward Beecher, the brother of Harriet Beecher Stowe, and a number of artists and writers, including John Greenleaf Whittier, Henry David Thoreau, Walt Whitman, and Ralph Waldo Emerson.

White northerners were not alone in their dangerous network to protect runaway slaves. They worked arm in arm with African Americans. Almost all of the approximately 450,000 African Americans living in the northern states were freed by the early 1850s. Most large cities, such as New York, Boston, and Philadelphia, had large black communities with populations ranging from 20,000 to 50,000 people, but significant settlements of freed blacks existed in several other northern states. Nearly 8,000 freed blacks lived in Connecticut in 1840. Rural Pennsylvania had more than 50,000 free blacks living in communities in Lancaster, York,

Williamsport, Harrisburg, Gettysburg, and other small towns. Their ranks were swollen over the years by some runaways who did not want to move all the way to Canada and managed to blend into the communities of freed men and women where they lived undetected.

Northern blacks played just as important a role as whites in the Underground Railroad. Local Vigilance Committees, publicly devoted to the antislavery cause through speeches and meetings, privately provided headquarters for the Underground Railroad. The few records that were kept show that blacks invariably made up at least half the committee membership and sometimes as much as three quarters, particularly in large cities. Freed black Robert Purvis served as the president of the Philadelphia Vigilance Committee. William Still, another African American, was the committee's longtime executive secretary. David Ruggles was in charge of the New York Vigilance Committee. Rev. Jermain Loguen, whose home and church in Syracuse, New York, served as depots, reportedly sheltered over 1,500 runaways in the 1850s. Foundry worker John Parker led raids into Kentucky from Ohio for fifteen years and claims he rescued more than four hundred slaves. Like their white counterparts, such as Coffin in Indiana and Rankin in Ohio, it was their responsibility to keep track of all correspondence, hide runaways, and provide transportation for fugitives from one city to another, a job they did superbly.

Blacks who lived in small towns worked just as hard as blacks in cities to assist runaways. Daniel Hughes, a towering 6'8" Pennsylvania man who lived near Williamsport, was part black and park Mohawk Indian. His wife was black. Hughes was a typical black member of the Underground Railroad. He worked as a lumber raftsman in Williamsport. His job was to sail rafts down the Susquehanna River to either Lancaster or Baltimore and then return. On his return he always brought from two to ten runaways with him, put in his care by Underground Railroad leaders in those cities. Hughes, like so many conductors black and white, followed carefully laid-out routes through the quiet Pennsylvania countryside, often traveling on old Indian trails, to bring his charges to Williamsport undetected. He hid some at his farm or at the homes or farms of others in the area, black and white, and then made arrangements for them to move north to Elmira, on the New York line, and then to Canada, sometimes using the commercial Williamsport and Elmira Railroad, whose abolitionist owner encouraged it. The northeastern area of Pennsylvania, which had over a dozen underground railroad depots, was evenly split between white and black members.

Black women were instrumental in the success of the railroad, too. Hundreds of them helped to hide runaways and move them from home to home and town to town. Sometimes an entire neighborhood of men, women, and children, would respond to an emergency (such as the "funeral train" in Cincinnati). Black women routinely sewed clothing, in different sizes, so that runaways sought in the clothes in which they escaped could change and avoid capture. Many black women, such as Charlotte Forten of Philadelphia, were instrumental in the formations of dozens of female anti-slavery societies in the 1830s. Lucretia Mott was just as influential in running the Philadelphia underground as any of the men in that city. Former slave Sojourner Truth, who wore a distinctive white turban, began to speak out against slavery in 1829, testifying to the terrible living conditions of slave women, and was soon invited to dozens of major anti-slavery rallies.

The most famous black woman in the Underground Railroad was Harriet Tubman, whose story has been told often. Tubman, after learning she was to be sold, escaped from her plantation on the Choptank River, in Maryland, in the 1840s, and made her way first to Philadelphia and then to Albany, New York. She did not want to leave the country and was determined to return to Maryland to liberate members of her family and friends. She went on eighteen daring raids into Maryland and brought out family members and more than eighty others. Tubman, who quickly became a legend in the anti-slavery movement, traveled to public anti-slavery meetings and turned up at rallies for abolitionists on trial or demonstrated on behalf of slaves held in jail for return trips South. Her daring rescue of runaway Charles Nalle in Troy, New York, caught the attention of the entire country.

Black and white Underground Railroad leaders were aided by black churches and their memberships. These churches were firmly established in northern communities by the 1840s, as part of the Second Great Awakening, and their ministers often hid fugitives in false rooms and closets in churches, in basements, or in nearby barns. Many ministers hid runaways in their homes or in the homes of parishioners.

The operation of the Underground Railroad was complicated in scope but rather simple in operation. Fugitives always seemed to know, via rumor, the location of Underground Railroad homes. They knew prearranged codes and signals to use at the houses: three rapid knocks on a door, the hooting sound of an owl, or a special verbal greeting, such as "I am a friend of a friend." They also knew which homes in a village were friendly because of certain signs they had heard about. Many members of the railroad kept single candles lit in an upstairs window. Others left an American flag flying from the front porch at night. In an ironic twist, one Ohio woman stuck a flag into the hand of the black jockey statue on her front porch.

The sheltering and feeding of slaves was dangerous. Once inside a home, slaves were hidden from marauding slavecatchers and local police. Most conductors merely hid slaves in upstairs bedrooms or in barns. Some, fearful of capture or harm, built false closets, secret rooms, and tunnels. Secretive transportation was difficult, however, and Underground operators had to be careful to make firm arrangements and move their passengers late at night. This was done with remarkable efficiency in an era of horses, buggies, and wagons. Local members would pick up slaves at a home and drive them to another house in another town on the railroad line. Someone there would care for them overnight, or for a few nights, and then move them somewhere else. The first conductor would mail letters ahead to people to watch out for new arrivals. The railroad had, by the early 1850s, become methodical, organized, and efficient.

This systematic success had always angered southern slaveowners and they passed local and state laws for years to prevent it. Virginia legislators were so worried about runaways that in 1723 they made it illegal for five or more slaves to talk together on a plantation. In 1770, Maryland passed a statute forcing anyone who aided a runaway to pay a fine of 550 pounds of tobacco. In 1833, the North Carolina legislature made assistance to a runaway punishable by death. In 1835, slaves in St. Louis were forced to observe a 9 P.M. curfew. Any slaves seen after that hour were given fifteen lashes and their owners fined. Any Missourian who attended an anti-slavery meeting was fined $10 if caught. Slaves seen at one were fined $10 and given ten lashes. A steamboat captain who took his ship over any river through any southern states was legally liable for any runaways found on his boat and could be fined and jailed. Frustrated by the steady exodus of runaways despite these laws, southern planters once again engaged in public crusades in the 1840s, contending there was nothing wrong with the slave system. Southern newspaper editors, politicians, and ministers again argued that African Americans could not survive alone and that their owners took care of their needs. They pleaded once more that not only southern whites, but whites in northern states, would lose their jobs if four million unskilled black laborers were freed.

Robert Toombs, a U.S. Congressman from Georgia who owned over one hundred slaves, and suffered runaways, as did U.S. Senator Jefferson Davis, later Confederate president, defended the institution of slavery for years, ever since the day in 1847 when Toombs rose up in the House of Representatives and demanded that southerners had a right to their "property," or slaves.

Toombs, like so many slaveholders, also said that slaves could not live free, that "when left to themselves are barely capable of maintaining their existence." He even chided northern congressmen, to their astonishment, that slaves lived better than white northerners. He charged, "He [slave] is entitled by law to ample food and clothing and exempted from excessive labor, and when no longer capable of labor, in old age or disease, his comfortable maintenance is a legal charge upon his master" and that "the nature of the relation of master and slave begets kindness which exist in no other relation of capital and labor."

Virginia planter George Fitzhugh, in 1850, argued, "The slaves are well fed, well clad, have plenty of fuel, and are happy. They have no dread of the future—no fear of want. The slaveholder is the least selfish of men . . . the institution of slavery gives full development and full play to the affections."

"The slaves are wronged?" wailed a southern minister from his pulpit. "They live with moral, intellectual, and civil improvement, a state of protection, comfort and happiness never known elsewhere in any period of the world's history."

Throughout the eighteenth century and much of the nineteenth, southerners managed to use their political influence in Congress to make any efforts by the anti-slavery forces to change federal laws on slavery futile. Southerner George Weston said accurately the federal government had always been neutral. Its leaders had neither tried to abolish slavery or expand it to the territories. Slavery existed because people wanted it, not because, as anti-slavery advocates suggested, it was too firmly established. To think otherwise, he wrote, was "a piece of shallow hypocrisy."

But the growing number of anti-slavery societies and abolitionist newspapers worried southern slaveholders. They were also concerned about two dramatic decisions of the U.S. Supreme Court. The high court ruled in 1841 that slaves who mutinied aboard the schooner *Amistad* could not be returned to slavery and were free men. Just a year later, in 1842, in *Prigg vs. Pennsylvania,* the high court frightened slaveholders when it ruled that state courts and police in northern states no longer had to honor the provisions of the 1793 federal Fugitive Slave Act, a law that forced them to cooperate with slaveowners seeking to retrieve runaways. The ruling resulted in dozens of personal liberty laws enacted by northern state legislatures which forbade the retrieval of slaves.

The efficiency of the Underground Railroad, especially after *Prigg vs. Pennsylvania*, the personal liberty laws and the anti-slavery effect of the Second Great Awakening, caused southern slaveowners considerable worry about their economic future. Cotton prices were rising weekly as European markets absorbed as many millions of cotton bales southern plantations could produce at the very moment when it seemed the courts, long the allies of the slave states, threatened to topple two hundred years of slavery.

Then, in 1846, the United States became entangled in a war with Mexico. American forces, led by General Zachary Taylor, defeated Mexican armies at Monterey and Buena Vista and, in victory, were awarded the northern provinces of Mexico, consisting of what is now New Mexico, Arizona, California, and parts of Texas, Utah, Nevada, and Wyoming. Southerners, fresh from a political victory in the admission of Texas as a slave state in 1845, clamored for the legalization of slavery in these huge new territories. The dispute over the new territories spilled into the halls of Congress in 1850. Northerners insisted that the new states of California, Arizona, and New Mexico come into the Union as free territories. Southerners were determined to bring those lands into the Union as slave territories and, at the same time, of paramount importance to them, force Congress to write a tough new law on fugitive slaves, which had to be enforced, to crush the Underground Railroad once and for all.

4

THE VIOLENT YEARS

On September 11, 1851, Edward Gorsuch, along with his son, nephew, and other relatives, rode to tiny Christiana, Pennsylvania, a village close to the Maryland border, to look for his two runaway slaves. They believed the slaves were hiding at the home of a black freedman, William Parker, whose house they imagined, correctly, was also a stop on the Underground Railroad. Area farmers had been told that the men might be searching for slaves. Their appearance on horseback on a road nearby prompted the farmers to sound a sharp, loud bugle and several horns as a warning.

The men carried writs signed under the new Fugitive Slave Act of 1850 and were accompanied by U.S. Marshal Henry Kline, who told the men that, according to law, he would help them apprehend the fugitives. They found the two fugitives hiding in the Parker home with several other runaways, read them the legal writs, and ordered them to return to Maryland. The runaways refused. A moment later, Castner Hanaway and some Quakers who lived in the area arrived and challenged the legality of the writs. As the argument with the slaveowners and the marshal grew longer, several dozen freed blacks and white farmers who lived nearby arrived with clubs and guns and surrounded the group. Everyone began shouting.

A shot was fired, someone was shoved, and a battle ensued. The slaveowners pulled out their guns and began firing at the blacks gathered at a distance of several yards, wounding three who, bloodied, stumbled away. Gorsuch was struck on the back of the head with a club and was shot and killed as he fell to the ground. His son, frantically coming to his aid, was

53

shot and wounded. The other slavecatchers fled and the runaways and Parker were whisked off on horseback, where they were eventually taken to Canada and safety.

The Underground Railroad had become a dangerous road. The bloody battle at tiny Christiana was the first fatal confrontation between members of the Underground Railroad and slaveowners. It came at the beginning of one of the most turbulent decades in American history, a decade that started and ended with a controversy over slavery, a period that saw the dissolution of the powerful Whig Party, the creation of the Republican Party, constant bloody clashes over slavery in the western territories, a dramatic conservative turn by the U.S. Supreme Court on slavery, and the political rise of an unknown young Illinois lawyer named Abraham Lincoln.

The Fugitive Slave Act was passed by Congress in 1850 to mollify southern politicians in order to gain their support for the complex Compromise of 1850, hammered out by Henry Clay and others to prevent the threatened secession of some southern states. Under the terms of the Compromise, California was admitted as a free state and the slave trade was abolished in the District of Columbia, concessions to northern politicians. The territories that are now the states of Arizona, New Mexico, Nevada, and Utah were permitted to decide for themselves whether they wanted slavery and a new Fugitive Slave Law, this one with sharp teeth, was enacted to placate the South. The new states and territories would fill in the map of the United States; the new fugitive slave law would tear it apart.

The new Fugitive Slave law overrode *Prigg vs. Pennsylvania* and all other state, county, and city laws and court decisions that prohibited state and local officials from aiding slaveowners in their pursuit of runaways. Under the harsh terms of the new law, owners and hired slavecatchers could travel into the northern states to retrieve runaways. Local governments not only could not stop them, but they had to cooperate. The law also permitted the pursuit, capture, and return of *any* former fugitive, no matter how long the former slave had lived as a free man in the North. The law also provided for stiff fines and prison terms for any freed blacks or white citizens who aided the runaways. The Fugitive Slave Act embittered the workers of the Underground Railroad, at whom it was aimed, but instead of frightening them into giving up their work, as intended, it strengthened their resolve.

The Compromise of 1850 began a decade of political, social, and cultural conflicts that shook the United States. Harriet Beecher Stowe, whose brother was a leader in the New England Underground Railroad, and who at times harbored fugitives herself, published *Uncle Tom's Cabin* in 1852, and the book, which outlined the horrors of slavery and made heroes out of Underground Railroad workers, became an instant bestseller. In 1856 Charles Sumner, a fiery anti-slavery U.S. Senator from Massachusetts, was nearly beaten to death on the floor of the Senate by a southern congressman. Another book, *The Impending Crisis in the South,* by southerner Hinton Helper, published in 1857, was a savage attack on the slave system and argued that many businesses in the southern states, even cotton plantations, could be run more efficiently with paid labor. Throughout the northern states, more abolitionist newspapers began to publish and anti-slavery societies grew in strength. The Underground Railroad grew, too, following the bloodshed in Christiana.

The major problem the workers on the Underground Railroad, and all abolitionists, struggled with in the early 1850s was their inability to convince the majority of northerners that their cause was just. Despite both debates over the 1820 and 1850 political compromises, residents in the free states did not see slavery as any real threat to them and were content to permit its continuance in the southern states where it existed. The abolitionist movement was also thwarted by the inability of its members to have any real success in politics in order to change public policy. The movement had eloquent speakers and some passionate ministers, but it had few people on its side in public office. Some abolitionists had won offices in the late 1840s as candidates of splinter groups, such as the Liberty Party and Free Soil Party (abolitionist Salmon P. Chase became governor of Ohio under the Free Soil banner), but the Democrats and Whigs still controlled most state and county governments and the national government. The abolitionists had mobilized a small, committed group of Americans, but they were unable to include significant numbers of the huge working class in the free states, a class of people growing rapidly as the industrial revolution expanded.

All of that changed in 1854 with the passage of the Kansas-Nebraska Act. The bill, sponsored by Illinois Democratic Senator Stephen A. Douglas, allowed residents of the Kansas and Nebraska territories, like those in other western territories, to decide for themselves whether they would allow slavery within their borders. The bill hit northerners like a thunderbolt. They suddenly realized that Kansas and Nebraska alone (the territories included what are now the states of Kansas, Nebraska, South Dakota, North Dakota, Colorado, Wyoming, and Montana) made up nearly 20 percent of the land in the United States. If slavery was introduced there it might also be introduced in the New Mexico and Utah territories, then in the far western territories of Washington and Oregon, and would soon be legal in two-thirds of the United States.

Reaction to the Kansas-Nebraska Act was swift. Abolitionists throughout the North held huge public rallies featuring the movement's best speakers and won tens of thousands of converts to the cause. More and more ministers, who were previously willing to leave slavery in the hands of God, now urged their congregations to see it as a moral evil. More Americans, in large cities and small villages, joined the Underground Railroad and pledged to help even more slaves escape to freedom.

The biggest effect of the bill, however, was to draw more and more moderates into the anti-slavery movement. The people entering the movement in 1854, horrified by the Kansas-Nebraska Act, were not zealous ministers and poets, but newspaper editors, bankers, and businessmen, men with substantial influence. They did not join the movement before 1854 because the issue did not seem important enough and, with the Whigs and Democrats dominant, they found no party to which they could give their allegiance.

Now, however, they had an issue and a home—the brand-new Republican Party. The new party sprang into existence as a direct consequence of the Kansas-Nebraska Act of 1854 at the same time that the old Whig Party was collapsing as its northern members, rebelling against its southern members over slavery, left the party. The Whig Party disappeared by 1854 and was immediately replaced by the Republican Party. The new party's leaders did not dance around the slavery issue, as the old Whigs and Democrats did. They were firmly against it. The establishment of the Republican Party also gave powerful old Whigs, such as New York Senator William Seward, a home. He and hundreds of former Whigs joined the Republican Party, giving it instant respectability and, in the elections of 1855 and 1856, substantial and immediate influence in Congress.

But the real strength of the party was the tidal wave of new members who, driven by the slavery issue, wanted to participate in politics. By the middle of the 1850s, the Second Great Awakening had faded as a powerful evangelical religious movement, but its converts began to see politics as a field in which they could achieve all of its moral and religious goals. They would use politics, particularly anti-slavery politics, to do God's work. The 1850s was a time, too, when young men began to break away from traditional farm life and seek careers in the growing cities. These young men saw the new party as the one in which they could have immediate influence.

Politics had also become entertainment. Gifted speakers would anger, enthrall, amuse, and inspire large crowds who gathered in fields lit with torches after long parades, led by bands playing newly written political songs, snaked through communities. Some of the best public speakers in the land were new Republicans, men such as Seward, Chase, and former Illinois Congressman Abraham Lincoln, who returned to politics in 1856 and joined the Republicans.

Many successful merchants and factory administrators who prospered as industrialization changed the face of the economy in the free states began to connect business success with moral responsibility. They came to believe that their prosperity was not merely a reward for hard work, but something that now required social or moral action on their part. The world was changing because of capitalism and those who profited from capitalism had to change it for the better, working to improve the conditions of people's lives. Nothing symbolized this view like the slavery issue and many newly successful businessmen saw work in the anti-slavery movement as a way to give back to society and say thanks for their own recent success.

The Republicans sensed a dramatic change in the philosophy of workers in the free states, too. Workers for many years accepted slavery because the system forced the blacks to occupy the bottom rung on the labor ladder. Their employers made them believe that they were better off as lowly paid white workers who were free. After all, no matter how little they were paid and how badly they were treated, at least they were white.

By the middle of the 1850s, workers, whether individually or as members of the growing labor unions, began to feel that the presence of slavery undermined their future. They believed slavery demeaned all workers, and felt they were treated like slaves, particularly in factories. Republican leaders jumped on this growing change of heart among workers and went farther, convincing white workers that no laborer should be treated as badly as a slave.

Further, the new Republicans told millions of white workers that they should be appalled to think that their bosses compared them to slaves if, indeed, slaves were such wretched creatures. Workers, who also felt that the slave economy hurt their chances for future success in a growing industrial world, embraced the Republican Party, finally giving the anti-slavery movement a party that reached out to everyone and that had a genuine chance to overturn two hundred fifty years of slavery. The success of the Republicans in the 1856 elections, when they captured control of the House of Representatives, thrilled abolitionists and workers on the Underground Railroad, who believed that the new Republicans could control both houses of Congress and perhaps even capture the White House in 1860.

Politics became very public and very confrontational in the 1850s, particularly after the Dred Scott decision of 1857, in which the U.S. Supreme Court ruled that slaves were not only property, but could be returned from a free state to a slave state by their owners. The decision upheld the Fugitive Slave Act and increased southerners' boldness in recapturing runaways. Confrontations erupted in many northern towns and cities. Nowhere was this battleground more apparent than on the Underground Railroad. The Christiana rebellion was just the first in a series of confrontations, some of them violent, arising from the passage of the Fugitive Slave Act. The conductors on the Underground Railroad were just as determined to protect runaways as slavecatchers, armed with the new law, were to capture them. The decade was filled with gun battles, rescue raids, and court fights, all taking place at the same time that the number of escaping slaves dramatically increased.

Southerners felt relieved that they finally had legislation to bring back slaves and halt the exodus of thousands more on the Underground Railroad. South Carolina planter William Pettigrew said that, "The South . . . has gained a great triumph" and Henry Clay told audiences, north and south, that although some might be opposed to the Fugitive Slave Act, in time they would see its benefits.

Many northern newspapers, while not directly condemning the Fugitive Slave Act outright, complained that it represented yet another congressional political victory for southern slavers. The editor of the *Boston Advertiser* wrote that residents of the free states were "entirely disgusted and disheartened in finding themselves placed in the unexpected position of being held to a compromise which is binding on but one side."

The Fugitive Slave Act was despised by the abolitionists. One anti-slavery minister, Charles Beecher of New York, wrote in a widely published sermon in 1850, "This law . . . is an unexampled climax of sin. It is a monster iniquity of the present age, and it will stand forever on the page of history as the vilest monument to infamy of the nineteenth century." New York Whig Congressman Amos Granger called it "a stain to our country." Governor Chase of Ohio, one of the Midwest's fiercest abolitionists and a lawyer who had defended several runaways himself, prophetically said that the law "will produce more agitation than any other which has even been adopted by Congress."

Many northerners opposed the federal act but believed there was nothing they could do about it. Anti-slavery public officials told crowds that as unpopular as it was, the Fugitive Slave Act had to be adhered to. Massachusetts Senator Sumner told people to obey it, but urged them to let their representatives know how they felt. "I counsel no violence. There is another power, stronger than any individual arm, which I invoke; I mean that irresistible public opinion inspired by love of God and man which, without violence or noise, gently as the operation of nature, makes and unmakes laws."

Most anti-slavery speakers disagreed with the law-abiding Sumner and told their audiences to disobey it. At large public rallies, dozens of state, county, and local abolitionist societies voted to disregard it. Many small villages passed statutes outlawing the capture of runaways, in direct defiance of the new federal law. Even the city council of Chicago approved statutes to nullify it. Most agreed with Theodore Weld, who called the Fugitive Slave Act a crime, not a law, and warned that God made all men his moral agent and that "he who robs his fellow man of this tramples upon right, subverts justice, outrages humanity, unsettles the foundations of human safety, and sacrilegiously assumes the prerogative of God."

Boston's Underground Railroad leader Theodore Parker growled in front of one crowd that he would do all in his power "to rescue any fugitive slave from the hands of any officer who attempts to return him to bondage . . . What is a fine of a thousand dollars, and jailing for six months, to the liberty of a man?" Philosopher Ralph Waldo Emerson told audiences that "this is a law which every one of you will break on the earliest occasion— a law which no man can obey or abet the obeying, without loss of self-respect and forfeiture of the name of a gentleman."

Perhaps the most forceful in his condemnation of the law, and determination to ignore it, was Frederick Douglass, the former slave, spirited to freedom on the Underground Railroad. Douglass had become one of the nation's most popular anti-slavery orators. He was constantly reminded that many congressmen did not worry about the law, that it would have little effect and wind up as a postal "a dead letter." He barked back that the only way to prevent it from becoming a "dead letter" was "to make a dozen or more dead kidnappers."

The ferocity of the protectors in the North was more than matched by that of the runaways in the South who quickly discovered that the uproar over the Fugitive Slave Act encouraged many southerners, who previously wrote off a few escaped slaves as a business loss, to hunt them down. The slaveowners now had the law on their side. The hunts were often limited by the owners' resources. Wealthy planters with one hundred or more slaves, several overseers, and a staff of white laborers could dispatch a posse after a runaway. Small farmers with only a few slaves or with a friend might chase a runaway themselves. Many pursued slaves intently through their own state, but gave up once the slave made it to a free state.

Their reluctance to follow slaves into northern states may have saved the life of the traveling ornithologist, Dr. Alexander Ross. He once rescued a young woman in Delaware, wrapping her in blankets and placing her in a prone position in the front of his carriage as he drove her toward Philadelphia. A short time later he heard the muffled sound of horses hooves somewhere in the distant darkness behind him. He drove on, certain he was about to reach the Pennsylvania border. When he was within a mile or two of the border, the men following him gained ground. He turned and saw two horsemen within two hundred yards. Ross bent down and reached for the two pistols he always kept loaded and within reach. He leaned out the side of the carriage and began firing at the men, who fired back. He hit one of the horses, which fell, and felt a bullet from the second man whiz past his head. He drove as fast as he could, his pistols discharged and useless, but the remaining rider pulled up and stopped.

One of the saddest stories of fugitives fleeing from slavecatchers took place in the winter of 1856, when a brutal cold wave caused the Ohio River to freeze over near Covington, Kentucky, across the river from Cincinnati. Runaways prayed for the river to freeze because it made crossing easier. Seventeen slaves left their plantations and stole their owners' large sled, pulled by a fresh team of horses. They rode all night, made it to the river undetected and managed to walk across, some slipping and some sliding on the thick ice and snow beneath their feet. Among the group was Robert Garner, his wife, Margaret, and their four children. They were spotted and soon found themselves trapped inside a house.

The house was surrounded by slavecatchers and the Garners refused to give up. Robert shouted that he was armed and Margaret told her husband that she would not let her children be taken back into slavery, that she would kill them before that could happen.

Robert tried to calm his wife, but was distracted as the men began to break through a living room window. He pulled out his revolver, aimed straight ahead and shot the first man who climbed through the window. Bedlam followed. Several men picked up a large pole and used it as a battering ram to knock down the front door. Robert Garner backed up a step as the men pushed through the door and began firing, hitting four of them. His wife's eyes widened as she saw the men rush in. Certain they would be returned to the plantation, and unwilling to let her children grow up in slavery, she turned to the right, grabbed a large butcher knife on a table and used it to fatally slash open the throat of her youngest daughter, the child she told her husband she loved the most, killing her. The men pushed her husband against a wall, grabbed his gun and then seized Margaret as she lunged at a second child with the knife, knocking the weapon to the floor before she could use it again.

A judge ruled that the Fugitive Slave Act, which permitted Margaret Garner's capture, superseded Ohio's statute on murder and the slave mother had to be tried under the federal law and, if found guilty, returned to her plantation in Kentucky. The 1856 trial attracted a large audience that jammed the Cincinnati courthouse on the morning of the trial. All eyes were on the twenty-three-year-old Margaret. She was an attractive mulatto woman, just over five feet tall, with Caucasian features on the upper part of her face and African features on the lower part. She had wide, arched eyebrows, bright eyes, and an intelligent, inquisitive demeanor about her. There was a scar on the left side of her forehead, a reminder that slaves don't talk back to overseers. She had a crisp, clean white handkerchief tied around her neck and a larger, bright yellow handkerchief wound as a turban around her hair. She held her nine-month-old baby in her arms; her small sons, aged six and four, sat on the courtroom floor next to her. Spectators strained to see them.

Among the spectators was Lucy Stone, a well-known abolitionist public speaker who drew large crowds wherever she appeared. It was rumored that she gave Margaret Garner a knife during a jailhouse visit and told her to kill herself rather than return to slavery. She did not do that, but when called to explain the rumor to the court, she delivered a passionate defense of the slave mother, brooding at the defense table.

She said she had made a deeply disturbing visit to the woman in her jail cell. She addressed the hushed courtroom audience, "I told her that a thousand hearts were aching for her, and that they were glad one child of hers was safe with the angels. Her only reply was a look of deep despair, of anguish such as no words can speak . . . The faded faces of the negro children tell too plainly to what degradation female slaves must submit. Rather than give her little daughter to that life, she killed it. If in her deep maternal love she felt the impulse to send her child back to God, to save it from coming woe, who shall say she had no right to do so?"

Her pleas fell on deaf ears. The judge, citing the Fugitive Slave Act, ruled that Ohio could not try her for murder and ordered that she be turned over to her Kentucky owner, who soon left Cincinnati with Margaret and her husband. Margaret's tragic story did not end there. The slave owner sold Margaret and her husband to a slavetrader who transported them down the Mississippi toward New Orleans, where they were to be hired out to yet another owner. Their riverboat was involved in a serious accident, and Margaret and her child, both manacled, were hurled into the river. Several men jumped in to rescue them, but the child drowned. The men said that when they got Margaret onto the deck of the ship and had to tell her the child was dead she wept . . . in joy . . . and said she was glad another of her children had avoided slavery and gone back to God. Margaret Garner was eventually sold to a slaveowner in New Orleans and died of typhoid fever two years later. (Garner's story was the basis for Toni Morrison's novel *Beloved,* recently a movie starring Oprah Winfrey.)

Many of the more dangerous escapes were made through single states with slavecatchers at the heels of the fugitives. The runaways, who devised clever flights, usually won the race. One of the more heated chases took place in Clear Springs, Maryland, in 1856. Owen Taylor and his wife Mary Ann, with their baby, his brother Otho and his wife and their two children, and a third brother, Ben, waited until their owner, farmer Henry Fiery, and his family went to sleep on Easter Sunday. They then met at the stables. Owen, a mechanic and wheelwright, had outfitted the master's large riding carriage to carry extra weight and bundles. He hooked up a team of the owner's fastest horses and put the women and children inside the carriage. He and his brother drove the carriage very slowly out of the stables and off the farm and then, as soon as they turned on to the main road, urged the horses to run north as fast as they could.

It wasn't long before Fiery woke, realized both his slaves and carriage were gone, and ordered slavecatchers to chase them. The Taylor brothers knew they would be pursued and that the pursuers would be looking for a carriage, so they devised a careful plan. The men drove the horses to the point of exhaustion to Harrisburg, Pennsylvania, and parked the horses and carriage at the rear of an inn, making it appear as if they were sleeping inside. The group then went to the Harrisburg rail depot and hid until a Philadelphia bound train arrived. They sneaked onto one of the baggage cars and traveled to Philadelphia, where they found members of the Underground Railroad, and safety. Back in Harrisburg, slavecatchers were still interviewing guests at the hotel.

Others, fearful of capture under the Fugitive Slave Act, traveled in large groups. The groups of runaways often arrived together at Underground Railroad stops and their protectors were often heartbroken by their stories. One of the saddest concerned Joseph Cornish. Over the years, through manumission and self purchase, Cornish had won freedom for his wife and five children, who lived nearby while he worked at the home of Captain Samuel LeCount, of the U.S. Navy, in Dorchester County, Maryland. Cornish was a hardworking member of the area slave community and was a very religious man, eventually becoming minister of the African Methodist Church in the Dorchester area, which served slaves and freedmen. In January 1856, Rev. Cornish learned that LeCount planned to sell him to a traveling slavetrader who would take him south, far away from his family. The minister learned of a group of slaves planning to flee Dorchester and he joined them, even though he had to leave his family behind.

Slaves were not only the targets of increased hunts, but victims of betrayal by some of the weaker workers on the Underground Railroad. The cotton business had become so profitable by the late 1850s, with nearly five million bales sold each year, that the value of slaves had dramatically increased. Slaveowners began to offer high bounties for captured slaves, as much as $2,000 for a pair (over $50,000 in today's money), and several were turned in by northern Underground Railroad conductors.

The betrayed fugitives did not go willingly and found that violence was a routine part of escape. Henry Predo, a huge, twenty-seven-year-old slave, led a group of seven others in a daring escape from their Buckstown, Maryland, plantation in 1857, only to be turned in by a protector he trusted, who received $3,000 for his duplicity. Predo and the others were taken to a local jail by the sheriff who forced them up the stairs, at gunpoint, to third-floor cells. Predo suddenly turned and smashed into the sheriff, knocking him to the floor. He told the others to run back down the stairs, but the sheriff was on his feet, gun in hand, trying to fire at them. The group raced down the stairs and saw an open door to the left. They burst into what was the sheriff's apartment.

"Murder! Murder!" screamed his terrified wife as the fugitives ran into the room, the sheriff in pursuit. Predo took a shovel leaning against the fireplace and used it to scatter coals around the room, which started a small fire on the corner of a rug. He then grabbed an andiron from the fireplace and used it to smash open a window, the glass hitting him in the face and chest. He hurried the other seven out the window and then leaped twelve feet to the ground.

The sheriff, his wife screaming, made it to the window a moment later and, seeing Henry start to get up from the lawn, aimed his pistol at him and fired. The gun misfired, however, and Predo ran to the fields with his friends before the sheriff could reload. All in the group escaped.

Robert Jackson and three others escaped from Martinsburg, West Virginia, in October 1853. They found protection in the northern part of the state in a barn owned by a man who told them he was in the Underground Railroad. He cooked the four a hearty breakfast, charging them one dollar, and then hid them in the hayloft of his barn. A few hours later he arrived with eight men, all armed with pistols and lariats. The four were brought out of the hayloft to the floor of the barn and, when they could not produce passes, were told they would be tied up and taken back to their plantation.

One of the runaways pulled out a gun. "Betrayer!" he yelled and shot the farmer, who dropped to the dirt floor. The eight slavecatchers turned toward the slaves. One man grabbed Jackson by the collar of his jacket. Jackson pulled a gun from the waistband of his trousers and shot him in the side of the face. Jackson pushed him away and drew out a sword he carried, trying to escape the barn by slashing wide circles in the air with the blade. He was shot by a second slavecatcher wielding a shotgun and fell near the door, bleeding badly. A second slave was shot in the face and then beaten to the ground with the butts of the pistols. The other two surrendered without injury and Jackson and the other wounded man were held prisoner at a nearby tavern until their wounds healed, but managed to escape with a rope supplied by a black woman who worked there as a cook.

There was no more safety for runaways at sea than on land as slavecatchers, armed with their writs and protected by the law, became bolder. Thomas Sipple and Henry Burkett, with their wives and two friends, were fearful of violence on the roads of Maryland when they decided to escape their Kunkletown plantation in 1857, so they saved their money and purchased a small rowboat for six dollars and set out across the Delaware Bay toward New Jersey. They did not get very far before they saw a much larger rowboat approaching, carrying several white men with shotguns.

The white man in charge of the group grabbed the chain of the fugitives' boat and tried to pull it close to his own rowboat. "This is not your boat. We bought this boat and paid for it," Sipple shouted.

A second white man pulled his flat wooden oar out of the water and swung it so hard at Sipple that it broke in two when it came down on his head, knocking him to the floor of the rowboat. Burkett then raised his oar and knocked the white man down. The pursuers, frightened as their boat began to tip beneath them, rowed backward as the escaping slaves rowed hard away from them. A few moments later, several of the white men aimed their shotguns at the fugitives and fired, hitting each of the four men and wounding them slightly. They continued to row faster and were quickly out of range as the frustrated slavecatchers turned back toward the Delaware shore.

Sea flights were as popular as land journeys. Schooners that criss-crossed the Great Lakes, particularly those operating on Lake Erie sailing from ports in Ohio and Pennsylvania to Canada, often carried fugitives who were sneaked on board by friendly seaman or an anti-slavery captain. Other schooners sailing across Lake Michigan and Lake Superior also secretly transported slaves. Ferries that crossed the narrow Detroit River often carried runaways from Michigan to Canada. Many others escaped by hiding on ships that carried cargo up and down the East Coast. These ships took slaves to Detroit, Chicago, Philadelphia, New York, Boston, and New Bedford. From there, slaves followed routes that brought them to Canada at entry points at Niagara Falls, Detroit, and Quebec and Montreal along the St. Lawrence River.

Slaves who escaped in the cargo holds of ships, a popular means of flight since the 1820s, began to encounter trouble, too, as slavecatchers, armed with their writs, started to force captains to let them search their boats in southern and northern harbors. One target were the vessels commanded by Captain William Fountain, of Boston. The well-known Fountain was a big man with an oversized head, large eyes, and thick, bushy black eyebrows. He had become a successful merchant captain for New England shippers who made frequent stops in Virginia ports to pick up cotton and tobacco.

Fountain sailed large cargo ships and found it easy to hide up to thirty fugitives on his vessels. The fugitives usually remained hidden during the voyage, but often had the run of the ship, particularly if it became frozen in ice on winter trips and all on board had to work to free it from the ice. On a typical voyage, Fountain would drop anchor at night at a desolate area a few miles outside of Boston, New York, or Philadelphia, depending on his destination, and lower the runaways with one or two seamen over the side in rowboats. They would row to shore and depart, undetected, and the next day the captain would sail into port.

Fountain did more than just sail runaways north. Records show that he also cooperated with freed black Underground Railroad workers employed at the docks to let them know he had room for prospective runaways. His operation was so complete, and his network so efficient, that he soon began to arrive in southern cities with lists of slaves to seek out for passage, their transportation already paid for by family or friends in the North.

Fountain had to halt the loading of a shipment of wheat in Norfolk in November 1855, when the mayor of the city and a group of policemen boarded the boat and told him they suspected that twenty-one slaves who had escaped from nearby plantations that morning were hidden on his ship. The mayor ordered the police to take long spears and thrash the bales of wheat in the hold in an effort to stab any fugitives hiding in them. They lanced several dozen bales of wheat without hitting or finding anyone. Next, he ordered the police to use their axes to slash open cabinets and sections of the deck where secret compartments might exist. The police hacked away for several moments as Fountain stood idly by, seemingly unconcerned by the search.

Finally, after establishing an uncaring demeanor, and as the police apparently came closer to the hiding place of the fugitives, the captain became angry. He told the mayor that the men were wrecking his ship and that if that was the purpose, he could do a better job of it himself. To the surprise of the mayor, the captain grabbed one of the axes from a policeman and raised it above his head.

"How about here?" he barked and slammed the ax down onto the deck with all of his strength, sending shards of wood flying, hitting several policemen.

He raised it up again. "Or here?" he shouted and then slammed the ax down again, sending up another shower of splinters.

The mayor stopped him, convinced there were no fugitives aboard. "We are barking up the wrong tree," he told the police and the men left the boat. The rest of the wheat was loaded and the officers began to search other boats, looking for the twenty-one escaped slaves. A few hours later, Fountain's ship sailed out of the harbor, the runaways safely below, hidden in storage bins.

Slaves began to run away in large groups—for protection in numbers against violence—and often carried guns and knives. Groups of ten or more slaves arriving at Underground Railroad homes in lower Pennsylvania were not uncommon in the late 1850s and one conductor was startled to open his door and find twenty-eight runaways in his front yard.

The stepped-up efforts of the slavecatchers did not reduce the number or boldness of the runaways or the effectiveness of the Underground Railroad. Several newspapers predicted, correctly, that the tough new law would backfire on the southerners who worked so hard to gain its passage. The editor of the *New York Tribune* wrote in April of 1851 that northerners "will burden its execution with all possible legal difficulties and they will help slaves to escape all the more zealously." What followed was a decade of political turbulence as the exodus of slaves from southern plantations grew larger and the battles to save them grew fiercer.

5

THE RESCUERS

Frederick Jenkins, nicknamed Shadrack, felt very comfortable living in the middle of the large black community in Boston, a city that also had the largest abolitionist population in America. He fled the Norfolk, Virginia, home of the U.S. naval officer who owned him in the spring of 1850 and, through that summer and winter in Boston he felt safe and secure. Friends got him a job as a waiter, which enabled him to pay rent, buy a new set of clothes, and even attend the theater once in a while. Life was good. Then, in February 1851, his owner, seething that his slave had run away, hired a slavehunter to go to Boston and find him. Since his owner was a military officer, he was careful to observe all the guidelines of the new Fugitive Slave Act. His hired hunter obtained the necessary papers and writs from a judge in Virginia, contacted a U.S. marshal in Boston, and went with him to arrest Shadrack, seen going to work, and arranged for deportation on February 15.

The runaway was immediately taken to the office of a commissioner appointed to hear fugitive slave cases under the new law. There the slave-hunter's papers were checked and approved and permission was granted for Shadrack to be returned to Norfolk. While this hearing was taking place, a large crowd of freedmen and white residents, including many of the city's leading abolitionists and underground leaders, gathered in the square outside the courthouse. A thin line of police tried to hold back the angry mob, but after a few minutes a wedge of more than one hundred men pressed hard against the police line and broke through. The men ran into the courthouse and burst into the hearing room. Several shoved the startled marshals aside and others seized the runaway, who was very pleased to see them, and pulled him from the room.

Before the police in the street had a chance to regroup, the men surrounding Shadrack took him out a side entrance of the building and, protected by a growing mob, hustled him down the street and over a bridge to Cambridge, where a borrowed carriage waited. Shadrack was put into the carriage and it began to race out of Cambridge. The mob filled the street behind it to prevent the police from pursuing it. The carriage was far out of Boston and headed for an underground safe house in the suburbs.

Shadrack's rescue was the first of several in the 1850s. The Underground Railroad leaders did everything more zealously then as the Fugitive Slave Act and Dred Scott decision threatened to end their effectiveness. The railroad leaders joined with local abolitionists, whether in large cities or small towns, to insist that slavecatchers show legal writs and then, even when they did, to tie them up in local courts in an effort to block the return of any captured slaves. Although it turned out to be a hopeless effort in most cases, it did serve to make prospective slaveowners aware that they now had to pay lawyers as well as slavecatchers and it probably convinced many that the total cost of a capture was not worth the value of the slave.

Judges and specially appointed fugitive slave commissioners, bound by the new law, had to permit the capture of runaways in free states. They also had to honor legal writs and, after proper judicial hearings, were compelled to let many of the slavecatchers return south with the runaways. The precedent was set in the very first fugitive slave law case in New York City, just weeks after the legislation went into effect in 1850. Slaveowner Mary Brown, of Baltimore, sent an agent to New York to bring back a runaway, James Hamlet. The runaway was legally apprehended and the slavecatcher showed his writ to the local fugitive slave commissioner, who sent Hamlet back to Baltimore (abolitionists quickly raised $800 to purchase his freedom). A month later, in Detroit, Michigan, precedent was set when a runaway was apprehended and taken to court by his captor and a federal marshal, despite a gathering of several hundred freed blacks who badgered the slavecatcher and marshal. The slave would have been sent back south, but friends raised $500 and purchased his freedom. In Indiana's first case, in November 1850, a local magistrate, checking writs, turned over a woman, her daughter, and grandson to a slavecatcher who took them back to Kentucky.

All fugitive slave law cases were heavily publicized. The abolitionist papers initially filled their columns with the trials and rescues, but by the early 1850s the large mainstream newspapers, whose editors were caught up in the anti-slavery crusade themselves, began to cover the cases, too. The enormous amount of coverage the cases received spurred leaders of the abolitionist movement and the Underground Railroad to push even harder for acquittals and rescues. Newspapers of the day often carried stories published in other newspapers, so stories about fugitive slave controversies in any northern state were read by people in all the states. This attention by the press was one of the key reasons why the abolitionist movement gained such prominence by the late 1850s.

Court proceedings involving runaways about to be sent back into slavery often attracted large and boisterous anti-slavery crowds and gained enormous publicity, even if the runaway was sent south. One of the first large public demonstrations took place at a hearing under the Fugitive Slave Act for Georgia runaway Thomas Sims, captured in Boston. As the hearing progressed and Sims appeared to be losing, a group of abolitionists, including Thomas Higginson, who would later gain fame as leader of an all-black regiment in the Civil War, plotted to rescue him from jail. They instructed him to leap from his third-floor jail cell window to a wagon loaded with mattresses to cushion his fall far below, but wondered if the prisoner would cooperate in the risky escape. Higginson said, "We were not sure that Sims would have the courage to do this rather than go back to certain slavery." The plot died when jailers cemented bars into Sims' cell window that night; a second attempt to free him from the boat assigned to carry him south after he lost the hearing went awry when the boat sailed before rescuers could reach it.

Another failed attempt to rescue a captured slave took place in 1859 in Ohio following the capture of a man named Jackson, whom a federal commissioner ruled had to return to his plantation. His departure from a jail in Zanesville created a riot and several hundred freed blacks and Underground Railroad workers charged the armed guards surrounding the runaway. Both sides exchanged gunfire and guards beat off the men attacking with clubs and hustled Jackson out of the state.

Sometimes runaways were freed but their protectors were not. Two entire runaway families were captured in Sandusky, Ohio, and taken to court. The town's mayor, F. M. Follette, perhaps confused or perhaps playing dumb, told the captors he had no reason to hold them but would turn them over to a federal magistrate. Within an hour, a large crowd of blacks and whites assembled at the mayor's office, and Rush Sloane, hired by the freedmen as a lawyer, demanded the release of the families because the mayor had not technically either arrested them or turned them over to a federal magistrate. The slavecatchers argued vehemently but when they were forced to explain why they had no writ, the fugitives' lawyer, ignoring the mayor, told the crowd to carry the families out of the building, which they did. The mayor said nothing and the families were taken to Canada, although Sloane was arrested for interfering and jailed for his actions.

Runaways were sometimes rescued in daring raids. Seven months after the liberation of Shadrack in Boston in 1851, another sensational rescue occurred in Syracuse, New York, as the city was crowded with delegates to the Liberty Party political convention and visitors to the annual Onondaga County Fair. A runaway named William Henry, known as Jerry, had escaped his Missouri owner and settled in Syracuse, where he lived in the free black community and worked as a cooper. He was seized on October 1, 1851, after the issuance of a proper writ, and taken before Fugitive Slave Commissioner Joseph Sabine. A group of several black and white men charged into the hearing room and rescued Jerry, battling their way out of the building trying to make their getaway. They were caught by city police and Jerry was taken to jail. The hearing resumed later that afternoon, while at the same time some of the nation's leading abolitionists, in town for the political convention, met to plan a rescue.

These men were convinced that a highly publicized rescue would not only free the runaway, but show the nation that the abolitionists and Underground Railroad leaders were a force to be reckoned with and that the attendant publicity would deter other slaveholders from trying to kidnap other runaways. Gerrit Smith, one of the leaders of the group, said, "A forcible rescue will demonstrate the strength of public opinion against the possible legality of slavery and this Fugitive Slave Act in particular. It will honor Syracuse and be a powerful example everywhere."

The men waited until the hearing was adjourned late in the afternoon and the marshals left the courthouse. Jerry was taken back to the local police station, where he would remain until the hearing resumed the following morning. A few hours later, a large mob of black and white men stormed the police station, guarded by only a few officers who were quickly overwhelmed, and freed Jerry. He was taken out of the building, put in a carriage and driven out of Syracuse, eventually to Canada.

Another successful rescue occurred in Oberlin, Ohio, in 1859 when a crowd of 200 men, women, and children, black and white, stormed a hotel where slavecatchers held runaway John Price, who had lived in the area for two years. They broke into the hotel room, grabbed Price, and hustled him downstairs to a waiting carriage that whisked him northward and to Canada.

Southern planters and politicians urged the federal government to prevent rescues and prosecute anyone who aided in them. One Louisiana senator, referring to the Boston rescuers as "a mob," said that slaves were like cows who had roamed into someone else's pasture and "should be returned upon demand." They were confident they would win this latest battle, too, because their political influence continued in both houses of Congress and in the executive branch. Slaveowners had always found friendly receptions at the White House.

Most of the early presidents owned slaves. James Polk, elected in 1844, owned several dozen. In 1841, while serving as governor of Tennessee, Polk received a letter from a British organization imploring him to abolish slavery. Indignant, Polk said the letter was "an impertinent and mischievous attempt on the part of foreigners to interfere with one of the domestic institutions of this state." Zachary Taylor, elected president in 1848, owned more than one hundred slaves on his Kentucky plantation.

His successor, Millard Fillmore, was from New York and not a slaveholder, but he supported the Fugitive Slave Act. In 1851, after the Shadrack case, he issued a proclamation that ordered "all well disposed citizens to rally to the support of the laws of their country, and requiring and commanding all officers, civil and military, who shall be found within the vicinity of the outrage, to be aiding and assisting by all means in their power in quelling this and other such combinations." Fillmore told every district attorney in the country to vigorously prosecute anyone who aided in the rescues, white or black.

The next two presidents, Franklin Pierce and James Buchanan, the latter taking office in 1856, followed their predecessors' policies. Pierce, who was from New Hampshire, told anyone who complained that as chief executive he had to follow the laws. Buchanan supported the Fugitive Slave Act and throughout his administration constantly ordered the Justice Department to cooperate with men retrieving slaves and force state and local courts to cooperate. President Buchanan was so emphatic in his support that in his very last State of the Union message, December 3, 1860, he

Fiery orator Wendell Phillips was a staunch abolitionist from Boston and one of the key speakers at the 1854 rally to protest the arrest and extradiction of runaway Anthony Burns. (Courtesy of the Society for the Preservation of New England Antiquity)

reminded Congress that the Fugitive Slave Act was "carried into execution in every contested case since the commencement" of his term and noted that in fifty-seven cases tried during his term of office, forty-five slaves were remanded back to their owners, twenty of them at U.S. government expense.

An example of the tenacity of White House and federal government support of the then four-year-old Fugitive Slave Act and a key moment in the battle against slavery occurred back in 1854 during the presidency of Franklin Pierce when yet another fugitive, Anthony Burns, of Virginia, was apprehended in Boston by his owner, Charles Suttle. When it appeared that Burns would be sent back to his plantation, a group of abolitionists broke up their meeting at Boston's historic Faneuil Hall and surged toward the federal courthouse, where Burns was held captive. Rocks were thrown through windows and axes were used to break down doors. A guard was killed in the struggle. Men reached the room where Burns was held, but could not get to him. The mayor of Boston ordered two companies of artillery to guard the courthouse and later that day President Franklin Pierce approved an order directing federal troops to surround the building.

Burns lost his case and a week later arrangements were made to move him from the courthouse to a ship headed to Virginia. City officials were determined that he would not be rescued. Burns was surrounded by two hundred armed guards as a carriage took him to the ship at the wharf for extradition to Virginia. Federal troops, again ordered by the president, joined more militia in holding back the crowds along the route and regrouped at the wharf to form a wedge of uniformed guards, weapons drawn, to protect the ship and get Burns aboard it. The guards had to carefully move his carriage through a throng of 50,000 angry Bostonians who lined the city's streets and hung out of second- and third-story building windows, shouting epithets at the slaveowner and the soldiers. Throughout Boston, stores were closed and a coffin hung from one building; thousands mourned as the ship prepared to sail.

The Burns trial and extradition under the Fugitive Slave Act, more than any other rescue or political event, even more than the Kansas-Nebraska Act, was the single most important turning point for many northerners who had little interest in slavery. The small, vibrant abolitionist movement had little political power, but the Burns trial would send hundreds of thousands of moderate Americans into the anti-slavery movement. As one Bostonian whose politics were changed forever as he watched federal troops march Burns to the wharf said: "We went to bed one night old fashioned, conservative, Compromise Union Whigs and waked up stark mad Abolitionists."

The federal government's determination to carry out the Fugitive Slave Act and to punish rescuers across the country was now also thwarted by the rising tide of public opinion against slavery, inside and outside the justice system. Many northern state legislatures, in the mid- and late-1850s, controlled by anti-slavery Republicans and anti-slavery Republican governors, passed more "personal liberty" laws which were supposed to protect slaves from capture. The state courts were supposed to uphold these laws. In the few contested cases between federal and state "personal liberty" laws, the federal law was always upheld, but the time-consuming bureaucratic chaos caused by the prosecution of state laws probably deterred more kidnapping forays by southerners. One popular tactic of anti-slavery state district attorneys was to arrest slavecatchers and agents of slaveowners, even when they had legal federal writs, on violation of personal liberty laws. None of the agents ever went to jail, but they were detained for weeks at considerable hotel and meal expense and wound up spending large sums of money for their legal defenses.

Most juries in northern states refused to cooperate with federal efforts to fine and imprison abolitionists and Underground Railroad workers who participated in the rescues of runaways who were arrested and scheduled for deportation. The lawyers for the rescuers, anti-slavery men themselves, were among the best in America. Congressman Thaddeus Stevens, later the leader of the Radical Republicans during the Civil War, speaker of the House, and the sponsor of the Reconstruction Act, defended several runaways and men and women who aided them and was chief counsel for the men involved in the Christiana, Pennsylvania riot. Two midwest lawyers who routinely defended fugitives and Underground Railroad workers were

Samuel Chase, later governor of Ohio and Lincoln's Secretary of the Treasury, and Rutherford B. Hayes, later President of the United States.

The Christiana case was a good example of a brilliant lawyer defending local farmers in front of a jury of their peers. The U.S. government indicted forty-five of the men involved in the killing of slaveowner Edward Gorsuch and charged them with treason. In a courtroom packed with spectators, Stevens argued forcefully that the men might have killed someone, but they were certainly not guilty of treason. Then he turned the entire case around. Calling the slavecatchers "outlaws," he told the jury that the men who killed Gorsuch were small farmers, like themselves, defending their land, families, and neighbors.

He said of the slavecatchers, "[They are] a gang of professional kidnappers. That they had not only upon one, but on two or three occasions, in the dead of night, invaded the houses of the neighbors, of white people, where black men lived, and by force and violence and great injury and malice, without authority from any person on earth, seized and transported these men away."

Then, he pointed at the defendants proudly and said that they were neither traitors nor murderers. Stevens told the jury, "We want to show that he [defendant] went there with pure and laudable motives, and we will undertake to show that what he did after he was there was honorable, humane and noble."

Following his eloquent defense, the jury acquitted the first defendant in the case and the government then dropped charges against the other forty-four. Eight men involved in the Shadrack rescue in Boston were indicted and brought to trial—four black and four white—and juries refused to convict any of them. The highly publicized rescue, in which a mob of abolitionists freed a runaway from a jail in Syracuse, brought swift government retribution. Indictments were brought against twenty-six men, twelve black and fourteen white. A jury did find the one man who directly attacked a policeman guilty, but charges against all the others were dropped.

Many legal officers, whether judges, district attorneys, or law clerks, aided the anti-slavery cause through inattention. All were bound to honor the Fugitive Slave Act and to hold civil trials for suits involving slaveholders seeking to recover the value of a slave harbored or rescued by men and women on the Underground Railroad. The suits were duly filed and recognized in many districts, but, oddly, court calendars always seemed to be full and suits were pushed back months and even years. The cases were either dropped by slaveholders, who got tired of lawyers' fees, or dropped by the courts.

Other judges and court officers helped the underground movement by doing little beyond routine procedures, which enabled them to delay slave-hunters in order to give runaways time to flee. Such was the case of a posse of slavecatchers in Michigan who managed to burst upon a Quaker Village in Cass County and abduct several dozen men, women, and children who had previously escaped from Kentucky. The men were soon surrounded by another posse of two hundred anti-slavery riders, who arrested the slave-catchers and freed their victims. A savvy local judge, following routine pro-cedure, ordered the Kentucky raiders held for trial without bail on kidnap charges brought by local underground leaders. The judge waited a few days, until the runaways were safely in Canada, and then held a quick trial at which all charges were dropped and the raiders were permitted to go back to Kentucky—empty-handed.

Some radical anti-slavery advocates carried out dangerous raids into southern and border states to rescue slaves, often using stops on the Under-ground Railroad to make their escape. The best known was John Brown, who orchestrated one of the most daring and highly publicized escapes in 1858. Just before Christmas, Brown met a slave who pleaded with him to free him, his wife, two children, and another man from a Missouri farm where they lived. Brown led two companies of men into Missouri and freed the five. While there, they learned of five other slaves at a nearby farm and rode through the night to bring them to freedom. During the struggle, one of Brown's men killed the slaveowner.

Brown decided to take the twelve liberated slaves all the way to Canada, a journey of over 1,500 miles, and informed men and women in the Under-ground Railroad in that part of the country of his trip. Eager for a chance to help the nationally famous abolitionist, they did all they could for Brown. Some helped him move his party of fugitives and men across the frozen Missouri and then into Iowa, where others arranged for them to board a train headed for Chicago. There, abolitionist Allen Pinkerton, the detec-tive who would later work for Abraham Lincoln, met them and escorted them to Detroit. The slaves and abolitionists hid out at safehouses in Detroit for three days and then, on March 12, crossed the Detroit River by boat. With Brown supervising the crossing, they arrived safely in Windsor, Canada.

The journey took nearly three months. Brown, who did little in secret, in contrast to others involved in Underground Railroad work, immediately wrote letters to newspapers describing his achievement. The raid not only heartened slaves and Underground Railroad leaders throughout the north, but alarmed slaveholders in the southern states, who increased security at plantations and even sold some slaves or transferred them to other, more southern, plantations to keep them out of Brown's grasp.

John Brown was a highly publicized white abolitionist. Other raiders were former slaves who had successfully escaped to free states or to Canada and wanted to liberate others. These included Josiah Henson, who frequently left the safety of Canada to rescue slaves in Kentucky, and John Parker, a black Ohio foundry worker who risked his life many times in bold raids into Kentucky to free slaves. Some runaways returned to liberate members of their family. Some staged these raids quickly, hiding in nearby woods or fields and getting word to family members to meet them during the night. Then, usually supplied with horses, they made their getaway, using stops on the underground to move out of the county and state. One runaway who left his family behind and missed them desperately even returned to slavery in Kentucky. He sorrowfully told his owner that he had no luck in Canada, that people there treated him badly, and he was unable to find work. "And," he went on, "those people called abolitionists that I met with on the way are a mean set of rascals. They pretend to help the niggers, but they cheat them all they can. They get all the work out of a nigger they can, and never pay him for it." At least on the plantation, he could live in some comfort and be with his family, he told the owner.

In order to make his complex plan work, the slave needed to prove he preferred the plantation. He lived there through the winter and much of the spring, working hard enough, and being obedient enough, that his owner seemed to believe he wanted to remain. Throughout his time he conspired with other slaves in planning an escape. In late spring, with his wife and children, he led a group of fourteen off the plantation and took them to a now familiar series of safe houses on the Underground Railroad into Ohio and then Canada.

Raiders were always in danger of capture and imprisonment as were any southerners suspected of aiding runaways. Although southerners supported their slavery-driven economic system, only twenty-five percent of them owned slaves. Many of the other seventy-five percent favored the system, but were indifferent about slavery. A few southerners were opposed to it and some of them, although only a handful, became the most secretive members of the Underground Railroad. Some urged slaves owned by harsh masters to try to escape and head north. Others became just as active at aiding escaping slaves as any leaders in the free states. When caught, they paid a high price, such as one southern conductor, a wealthy merchant named Jones (a pseudonym) who lived in Louisville, Kentucky, near one of the slave markets.

Slaves were kept in Louisville for several days before and after their being purchased and transportated to a new home. During this time, some escaped and found temporary protection in the homes of freed blacks or in the woods behind slave quarters on nearby plantations. They were put in touch with Jones, who was opposed to slavery. Jones moved them out of Louisville in an expensive stateroom on the packet boat that traveled the Ohio River between Louisville and Cincinnati. He turned the key over to a runaway, or to a group of runaways, who would remain in the private room, undetected, until the boat reached Louisville. While they were en route, Jones wrote underground leaders in Louisville that several "packages" were headed their way and could be picked up at the wharf on the day the boat was due to arrive. Jones usually aided in the escape of between twenty and thirty runaways a year.

Jones paid for slaves' passage for several years but was eventually found out, arrested and, after two trials, sent to prison for two years. His lawyer appealed and won a third trial, but Jones was unable to make bail. In poor health, he did not think he could live much longer. His Underground Railroad friends in Ohio came to his aid, raising the bail money, freeing him from jail, and moving him to Cincinnati, where they convinced him to skip his third trial and go into hiding.

Others who aided slaves were not so lucky. One Kentucky man who worked to free slaves, Calvin Fairbanks, was captured in 1845 and sentenced to four years in prison. Later, in 1858, he was convicted of aiding fugitives again and given an eleven-year term, but was paroled in 1864.

The runaway slaves who settled in Canada and the free states—freed black men and women, college students, the abolitionist leaders, John Brown and his raiders, the Underground Railroad workers, and hundreds of men and women involved in the anti-slavery cause—had, by the late 1850s, made slavery the single most divisive issue in the United States. Unable to attract the attention and support of powerful politicians for over two hundred years, the anti-slavery movement soon found important champions on the national political scene who were no longer hesitant to speak out against it.

One was William Seward, the former governor and then U.S. senator from New York, who frequently harbored fugitives at his Auburn, New York, home. He had become the best-known public figure in America by 1858, when, in Rochester, New York, he said that slavery would shortly bring about an "irrepressible conflict" that would engulf the nation. He told the crowd that people no longer could keep quiet about their hatred of slavery, as they had for generations. "I know, and you know, that a revolution has begun," he said of the anti-slavery crusade, "and all the world knows that revolutions never go backwards."

Another was former congressmen Abraham Lincoln of Illinois, a long-time opponent of slavery, which he called "a moral, social, and political evil." Opening his campaign for the U.S. Senate in Illinois in 1858, he told the Republican Convention, "A house divided against itself cannot stand. I believe this government cannot endure, permanently half slave and half free . . . It will become all one thing or all the other. Either the opponents of slavery will arrest the further spread of it, and place it where the public mind shall rest in the belief that it is in course of ultimate extinction; or its advocates will push it forward, till it shall become alike lawful in all the states, old as well as new—North as well as South."

Two years later, on November 6, 1860, Lincoln was elected the sixteenth president of the United States. Shortly after his election, the first five of what would eventually be eleven states seceded from the Union to form the Confederate States of America. The new country carved out of the southern states vowed to protect slavery under states' and property rights' doctrines and to go to war if necessary. On April 12, 1861, one month after President Lincoln urged the southerners to return to the Union in his first Inaugural Address, Confederate forces bombarded Fort Sumter, in the harbor of Charleston, South Carolina, to ignite the Civil War.

Slavery continued in the southern states during the first few years of the Civil War, but on January 1, 1863, Lincoln's Emancipation Proclamation, which freed most of the slaves in the United States, went into effect and most of the four million men and women in bondage became free; all were freed by the end of the war. After the war, with the passage of the thirteenth, fourteenth, and fifteenth amendments to the U.S. Constitution, they became full citizens of the United States. The Underground Railroad had made its last trip.

The *Amistad* Africans lived in this wood-frame dormitory, built just for them, in Farmington. The man who built it, Austin Williams, was one of the underground leaders in the village.

Opposite   The *Amistad* Africans spent several months in Farmington, Connecticut, as abolitionists worked to raise money to return them to Sierra Leone, in Africa. They arrived to a packed reception at the First Church of Christ Congregational, a hub of anti-slavery activity. (Photo by Author)

PART II: THE TRAVEL GUIDE

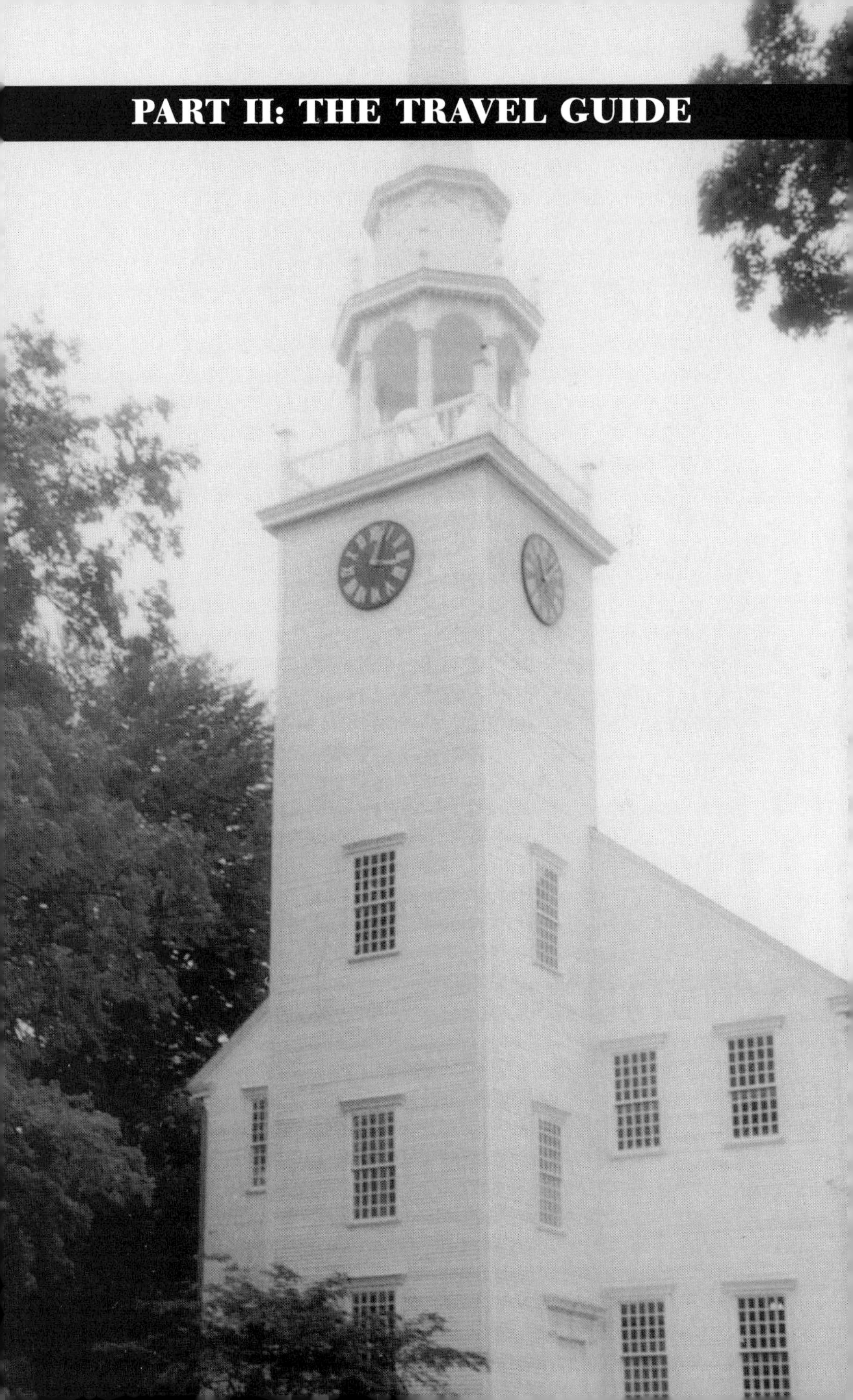

INTRODUCTION

Americans' interest in visiting historical sites to remind them of their country's past is not new. Each year, millions of Americans take day or weekend trips or vacations to visit such places as Bunker Hill, in Boston, Independence Hall, in Philadelphia, the Lincoln Memorial, in Washington, D.C., Gettysburg, Pennsylvania, The Alamo, in San Antonio, and restored historic seaport centers in Baltimore, Charleston, and Savannah. They visit the houses of famous figures in the nation's history, such as the homes of Abraham Lincoln, George Washington, Andrew Jackson, and Thomas Jefferson.

Until recently, there has been little interest in visiting sites of the Underground Railroad because few were identified and restored. No national organization made recognition of the Underground Railroad part of its mission. Although books have been written about the Underground Railroad, most Americans still know little about it.

There were always some public Underground Railroad sites and they always intrigued tourists. Everyone who dined at the Dobbins House restaurant, in Gettysburg, over the years was touched by the secret room there where slaves hid, which the proprietors proudly display. The story of the runaway slave girl who lived at the Kelton House, in Columbus, Ohio, and was married there has warmed the hearts of visitors since the 1970s.

For years, owners of taverns or restaurants that once served as underground stations showcased their fake closets and trap doors to visitors. "Every single person who hears the story of our hideaway in the cellar is enchanted by it and when I pull up the trap door in the middle of our dining room there are gasps from all," said Bill Foakes, manager of Randell's Ordinary Inn, an Underground Railroad site turned into a restaurant

This hideaway at Randell's Inn in North Stonington, Connecticut, was originally built as a food cellar. It was renovated as a tiny room beneath the farmhouse kitchen in the 1830s. The abolitionist owners covered it with a rug and table. (Photo by Author)

in North Stonington, Connecticut. But the number of open underground stations was few and public interest slight.

Since the early 1980s, however, interest in the underground has increased dramatically. The era following the Civil Rights movement of the 1960s and 1970s saw the publication of hundreds of books about African-American history. The mid-1970s televison series *Roots* and later films such as *The Biography of Miss Jane Pittman, Glory, The Color Purple, Amistad,* and *Beloved* gave Americans a new understanding of the history of African Americans. The 125th anniversary of the Civil War, 1986–1990, resulted in many new works about the Civil War era and slavery. Ken Burns' PBS-TV series on the Civil War gave Americans a compassionate look at the suffering of slaves. Television now has the History Channel and several cable networks that feature weekly series on the Civil War history era.

Said Georgeanne Royter, director of Kelton House, in Columbus, Ohio, "I think that there is tremendous interest in American history today, and, added to that, great interest in the stories never fully told, such as African-American history and women's history. The Underground Railroad is part of that story and people seem to want to learn all they can about it."

There is a feeling, too, that Americans may be able to solve the problems of the present by looking to the past. "Here was a time when blacks and whites worked together, risking their lives, for freedom. Many feel that we can use those lessons to bridge the racial gaps in the country today," declared Iantha Ganntwright, associate director of the National Parks and Conservation Association, which helped form the National Network to Freedom, a civic group to promote the study of the Underground Railroad.

"The white and black people who ran that railroad showed incredible courage. Today, we look back at what they did and know that we can do it again," said Gerald Johnson, director of Kanisha House, a community center in Elyria, Ohio, located in an 1840s underground home.

These events created a groundswell of interest in the Underground Railroad, perhaps the last great untold story of the nineteenth century. A federally funded, $60 million national center and museum for the Underground Railroad in Cincinnati, Ohio, is now in the planning stages and will open in 2002. Eleven states now have Underground Railroad asso-

This is one of the hundreds of letters written in the 1890s to Ohio State professor Wilbur Siebert from underground organizers detailing their illegal operations. (Courtesy of the Ohio Historical Society)

This home of abolitionist John Holyoke in Brewer County, Maine, was believed to be an underground station by local historians but they could not prove it and prevent the state from demolishing it for a highway expansion. When the house was knocked down, workers found underground tunnels and clothing in the rubble. (Courtesy of the Brewer County Historical Society)

ciations. People connected to underground research and tourism formed the National Network to Freedom. Most states now showcase underground sites in their tourism brochures and many county and local travel offices offer tours of underground homes. Dozens of county and local historical associations now highlight their underground stations and also offer tours. The National Park Service took the Underground Railroad under its wing in the 1980s and its employees have done extensive work in restoring sites and promoting the underground from coast to coast. And, in 1998, President Clinton signed a bill that gives $500,000 a year for at least three years to the Park Service to promote its Underground Railroad sites.

The Underground Railroad was a secret organization and membership in it was against the law, so it has always been difficult to determine how many actual stations were used. Exhaustive research in the 1890s by Dr. Wilbur Siebert, of Ohio State University, which included documents from the underground leaders themselves, showed 250 sites in Ohio alone. Siebert claimed that Maine had over 50 sites and Pennsylvania more than 100. Work by historian Charles Blockson, of Temple University, Philadelphia, for the National Park Service in the 1980s uncovered many more sites.

Determining whether an old home was an underground station has always been difficult. Some old houses whose owners hoped were underground stations were not. Many of the unusual open spaces in people's basements were not slave hideways but old closets. The trap doors in kitchen floors were not entrances to hideaways for runaways but common cellars. Odd-looking rooms shoehorned into attics were not spaces where runaways took refuge from slave hunters but extra bedrooms for children. However, other homeowners who had no idea their house had any history discovered genuine hiding rooms, false basements, and tunnels during renovations to add a bedroom or garden. Some even found remnants of fugitives' clothing and collections of abolitionist newspapers.

Many homes in addition to those on Siebert's list have been recognized as probable underground sites through the use of different, modern historical tools. No records were kept of individual homes in most towns, but historians have used family diaries and letters, newspaper clippings, computer-based genealogical searches, and local oral histories to pinpoint underground stations with reasonable accuracy.

Over the years, many underground stations disappeared the way all buildings disappear. Some were demolished to make way for housing developments, some burned, and some were victims of the wrecking ball to make way for interstate highways. Some very old buildings were simply razed by their owners and replaced with new housing. Brittle old barns, hideways long ago, were knocked down and replaced by modern structures. One-hundred-year-old escape tunnels were filled up with dirt and rocks. Little was done to preserve these sites.

"It is very sad to see an old building, a building that might have been part of history, destroyed for a road or a bridge," said Brian Higgins, head of the Maine Underground Railroad Association. "An 1850s building we strongly suspected was an underground station was torn down to make room for highway expansion and in the rubble we found tunnels and clothing that surely belonged to slaves on the run."

While there was little support for underground site preservation in the past, there is considerable support today. "People are realizing the need to preserve Underground Railroad heritage now just as they realized the need to save colonial era sites and Civil War sites," said Kevin Cattrell, who works for the Schoellkopf Geological Museum in Niagara Falls, New York, and conducts Underground Railroad tours in the area. David White, head of the Connecticut Historical Commission, agrees. "I think, too, that people are starting to see that their story is the story of all the people, black and white," he said. Newspaper columnists have joined historians in the battle for preservation. One of them is Joe Blundo, of the *Columbus* (Ohio) *Dispatch*. He argued in one of his 1998 columns that more federal and state support was needed not only to run existing public underground homes, but to repair recently discovered, quite shabby sites. In an emotional column about the need for preservation of underground sites, Blundo wrote that "the homes of the brave are falling down."

Today, there are approximately 350 standing sites, whether museums, restaurants, inns, office buildings, farms, churches, or private homes. More are uncovered each year. The Maine underground group has targeted 55 additional sites that might have been stations and a group in Ohio has a list of nearly 200 prospective sites in 88 different counties. A Kansas group is studying dozens of possible sites.

Most of these sites are private homes. The men and women who live in them now feel a deep sense of history. "The thing that struck me was just how brave these people were. The family in my home risked their lives and huge fines to protect slaves, people they did not know and would never see again," said Ron Bernard, who lives in an underground station in Farmington, Connecticut. "And, most important, they never saw themselves as heroes, just people helping other people in trouble."

That sense of the past lives with all homeowners. "Sometimes I'll just open the trap door to the basement hideaway and stare down there. It gives me goosebumps," said artist Robin Hay, of Farmington, Connecticut. Homeowners often plunge into local history. "We have found dozens of letters, diaries, and documents that bring to life the history of this place," said Sue Brewer, who lives in an underground home in Sheffield, Ohio.

Tour guides at public underground sites claim people are surprised and awed by the stories they tell. "When I explain that a barn across the way was used as an underground hideaway, and that Mark Twain's in-laws hid slaves, I can see the eyes of the people widen," said Richard Koch, a guide at the Mark Twain Home in Hartford, Connecticut.

The biggest impact is on children. "We get over 2,000 schoolchildren a year who tour the home with their teachers and to them it is an introduction to a whole new world," said Janice McGuire, of the Levi Coffin home, in Fountain City, Indiana. Some children already know some of the story, though. "I'll start talking about Frederick Douglass or Harriet Tubman, and little fourth-graders will tell me they know all about them," said Ruth Schwaegerle of Oberlin, Ohio, who is a guide at an underground home there. "I'm so encouraged that the children know part of the story through school."

How to Use the Guide

This guide pinpoints the known probable underground sites, private and public, based on the most current available research from local, county, and state historical societies. The sites are divided into six geographic areas: Northeast, Atlantic, Midwest, West, South, and Canada. Each area is then broken down into separate states and then into cities and towns, with street addresses where possible. It also lists, where available, organizations such as historical societies or tourism offices that can offer assistance. Tours are offered of individual houses, collections of homes, and, in some cases, entire towns. Tour offices are listed, with phone numbers. The purpose of the guide is to outline day trips, places to visit on weekends, or vacations for readers, particularly families, interested in the Underground Railroad. The guide enables you to select key sites and plan a comprehensive trip. This structure was devised by the author, who has visited many of the sites himself.

Where possible, local histories are added to the physical descriptions of the homes or businesses listed in the guide. In addition, short biographies accompany the homes of the famous participants, such as William Seward and John Brown. Within the appropriate geographic areas, stories of famous slave rescues by freedom-minded crowds are included, along with accounts of men and women who secretly rescued hundreds of slaves, such as Harriet Tubman and John Parker. There are stories about underground leaders, men like Levi Coffin and the Rev. John Rankin and women like Laura Haviland. Also included are stories about critical events in the story of the Underground Railroad, such as John Brown's raids in Missouri and Kansas, the capture of the *Pearl* and the *Amistad* and their slaves, the secret underground work of abolitionist newspaper editors and writers, such as John Greenleaf Whittier and Henry David Thoreau, and the death and imprisonment of underground leaders. The guide will not only alert readers to underground sites they can visit, but add much history about this rich, yet largely untold chapter of the American story.

THE UNDERGROUND RAILROAD
IN THE NORTHEAST

C A N A D A

Lake Huron

Toronto   Lake Ontario   NEW
                           Syracuse
                    Rochester   Auburn
St. Catherines Lewiston   Peterboro
            Niagara Falls
Ft. Erie   Ithaca
            Buffalo
                    Peterboro

Dresden
            Jamestown
Lake   Erie
Erie   New Richmond
Windsor   Williamsport
Amherstberg   Muncy

                Bellefonte   Pottsville
        New Castle   Milroy
            Smithport   Harrisburg
        Beaver Falls
            Pittsburgh   PENNSYLVANIA
OHIO
        Washington   Gettysburg
    Brownsville Mercersburg

Ohio River

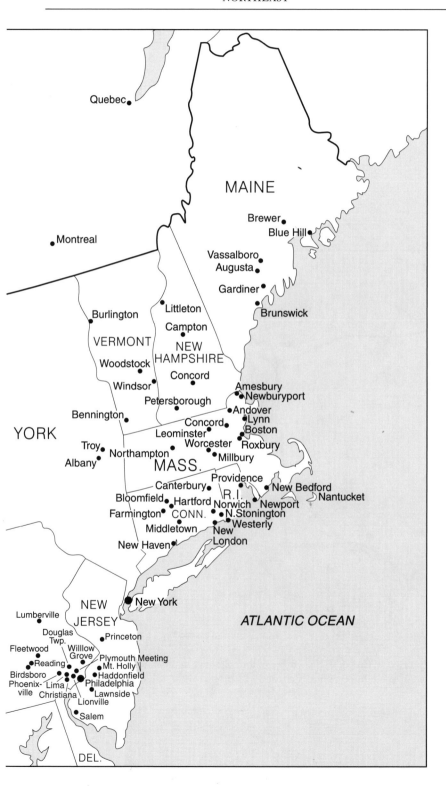

Quebec

MAINE

Montreal

Brewer
Blue Hill

Vassalboro
Augusta

Gardiner

Burlington

Littleton

Brunswick

Campton

VERMONT

NEW
HAMPSHIRE

Woodstock

Concord

Windsor

Amesbury
Newburyport

Petersborough

Andover

Bennington

Concord
Lynn
Boston

YORK

Leominster
Worcester
Roxbury

Troy
Northampton
Millbury

Albany

MASS.

Providence

Canterbury

New Bedford
Nantucket

Bloomfield
Hartford
R.I.
Norwich
Newport

Farmington
CONN.
N.Stonington

Middletown
Westerly
New
London

New Haven

NEW
JERSEY

New York

ATLANTIC OCEAN

Lumberville

Douglas
Twp.
Princeton

Fleetwood
Willlow
Grove
Plymouth Meeting

Reading
Mt. Holly

Birdsboro
Haddonfield

Phoenix-
Lima
Philadelphia

ville
Lawnside

Christiana

Lionville

Salem

DEL.

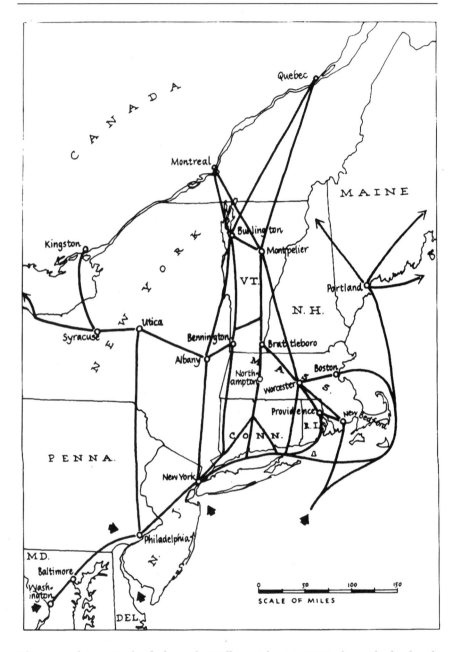

This map of New England, drawn by Wilbur Siebert in 1894, shows the land and sea routes of the Underground Railroad. (Courtesy of the Ohio Historical Society)

NORTHEAST

Connecticut

Connecticut had one of the busiest undergrounds in America because of its location and its large anti-slavery community. There were two main routes through the state. The first started at the seaport of New London, where slaves hidden on ships from southern states disembarked and fled to local safehouses before traveling westward to Old Saybrook to board local steamers for underground stops on the Connecticut River or north on the Thames River from New London to Norwich, Canterbury, Lebanon, Willimantic, Hampton, Putnam, and then to Worcester, Massachusetts. A second line, the most popular, started at the southeastern corner of the state, at Stamford and Wilton. Runaways would travel there on trains with forged papers or by wagons through Westchester County, in New York. They were taken from these towns to the seaport of New Haven, where they were put on another route north that took them to safe houses in Middletown, North Guilford, Meriden, Southington, Berlin, New Britain, and then Farmington. Runaways arriving via ship in New Haven were taken on this same route to the small village of Farmington, which had over a dozen safehouses. Farmington was one of the nation's major underground switching stations because it was located at the intersection of several major turnpikes and the terminus of the Farmington Canal. From this quiet little village on the banks of the Farmington River fugitives were sent on several different routes out of the state. One took them east to Hartford and then north into Massachusetts. Another brought them to Bloomfield, and the home of U.S. Senator Francis Gillette, and then north. Another took them west to Torrington, birthplace of John Brown, then to Winchester and Norfolk and then into Massachusetts and to the town of Northampton. Another route out of Farmington went through the small villages of Avon, Simsbury, Granby, and West Suffield.

* * *

Amistad

In 1839, Mendi Africans, captured in their homeland, mutinied aboard the Spanish schooner *Amistad*. They were on their way to a South American slave market in Guanaja, Honduras. The Africans, mostly strong men in their twenties, overpowered their guards, killed the captain and cook, and seized the ship in a bloody battle. The 36 remaining slaves ordered the only three Spaniards who did not flee the ship into rowboats. The three remaining crewmen agreed to sail the *Amistad* to Africa, but the Spaniards tricked them and sailed to Long Island sound, off the coast of Connecticut. The ship was seized by a U.S. Navy revenue cutter and taken to New London, Connecticut, where the Africans were arrested and charged with piracy and murder. As soon as the seizure of the ship was made public, the Cubans who purchased the slaves sued to have them returned to Cuba.

The Africans were taken to a jail in New Haven to await trial. Within three days of their arrest, the leaders of the abolitionist movement in New England began efforts to free them. A special *Amistad* committee was formed consisting of Reverend Joshua Levitt, an abolitionist editor, Reverend Simeon Jocelyn of New

Cinque was the leader of the Africans on the *Amistad* who mutinied and tried to sail their slave ship to Africa but were captured in Long Island Sound. The U.S. Surpeme Court set them free after a spirited defense by former President John Quincy Adams. (Courtesy of the New Haven Colony Historical Society)

The first *Amistad* trial, at which the captured African slaves were acquitted, was held at the Old State House in Hartford, Connecticut. (Photo by Author)

Haven, and Lewis Tappan, a wealthy New York businessman and abolitionist leader. They engaged lawyer Roger Baldwin to represent the Africans. Since none of the Africans spoke English, Baldwin, with the help of Yale professor Josiah Gibbs, located James Covey, a seaman, who spoke Mendi, to help as an interpreter.

The Africans' trial began in January, 1840 and their leader, Cinque, through the interpreter, gave an emotional defense of himself and his colleagues, charging that they had been illegally seized and sold into slavery. "We are men, too," he declared. U.S. District Court Judge Andrew Judson was impressed by Cinque and Baldwin and ruled that the Africans were free men, not slaves, and therefore could not be returned to their owners in Cuba. The defendants were jubilant and, outside, throughout Hartford, church bells rang to greet the news.

The euphoria of the defendants and the abolitionists in New England was short-lived, however, because the government of Spain still insisted that the Africans were "cargo," not people, and had to be returned. The case then went to the U.S. Supreme Court. Fearful that the highest court in the land would be influenced by international and domestic politics, the *Amistad* Committee convinced former President John Quincy Adams to aid in the defense of the Africans. Adams gave a brilliant summation to the high court, in which he said that Cinque was right to mutiny against the men who captured him, just as men throughout history were right to fight oppression. The Supreme Court then upheld the lower court ruling, freeing the *Amistad* Africans.

The freed blacks, in prison for two years, could not return to Africa until money was raised to pay for their expensive passage. Abolitionists wanted to place them in a community where they could be protected by anti-slavery residents, be housed, fed and clothed properly, and have religious guidance until funds could be found. They also sought a town close to main turnpikes and waterways so that Cinque and others could travel with the abolitionists to fund-raising meetings throughout New England. And so on March 19, 1841, the Africans headed for Farmington, Connecticut, a village of 2,000 people on the banks of the Farmington River. A winter storm had just swept through the central part of the state and when the freed Africans arrived in town the little village was covered with a white blanket of snow.

Amistad Tourism: The premier of the movie, and its release on videotape, has spurred nationwide interest in the *Amistad* story. Connecticut now offers several exhibits concerning the Mendi prisoners and a variety of local and statewide tours are available. Since the premiere, several exhibitions concerning the *Amistad* story have opened on a permanent basis. One is at Battel Chapel, College Avenue, Yale University; another can be found at the Connecticut Historical Society, One Elizabeth Street, Hartford; and a third is housed in the Wadsworth Atheneum, 600 Main Street, Hartford. An acting troupe stages a thirty-minute dramatization of the *Amistad* trial at its original site, the Old State House, Central Row and Main Street, Hartford, each Tuesday at noon and Thursday at 1 p.m. A statewide tour of *Amistad* sites, coordinated by several tourism agencies, offers visitors a three day, two night package. *For information: Greater Hartford Tourism: 1-800-793-4480, Mystic & More Tourism: 1-800-863-6569, or Greater New Haven Tourism: 1-800-332-7829.* The *Amistad* sites are part of a larger program called Freedom Trail, which also honors the Underground Railroad and the state's African American heritage. *For information on the Freedom Trail: Connecticut Historical Society: 860-566-3005.*

* * *

FARMINGTON

It was a chilly evening on March 19, 1841, as hundreds of Farmington townspeople packed the First Church of Christ, Congregational, awaiting the arrival of the 36 African men and three young girls recently freed by the U.S. Supreme Court in the celebrated *Amistad* slavery case. The people of Farmington had volunteered to house the Africans until fund-raising groups, some led by the town's underground railroad leaders, earned enough money to send them back to Sierra Leone. The freed slaves came through town in a procession of large sleighs. They were bundled up under furs and blankets as the sleighs, pulled by teams of horses, moved down Main Street toward the church.

The front double doors of the church were flung open and the Africans, led by Cinque, marched in with their Farmington hosts. They shook hands as they proceeded down the main aisle. Everyone surged forward in their pews, the people on the three-sided second floor balcony leaning over the brass rails to look at the freed men and girls.

The members of the church, many of whom were abolitionists and underground organizers, adopted the 39 African men and girls until they could raise enough money to book boat passage back to their homeland. Dozens of townspeople worked collectively to aid the black strangers they knew absolutely nothing about except that they needed help. Some men in town, led by abolitionist lawyers John Norton and John Hooker and businessmen Samuel Deming, raised money throughout New England for the freed slaves' voyage home. They often brought Cinque with them to lecture, through an interpreter. His commanding presence impressed the abolitionist groups whom he addressed and substantial funds were raised at these meetings. Women in town sewed clothes for them. A local tailor made twenty-five pairs of pants for the African men. Three families took in the three small girls. Businessman Austin Williams donated land for a dormitory, which was built after funds were raised in town. Samuel Deming opened a school for the Africans above his general store.

The *Amistad* Africans enjoyed giving acrobatic shows to townspeople. Cinque would stand at the top of the porch stairs at John Norton's home, which overlooked a large lawn that sloped away from the house, and then would somersault his way down the stairs and across the entire lawn to the delight of Norton's children and their friends. Although they never learned much English, they were able to entertain their hosts and the townspeople through elaborate pantomime. They were responsible and respectful, appreciative of the many kindnesses toward them, and made the people of Farmington proud to have known them.

The stay of the *Amistad* Africans encouraged the people of Farmington to become more involved in both the public anti-slavery movement and the secret world of the Underground Railroad. The town had several underground workers before the arrival of Cinque and his colleagues who hid slaves in their homes and moved them north to Massachusetts on the Farmington Canal or by wagons to other communities. Abolitionists in Farmington formed their own anti-slavery society in 1836 and the women in town formed a separate anti-slavery society, but the arrival of the *Amistad* slaves in 1841 energized the people of the small Connecticut village to become deeply involved in the underground.

From 1841 until the start of the Civil War, Farmington not only served as the "grand central station of the underground," as it was nicknamed by abolitionists, but as one of the busiest underground stations in America and one of the few, along with towns such as Oberlin, Ripley, and Xenia, in Ohio, and Fountain City, Indiana, in which a large number of residents took risks to contribute to the work of freeing the slaves. The town had a population of 2,000 in the 1840s, and 110 of the people, about 15 percent of the adult population, belonged to the local anti-slavery society. At any time from 1841 to 1861 there were more than a dozen frequently used safe houses in town and a well organized network of men, women, and children who kept a lookout for strangers who might be slavecatchers, including the young daughter of Horace Cowles, Mary Ann, who, when she saw someone she did not know riding down Main Street, would begin to sing, casually but loudly, a particular children's song that everyone in the neighborhood knew was a coded warning.

Underground organizers in the town were wary of their neighbors as well as strangers. Even though many in town were abolitionists, there was a large contingent of anti-abolitionists, too, who were offended by the more than 100 freed blacks living in Farmington. These men and women formed anti-abolitionist groups that held public meetings and one even shattered a window at the Congregational Church when he threw a rock at an abolitionist minister preaching there.

Farmington's location, at the terminus of the busy canal and the intersection of several well-traveled turnpikes, made it a geographically perfect place for the work of the underground. The community's underground leaders, Austin Williams, Stephen Cowles, Elijah Lewis, Timothy Wadsworth, and Samuel Deming, were all young men when the *Amistad* Africans left in 1841, and were able to carry on their underground work for twenty more years. The underground organizers and their colleagues in Farmington developed sewing circles to make clothes for runaways, had easy access to wagons in the farming area and, through business contacts throughout Connecticut and Massachusetts, could maintain close ties with underground leaders in different towns. Most of the Farmington underground leaders were also financially comfortable businessmen and lawyers who had money to give fugitives on the run—all of which combined to make Farmington the East Coast's leading underground center.

There are two excellent tours of the *Amistad* and Underground Railroad sites in Farmington. One is conducted by staffers at the *Farmington Historical Society: 860-678-1645*. Another is sponsored by *Heritage Trails: 860-677-8867*.

First Church of Christ, Congregational
75 Main Street, Farmington, Connecticut
Open to the public

The white wood frame church and its tall steeple anchors Main Street. The church also served as a meeting hall for the community in the 1840s. All the village's New England style "town meetings" were held there and local boards and organizations met there to conduct their business. The local court was held at the church, with the judge sitting at a table just beneath the ornate pulpit. The *Amistad* Africans arrived at the crowded church on the evening of March 19 and left town after a farewell meeting at the church in November. Meetings to induce members of the congregation to house, clothe, and feed the Africans were held there. The final fund raiser, at which church members donated $1,200 (a large sum at the time) was also held there. Their emotional farewell meeting was attended by more than 1,000 people. The interior of the church was packed with people and all the aisles were filled. Several hundred people stood outside the church, listening to the speeches through open doors and windows.

The church itself and its fiery anti-slavery minister, Noah Porter, leader of the church community from 1806–1866, were never part of the underground, but all of the underground leaders were members of the congregation. They gathered casually on the large tree-lined lawn after services each Sunday and while others talked about the weather, they planned the risky escapes of slaves hidden in town that week.

Slaves hid in the home of Timothy Wadsworth in Farmington and fled to a secret hiding space in the basement, behind a chimney, if there was danger of capture. (Photo by Author)

Timothy Wadsworth House
340 Main Street, Farmington, Connecticut
Private home

The home, now owned by a local artist, had a crawl space under its rear wing that led to a small hiding space behind two stone walls in the basement. The hideaway was only two feet wide, about twelve feet deep and six feet high, but it was enough to protect someone if slavecatchers arrived at the home. "We imagine the runaways simply lived inside the house until they could be moved and were only sent down into this space when someone was after them," said current owner, artist Michael Ariezza. "Every time I see the space it reminds me of the lengths people went to in order to be free."

Horace Cowles House
27 Main Street, Farmington, Connecticut
Private home

One of the three *Amistad* girls lived with the Cowles family in 1841 in the two-story Georgian style home. Horace Cowles, a lawyer and state legislator, died the following year, and his son, Stephen Cowles, returned from Hartford, where he was editor of the *Charter Oak,* an abolitionist newspa-

As a child Mary Ann Cowles sat on the porch of this home in the middle of Main Street in Farmington and would begin to sing a familiar song to warn runaways if she saw strangers riding or walking through town. (Photo by Author)

per, and moved into the house. He soon joined the Underground Railroad, harboring slaves in the large, two-story wood frame home until the Civil War. His young daughter Mary Ann sat on the front porch most of the day watching for strangers riding or walking down Main Street and began to sing a particular song to alert slaves in the area to seek out their hideaways. Cowles became a local banker and community leader and was an underground organizer for twenty years.

"Living here gives you a sense of history, a reminder of how people worked together, at great risk, not just for a month or year, but several generations, to do what they thought was right," said Ron Bernard, the current resident and president of the Farmington Historical Association.

Samuel Deming House
66 Main Street, Farmington, Connecticut
Private school

Deming, along with John Norton and Austin Williams, was responsible for bringing the *Amistad* Africans to Farmington. Later, with others, he ran the underground in town, hiding slaves in his large, two-story home. The outspoken Deming, a wealthy farmer, was also a leader of the town's anti-slavery society and represented the county in the state legislature. The home is now part of the internationally renowned Miss Porter's School for Women.

Deming's Store
2 Mill Lane, Farmington, Connecticut
Open to the public

Today called the Village Store, Deming's Store was a general store in 1841. It was located next to Deming's home and later moved to this location. The underground leader renovated the top right half of the building into a large one-room school for the *Amistad* Africans. They were tutored there six mornings a week. The African men slept in the room at night until a dormitory was built for them. Lawyer John Hooker, brother-in-law of Harriet Beecher Stowe, used the other half of the second floor for his office.

Austin Williams House
127 Main Street, Farmington, Connecticut
Private home

Williams was a hard-working entrepreneur. He started off as a clerk in a local grocery store but in his twenties opened his own store. He then moved into the lumber business, building a lumberyard on the Farmington Canal that became quite profitable. Next, he opened a large, successful wholesale dry goods store in New York City. One of the town's leading abolitionists and underground leaders, Williams lived on a seven-acre parcel of land with a large meadow on its western end. He donated part of it for a large, two-story wood dormitory, paid for by local contributions, where the *Amistad* men lived for the last six months of their stay in the town. There was a large meadow west of the two-story, wood frame home of Williams where the Africans exercised each afternoon and played games. Shortly after his visitors left in 1841, Williams became an underground leader and doubled the size of the dormitory where he built an office for himself. Beneath the office was a secret, 20-foot-long by 20-foot-wide and 10-foot-deep stone, walled room, entered through a trap door in the office. The trap door was hidden by rugs and furniture and dozens of slaves hid there from 1841 until the Civil War. After the war, Williams used the building as an employment office for freed blacks living in the Farmington area.

The people who have lived in the office, now an apartment, enjoyed being a part of history. "I love history and old things and the idea of actually living in an underground railroad station, and where the *Amistad* Africans lived is very special to me," said artist Robin Hay, one of the residents. "Everyone who visits me is intrigued by the secret room."

Elijah Lewis House
738 Farmington Avenue, Farmington, Connecticut
Private home

Lewis, a successful farmer and another underground leader, housed slaves whenever they were traveling through the area in his two-story, white clapboard home, surrounded by a neat white picket fence. If strangers were spotted in town, he ordered the slaves to squeeze into a small hole in the side of his chimney and temporarily sealed them in with a large stone until the danger passed.

Riverside Cemetery
Garden Street, Farmington, Connecticut
Open to the public

Deming, Norton, and Williams are buried here. In the summer of 1841 the Africans interred one of their own, a teenager named Foone, who, despondent from two years of jail and trials and uncertain if he would return to Africa, drowned himself in the Farmington Canal. Adjacent to the cemetery is the town meadow, where the Africans were given ten acres of farmland to raise their own crops for food.

Noah Porter House
116 Main Street, Farmington, Connecticut
Private home

Noah Porter served as minister at the Congregational Church for sixty years. His daughter Sarah founded Miss Porter's School, which became a well-known private women's academy. A leader in the anti-slavery movement, Porter was host to Margru, one of the young African girls staying in Farmington. She lived with him and his family for eight months and was treated like any other girl in the village.

Art Guild
Church Street, Farmington, Connecticut
Private home

The large building was used by abolitionists for their meetings and, ironically, by anti-abolition groups that surfaced from time to time in Farmington.

Barney House
11 Mountain Spring Road, Farmington, Connecticut
Open to the public

The Barney House is now an elegant conference center owned by the University of Connecticut and the site of many weddings. Abolitionist leader John Norton lived there in the 1840s. The grandson of a governor of New York, Norton amassed a fortune as a young man through the operation of various stores in Albany. He became a large stockholder in the New York Central Railroad and served as its president. He moved to Farmington in the late 1830s and built Barney House which, then, as now, was surrounded by huge sprawling green lawns. Most of the operations involving the care of the Africans were coordinated by Norton, who became a close friend of Cinque, lovingly described as "the black prince" by Norton's young son Charles. Cinque raced to Barney House to tell Norton of Foone's drowning.

BLOOMFIELD

Francis Gillette Home
511 Bloomfield Avenue, Bloomfield, Connecticut
Private home

Gillette's home near Hartford, his first and main residence, was one of his two safe houses on the underground line that ran from New York through the State and up into Massachusetts and Vermont to Canada. Gillette came from a wealthy family and founded a company that later became Phoenix Mutual Insurance. He was deeply involved in the anti-slavery movement and politics. Gillette was elected to the state legislature in 1832 and 1838 and twice sponsored bills to permit blacks to vote. He joined the anti- slavery Liberty Party as soon as it was formed and was its candidate for governor of Connecticut several times in the 1840s and early 1850s. In 1854, a coalition of Free Soilers, Whigs, and temperance voters in the state legislature sent him to the U.S. Senate, where he proudly voted against the Kansas-Nebraska Act.

In 1853, Gillette, a second cousin of Harriet Beecher Stowe, and his brother-in-law purchased a 100-acre farm near Hartford, divided it into residential streets, and turned it into one of the most distinguished neighborhoods in America. It soon became home to Joseph Hawley, a U.S. Senator, Charles Warner, editor of the *Hartford Courant,* and authors Mark Twain and Harriet Beecher Stowe. Gillette built a house for himself there, with a large barn in the rear. Fugitives were sheltered in the barn and then, aided by Gillette and underground workers in Hartford, taken to other safe houses on the road north. Gillette harbored runaways in rooms throughout his large home. Gillette's son, William, became one of the country's most popular late nineteenth century playwrights with works such as *Secret Service*, a Civil War spy thriller. *For further information: Winterbury Historical Society 203-243-9392.*

CANTERBURY

Prudence Crandall School and Museum
Routes 14 and 169, Canterbury, Connecticut
Open to the public

Crandall, a devout Quaker, opened a school for African-American girls here in 1833 and was immediately the target of widespread abuse by her neighbors. Farmers filled her well with horse manure, grocers refused to sell her food, and local doctors would not treat her sick students. Local police finally arrested her and she spent a night in jail. Defended by some of Connecticut's best lawyers, she won her case when the State Supreme Court dismissed it. She attempted to continue the school, housed in a Federal-styled two story building, in 1834, but shut it down following an attack by an angry mob of men who broke most of the building's windows. Slaves were not harbored at the school itself, but they probably found refuge at Crandall's father's nearby farm. In 1995, the Connecticut State Legislature voted Prudence Crandall an official State Heroine. *For further information: Canterbury Historical Society 203-546-6482.*

HARTFORD

Mark Twain House
351 Farmington Avenue, Hartford, Connecticut
Open to the Public

This is the three-story, nineteen-room Victorian mansion of Samuel Langhorne Clemens, who chose the name Mark Twain. Dotted with balconies and chimneys, it is a gem of gilded age architecture. Edward Potter built the mansion for Twain in 1874 at a cost of $120,000 (several million today). The house is a tribute to the tall, red haired, well dressed, cigar smoking (30 a day) writer who turned the huge, dark, structure into a playhouse for himself and his family.

Writer and humorist Mark Twain lived in this Hartford, Connecticut, home in the late nineteenth century. Twain's novel *Huckleberry Finn* told the story of a runaway slave, Jim, and the boy who aided him, Huck, in Hannibal, Missouri. Twain's in-laws were underground station keepers in Elmira, New York. (Courtesy of Mark Twain House)

Twain and his wife lived in the home with their four children, eleven cats, four dogs, and a black freedman named George who was a hopeless gambler and often hid his winnings under his mattress. Twain humored his children whenever he could, attending plays they staged in the nursery and building a telephone system so that they could talk to "Santa Claus" at the north pole, a Santa with a Missouri accent. He trained several of his cats to sit on top of the pockets of his billiard table, located in the study where he wrote his novels, and the cats would brush back cue balls to save him work.

Twain entertained writers, politicians, and explorers in his home, regaling them with stories of his days in the wild west, his journeys on the Mississippi as a boatman, and his travels in Europe. The hot-tempered writer also fumed at the gas company, whom he constantly accused of trying to poison him with noxious odors, and the phone company, to whose local manager he sent unflattering "report cards" concerning their service. Amid his rantings, wild stories, cigar puffing, and pool shooting, Twain managed to write *Huckleberry Finn, Tom Sawyer, A Connecticut Yankee in King Arthur's Court, The Prince and the Pauper, Innocents Abroad,* and other stories in the home.

Twain grew up in Hannibal, Missouri, where the Underground Railroad thrived. He never participated in the Underground Railroad, although he was constantly aware of it. As a child he heard many stories about runaways in the slave state of Missouri and sat in court for several days at age six when his father was part of a jury that found men guilty of violating the original Fugitive Slave Act. His Hartford home was situated on the banks of a river and from his third floor study Twain could look down on the old barn that served as an underground railroad station in the 1850s. The biggest underground and abolitionist influence on him was his wife, Livy, and her family, the Langdons, of Elmira, New York. The Langdons were important members of the New York underground and hid slaves for years in tunnels beneath their large home there. All of these connections led Twain to write *Huckleberry Finn,* the story of runaway slave Jim and his young friend Huck, in his Hartford home.

Tours are given by well-informed and witty guides who provide visitors with a behind the scenes look at the man as well as the home. The best time to visit the home is in mid-July, when the city of Hartford celebrates its annual Mark Twain Days with a weekend of festivities. *For further information: 860-247-0998.*

Harriet Beecher Stowe Center
71–77 Forest Street
Hartford, Connecticut
Open to the public; Tours

Stowe, the author of *Uncle Tom's Cabin,* who lived in several towns during her career, moved to this home at the invitation of her cousin, John Hooker, in

Harriet Beecher Stowe's novel, *Uncle Tom's Cabin,* published in 1852, chronicled the horrors of slavery and was based on a true story. Stowe herself was an underground leader, hiding numerous slaves and their families in her Cincinnati home in the 1840s. (Courtesy of the Stowe Center)

Stowe's last home was in Hartford, Connecticut. Many said that
Uncle Tom's Cabin helped bring about the Civil War, the conflict
in which Stowe's son was killed. (Courtesy of the Stowe Center)

1873, and remained until her death in 1896. It was part of the farm Hooker
and his brother-in-law, Francis Gillette, purchased in 1853. Today, the
restored three-story home, surrounded by gardens and next door to the
Mark Twain mansion, is a museum and library with large collections of
nineteenth century writings and a fine repository of works on women's and
African American literature.

The home is a good example of Victorian architecture and living conditions. One of the highlights of the tour is the west parlor on the first floor,
where visitors can see the desk where Stowe wrote *Uncle Tom's Cabin.* She
received substantial royalties for that book (it sold over two million copies),
which made her a rich woman with homes in Connecticut and Florida,
where her family vacationed six months each year. She did not share in the
profits from any of the dozens of plays and films made from the novel or
the hundreds of souvenirs, fans, and wallpaper produced by others to cash
in on the phenomenal popularity of the book. Stowe wrote 30 books, many
of them at her home in Hartford.

She had a boisterous relationship with her neighbor, the zestful Twain.
He frequently accused her of sneaking into his greenhouse and stealing his

flowers and she continually upbraided him for telling too many raucous stories to her friends and appearing at her parties not properly dressed (when accused by Harriet of not wearing the proper shirt collar and tie to a dinner, he angrily mailed her a collar and tie. She shot back with a telegram informing him that Mark Twain would probably be a more pleasant guest if only the collar and tie, and not its owner, sat at the table).

The great sadness in the author's life was the death of her son Fred in the Civil War, a war started, historians assert, in a heated public climate created in part by the success of *Uncle Tom's Cabin*. From the end of the war until her final days, she would stare at any U.S. soldier in uniform, somehow certain it was her long lost son. Today, the Stowe House is a popular Hartford Museum. *For further information: 860-525-9317.*

Old State House
800 Main Street, Hartford, Connecticut
Open to the public

The two story red brick Old State House, an architectural gem and a National Historic Landmark in the heart of downtown Hartford, was the site of the first of the *Amistad* trials. Today it serves as a museum and twice a week, on Tuesdays and Thursdays, a local troupe of actors re-creates the *Amistad* trial there for visitors with a spirited thirty-minute play.

North Cemetery
North Main Street, Hartford, Connecticut
Open to the public

North Cemetery is the final resting place for a number of African Americans who served in the Union Army during the Civil War. There are scattered graves throughout the cemetery for Union veterans from different parts of New England who died in the Hartford area and, in the center of it, resting places of a half dozen soldiers who served in Connecticut's all black 29th Connecticut Volunteers.

NEW HAVEN

United Church-on-the-Green
Temple and Elm Streets, New Haven, Connecticut
Open to the public by appointment

The pre-Civil War pastors of the elegant, red brick church with its towering white steeple on the New Haven green, next door to Yale University,

The United Church on the Green in New Haven, Connecticut, like so
many places of worship, was an underground station. (Photo by Author)

were all workers in the underground. A booming community whose population jumped from 15,000 in 1840 to nearly 40,000 in 1860, New Haven
housed a large black community whose members were freed by Connecticut's anti-slavery legislation. One church pastor was the Reverend Simeon
Jocelyn, brother of the artist who painted the portrait of Joseph Cinque,
head of the *Amistad* slave mutiny, who raised money for the defense of the
Amistad mutineers. Rev. Jocelyn preached against slavery at the United
Church and, on his own, founded an African-American church in another

part of town. Jocelyn was also head of the New Haven Anti-Slavery Society. Another pastor, Reverend Sam Dutton, hid runaways in the attic of his home on College Street, two blocks from the church. Runaways, and members of Dutton's family, were instructed to admit other fugitives if they gave a special knock on the rear, kitchen door. Dutton and others secretly organized the group of Connecticut men who raised money for what later became John Brown's raid on Harper's Ferry. *For further information: 203-787-4195.*

Amistad Monument
City Hall, 165 Church Street, New Haven, Connecticut

The monument, dedicated in 1992, is a fourteen foot high, three-sided relief depicting scenes from the *Amistad* mutiny, an historic incident in the story of slavery given much prominence in 1997 when the story of slave leader Cinque and his followers was made into a movie by director Steven Spielberg. The bronze sculpture, which draws thousands of passers-by each year, was designed by Ed Hamilton. It stands on the site of the New Haven jail where the *Amistad* mutineers were imprisoned and overlooks the New Haven green and, on the other side of it, the United Church-on-the-Green.

Center Church
250 Temple Street, New Haven, Connecticut
Open to the public

The congregation of worshippers at Center Church was one of the most vocal in its support of the *Amistad* captives in 1839. Members of the church, some connected to the Underground Railroad, already flourishing in the state, contributed hundreds of dollars to the slaves' legal defense fund.

Battell Chapel
Elm and College Streets, Yale University, New Haven, Connecticut
Open to the public

Theology professors and students at Yale were also instrumental in raising funds for the *Amistad* mutineers. The chapel, just a few blocks from the New Haven Green, contains an *Amistad* exhibit.

Long Wharf
Long Island Sound, New Haven, Connecticut
Open to the Public

Long Wharf was the largest docking area for ships arriving in New Haven, a major seaport in the nineteenth century. Over the years, hundreds of slaves, stowaways on ships leaving southern ports, disembarked at Long Wharf, where they were met by members of the local underground and hurried to safe houses in the city. The *Amistad* was sailed to Long Wharf. A civic organization is raising funds to build a replica of the *Amistad* and have it permanently docked there. *For further information: New Haven Colony Historical Society 203-562-4183.*

MIDDLETOWN

Benjamin Douglas House
111 South Main Street, Middletown, Connecticut
Private home

Douglas was one of the underground leaders in central Connecticut and, unlike many, a very public man. He owned a pump works in town and shares in a shipping company. Douglas, one of the founders of the local anti-slavery society (there were approximately 200 freed black residents in the town in the late 1850s), served as mayor of Middletown from 1850 to 1856 and lieutenant governor of Connecticut from 1861–1862. He harbored many slaves in his large, two-story colonial home. Douglas had his attackers and on at least two occasions was nearly hit with bricks hurled through the windows of a church where he was attending an anti-slavery meeting.

His closest brush with harm did not come in Middletown, but in New York City in 1863. Douglas was in Manhattan on business when the draft riots began there in July, 1863, claiming over 100 lives. African Americans in the city were targets of unruly mobs, whose members hung or shot them. Douglas found himself faced with a fleeing runaway, Ephraim Dixon, and a mob looking for him. He hid Dixon in his hotel room and the next day hustled him, his face covered with a coat collar pulled up high, aboard a ferry and hid him in a stateroom he rented. The abolitionist and the runaway sailed to New London and then traveled to Middletown, where Douglas put him up in his home for several days.

Also in Middletown is the West Burying Ground in Washington Street Cemetery, where a number of soldiers who served in the all-black 29th Connecticut Volunteers in the Civil War are interred. Middletown was the site of one of the largest rallies to protest passage of the Fugitive Slave Act in 1850. *For further information: Middlesex County Historical Society 203-346-0746.*

NEW LONDON

11 Hempstead Street, Hempstead Historic District,
New London, Connecticut

Freed African Americans (and some slaves) had resided in New London
since the 1680s. The blacks and whites in town all lived in the shadow of
the wealthy Hempstead family. Descendants of the abolitionist family
owned a number of homes and property on their vast estate. Working with
a realtor and fellow abolitionist, Savillion Haley, they sold several homes
and dozens of parcels of property to blacks at affordable prices in the 1840s
in order to increase the size of the African American population in town. By
that time New London had its own abolitionist newspaper, the *Slave's Cry*,
its own anti-slavery group, and several churches whose ministers preached
against the evils of slavery. Several underground safe houses were established in New London because it was a jumping off point for fugitives traveling along the shoreline to routes north into Massachusetts and Vermont.

New London was also a port at the mouth of the Thames River, which
carried ships northward to Norwich and some smaller river towns. Many
fugitives stayed a single night in New London and were then put on steamers that took them up the river or were moved to Old Saybrook and traveled up the Connecticut River. New London was also one of New
England's major shipping stops and many slaves hid on schooners from
southern states and sneaked off at New London. In a famous 1859 incident, a slave trying to sneak down a ship's gangplank in New London was
spotted by its captain, chased, and captured. Word of the chase spread
quickly through town and within minutes Judge John Brandegee, who
presided over the local police court, arrived on the scene surrounded by
two dozen of the city's most prominent citizens, all ardent abolitionists. The
captain argued, correctly, that the slave had stowed away on his ship illegally, had no papers and, under the Fugitive Slave Act, had to be turned
over to him for return south.

The Judge listened to his argument and then turned to the slave. "Do
you wish to stay here or go free?" the Judge asked him. The slave said he
wanted to go free.

"Go then!" the Judge shouted, raising his hand and pointing that he
should run. The slave nodded thanks, turned, and started to run. The Judge
and the two dozen citizens then formed a large line across the road as the
Captain and his men stepped forward to chase the runaway. Outnumbered
and wary that a judge might jail him and impound his ship, the Captain

backed off and returned to this vessel. *For further information: New London County Historical Society 203-443-1209.*

NORTH STONINGTON

Randall's Ordinary Landmark Inn
Route 2, North Stonington, Connecticut
Open to the public

Like some Connecticut farmers, Darius Randall came from a family of slaveholders. His family owned slaves from the time they started their 1,500-acre farm in the southeastern corner of the state until the Connecticut legislature outlawed slavery. Darius became an abolitionist and built a fourteen foot deep, eight foot by ten foot stone-walled root cellar under his house. It could be reached by a trap door in the kitchen, where he stored produce. In the early 1830s he began to use it to hide runaways who arrived at the door of his two story, brown wood frame home. Runaways would stay in an upstairs room most of the time, but climb down a shaky wooden ladder into the root cellar if any strangers were noticed on nearby roads. Mrs. Randall then placed a rug over the 3½' by 2½' trap door and, with help from her husband or children, put the dining table and chairs over the rug.

Today, the Randall home is a popular bed and breakfast inn and all of its guests are intrigued when they are shown the trap door and the root cellar. "People have heard stories about how runaways were hidden and how the underground operated, but when they actually see it, and peer down into that dark, damp hideaway, it hits them how dangerous this whole operation was and what people, black and white, risked for freedom in this country," said William Foakes, the manager of the Inn. *For further information: North Stonington Historical Society 203-535-2496; Randall's Ordinary Landmark Inn 860-599-4540.*

WILTON

The Ovals
36 Seely Road, Wilton, Connecticut
Private Home

William Wakeman, one of several Wakeman men and women involved in both the Wilton Anti-Slavery Society and underground, was a bold operator who often transported fugitives hidden under a large canvas in the back of his wagon in the middle of the day. He concocted an elaborate "hardware store" scheme and for years wrote notes to underground operators throughout the state concerning his transportation of varied hardware "goods" and "packages," who were runaways. Wilton, in the southwestern corner of Connecticut, was one of the first stops on the underground for runaways heading north from New York City. *For further information: Wilton Historical Society 203-762-3950.*

OXFORD

Washband Tavern
90 Oxford Road, Oxford, Connecticut
Private home

The Washband family ran a tavern in this home for 125 years and, amid constant deliveries, found it rather easy to hide slaves in the tavern back rooms and in a secret room inside their cellar. A Washband woman working with the underground in the 1850s kept a diary, one of the few in existence in the country, in which she chronicled how her family hid fugitives. *For further information: Oxford Historical Society 203-888-0363.*

MANCHESTER

Wadell House
465 Porter Street, Manchester, Connecticut
Private home

The Wadells had an obscure outbuilding where they stored tools and equipment. Beneath it, connected by a hidden trap door, was a stone cellar they built expressly to hide fugitives. Another hiding place was in the attic of the main house. *For further information: Manchester Historical Society 203-643-5588.*

SHERMAN

Levi Stuart House
Route 39, Sherman, Connecticut
Private Home

An abandoned wooden cabin used by Levi Stuart while he built his two-story wood frame main house later served as a hideaway for slaves. The cabin is gone but the house still stands. Local historians were able to identify it from old blueprints of the estate kept by the Stuart family. *For further information: Sherman Historical Society 203-354-3083.*

OLD LYME

Samuel Peck House
Lyme Street and Beckwith Lane, Old Lyme, Connecticut
Private home

The Pecks built a secret room next to the chimney space on the third floor of the house where slaves could hide if strangers were spotted in town. It is unknown when the Pecks began to hide slaves. The home was moved to Old Lyme from another location in 1819. *For further information: Lyme Historical Society 203-434-5542.*

GUILFORD

James Davis House (today the Sachem House Restaurant)
Goose Lane, Guilford, Connecticut
Open to the public

George Bartlett owned this home before the Civil War and hid slaves in his cellar before other underground workers in the area transported them to New Haven in wagons. Today the old home, originally a smaller farmhouse, is a public restaurant. *For further information: Dorothy Whitfield Historic Society 203-453-9477.*

NORWICH

Verney Lee House
118 Washington Street, Norwich, Connecticut
Private home

The Lee home, a handsome three-story dwelling, at one time had an underground tunnel that connected its cellar to the nearby Thames River. Runaways were taken by boat to a small landing near the woods behind the home and then hurried to the concealed tunnel entrance and into the cellar of the house, where they were welcomed by the Lees with food and clothing. *For further information: Society of the Founders of Norwich 203-887-0881.*

NORFOLK

Amos Pettibone Home
Colebrook Road, Norfolk, Connecticut
Private home

Deacon Pettibone's large, two-story white clapboard residence was a major stop on the underground in the western part of Connecticut. He was proud of his work and not afraid to tell neighbors what he was doing. Documents reveal visits by neighborhood children to his cellar, where he hid slaves. Pettibone introduced children to the runaways and often showed them ankle scars from chains or scars on the backs of slaves from whippings to provide examples of the horrors of the institution. *For further information: Norfolk Historical Society 203-542-5761.*

BURLINGTON

Hinnan House
Route 4, Burlington, Connecticut
Private Home

The Hinnan House was built in 1740 and served as a local tavern in the 1790s. It is unclear when the two-story, brown clapboard home became an underground station. The owners built a false floor in their attic and a room under it to house three people.

For more information on sites in the state: Connecticut Historical Commission 860-566-3005.

Massachusetts

Fugitives reached Massachusetts by both land and sea. The favored land route was up from Connecticut. Most arrived via a Connecticut River valley line that emanated from the busy town of Farmington, then continuing their way to Northampton, Massachusetts, and then into Vermont. Others left Connecticut's eastern towns for Worcester, where they were switched to another underground route that carried them to Burlington, Vermont. Sea routes were the most popular, however. Ship captains landed runaways at Nantucket Island, Cape Cod, and the ports of Fall River, New Bedford, Salem, Newburyport, and Boston. Runaways taken to Fall River, New Bedford, Cape Cod, and Nantucket were directed overland to Worcester and then Canada. Slaves who arrived in the other ports were housed, clothed, and fed and then moved on through the northeastern part of the state to Vermont and New Hampshire. Many slaves remained in Boston and were assimilated into the large black community there.

* * *

The Poet Laureate of the Underground Railroad

Most Americans know John Greenleaf Whittier, the poet laureate of New England, as the marvelously gifted, lyrical poet who wrote *The Barefoot Boy* and *Snow-Bound,* the volume of verse about small town and farm life in New England in winter. Whittier lovers may also have read his collections of poems that celebrated his faith in God and in the common people, such as *Home Ballads* and *At Sundown.*

Whittier was so accomplished that on the day he celebrated his twenty-fifth birthday he had already published more verse than Lord Byron at that same age. He went on to publish a dozen volumes of poetry, collections of poetry, and hundreds of individual poems that appeared in the country's most influential newspapers and magazines. Millions of Americans seeking the comfort of quiet life in his warm poetry have read his works in the more than one hundred years since his death and each year thousands visit his home in Amesbury and his nearby farm in Haverhill, twenty miles outside of Boston. Few Whittier lovers realize, however, that the passionate Whittier was not only one of the finest poets in American history, but a hot-blooded abolitionist and one of the most successful operators in the Underground Railroad.

A Quaker from birth in 1807, Whittier grew up on a farm in Haverhill before moving to his Amesbury home in 1836. He was a close friend of William Lloyd Garrison, who founded the nation's first abolitionist newspaper, the *Liberator,* in 1831, and helped bail Garrison out of jail in 1829 when the latter was arrested for accusing a sea captain in an editorial of participating in the slave trade. Garrison, who knew how important the press was in the anti-slavery movement, urged the gifted young Whittier to turn his pen from poetry to politics. The poet, who always hated slavery, published his first anti-slavery pamphlet, *Justice and Expediency,* in 1833, reminding readers of the power of the press as he wrote, "The burning, withering concentration of public opinion upon the slave system is alone needed for its total annihilation."

A tall, thin man with a square forehead, Whittier dressed in Quaker clothing and always wore the traditional black frock coats. He plunged into the abolitionist movement with the same devotion he had to his poetry. One of the founding members of the American

John Greenleaf Whittier, the famous poet, was also an abolitionist newspaper editor and often hid slaves in his Amesbury, Massachusetts, home. (Courtesy of the Society for the Preservation of New England Antiquity)

Anti-Slavery Society at its Philadelphia Convention in 1833, Whittier wrote the ringing national appeal of the New England Anti-Slavery Society in 1834. That same year he began to appear at anti-slavery society meetings all over the East Coast, sometimes applauded and sometimes criticized by townspeople who did not want slavery to become a hot political issue (he was once pelted with eggs by passersby who saw him addressing an anti-slavery group gathered in a garden). He began to turn out dozens of poems condemning slavery. Whittier was at his best as he galvanized the anti-slavery movement when he wrote of slaveowners, "Thou hast fallen in thine armor," in the very first poem ever published in the *Liberator.*

The poet, who had such a gift for words, soon became the editor of an abolitionist newspaper in Philadelphia, the *National Enquirer,* and regularly wrote poems for its pages, including one of the most famous anti-slavery poems of the era, "The Farewell of a Virginia Slave Mother." His pen was just as sharp when writing prose politics and in a strident editorial he called for the immediate elimination of slavery, charging, "It is no evil to be mitigated, but a crime to be abolished."

He was hated by slaveowners and residents of Philadelphia opposed to the abolitionist movement and in late 1837, following the murder of editor Elijah Lovejoy in Illinois, the poet was warned that all abolitionist editors were in danger. His friends were right. In March, 1838, an angry mob stormed the building in which the *National Era* was published and burned it to the ground. The torching of his offices delayed Whittier only temporarily, and within a year he was back in Philadelphia as the editor of another abolitionist paper, the *Freeman,* and later, in 1847, became a contributing editor to the *National Era,* one of the largest abolitionist papers, and wrote for it until the Civil War.

Throughout the 1830s, 1840s, and 1850s Whittier produced hundreds of anti-slavery poems and many were collected into published volumes. He was considered not only the best poet in the anti-slavery movement, but one of the most eloquent columnists and editorialists. His work did not subside with the beginning of the war. He composed perhaps his finest poem, "Barbara Frietchie," early in the war and went on to write hundreds more, most calling for immediate emancipation of the slaves. Two volumes of his anti-slavery poems, *In War Time* and *National Lyrics,* were published during the war.

One of his poems, "Ein' feste Burg ist unser Gott," was turned into a song and sung by the Hutchinson Singers, a New England black family singing group, who performed it at dozens of army camps and at the White House (friends of Whittier claim that the song, which Lincoln loved, was a major factor in the President's decision to issue the Emancipation Proclamation several months later). The song concluded with the lines:

> But blest the ear
> That yet shall hear
> The jubilant bell
> That rings the knell
> Of slavery forever!

Throughout this period, from his appearance at the American Anti-Slavery Convention in 1833 to the start of the Civil War, when he was such a public editor and poet, Whittier had a private career, too—the underground. Like so many others in the Boston area, he did not believe that mere words were enough to end slavery. His Amesbury home was a permanent stop on the underground line that ran out of Boston and north toward Canada. Slaves were hidden in the bedrooms of the house or in a barn. Whittier did not keep records, but others in the Boston underground claimed over one hundred slaves were harbored by the country's acclaimed poet.

Late in life, when assessing his position as one of world's most heralded poets, Whittier scoffed and, in assessing his priorities, said, "I set a higher value on my names appended to the Declaration of Anti-Slavery Sentiment in 1833 than on the title page of any book."

* * *

Boston

* * *

Their Pens Were Mightier Than Swords:
The Abolitionist Press

I am aware that many object to the severity of my language, but is there not cause for severity? I *will be* as harsh as truth, and as uncompromising as justice. On this subject, I do not wish to think, or speak, or write, with moderation. No! No! Tell a man whose house is on fire to give a moderate alarm; tell him to moderately rescue his wife from the hands of a ravisher; tell the mother to gradually extricate her babe from the fire into which it has fallen— but urge me not to use moderation in a cause like the present? I am in earnest. I will not equivocate. I will not excuse. I will not retreat a single inch. AND I WILL BE HEARD.

> —William Lloyd Garrison, the *Liberator*, first issue, 1831

Garrison's rousing first editorial set the tone not only for the *Liberator*, but for all of the dozens of abolitionist newspapers that began to appear in the United States. Prior to starting the *Liberator* with no capital and so little money that he had to sleep at the newspaper office, Garrison worked for the first true abolitionist paper, Benjamin Lundy's the *Genius of Univeral Emancipation*. He gained national notoriety in 1829 when he was jailed in Baltimore after being charged with falsely accusing a sea captain of participating in the slave trade. He became convinced that the abolitionist movement was powerful enough to support a national newspaper. The *Liberator* started slowly, but Garrison had won over enough influential anti-slavery advocates and underground leaders to keep it going in its early years. The development of the steam press and other advances in technology in the early 1830s permitted the paper to greatly reduce its costs and flourish. It was circulated all over the northern states.

The newspaper quickly became the leader in the abolitionist press and Garrison the unquestioned early leader of the entire anti-slavery movement with his policies of immediate freedom for enslaved blacks and the secession of northern states. He was a non-

William Lloyd Garrison founded the first widely read anti-slavery newspaper, *The Liberator*, in 1831. (Courtesy of the Society for the Preservation of New England Antiquity)

violent man and refused to urge Congress to outlaw slavery or abolitionists to harm slaveholders. He hoped that slaveowners' consciences, pricked by the *Liberator*, would convince them to give up their slaves. As the abolitionist press and anti-slavery movement grew, however, militants began to lead it and Garrison lost much of his influence.

More than any other single factor, the abolitionist press drove the anti-slavery movement throughout the 1840s and early 1850s. Advances in technology enabled many small printers, and those without any printing experience, to start anti-slavery newspapers. They were not only published in large cities such as Boston and New York, but in small towns like Fayetteville, New York and Oberlin, Ohio. There was the *Friend of Man* in Utica, the *Christian Examiner* and the *Emancipator* in New York City, the *Herald of Freedom*, the *Green Mountain Freeman*, the *Voice of Freedom*, the *Spirit of '76*, *Liberty Herald*, the *Bennington Gazette*, and *Vermont Star* in Vermont, the *National Era* in Philadelphia, the *North Star*, Frederick Douglass's paper in Rochester, New York, and the *Observor* in Alton, Illinois.

The abolitionist papers had no precedent in America, where the mainstream newspapers were all owned or run by political parties. They would have no copiers until the 1960s, when the anti-Vietnam War movement gave birth to several dozen underground, counter-culture publications. All of the abolitionist newspapers were privately financed and each was produced by a single editor and one or two friends or family. The papers had little advertising and relied on subscriptions that were often unpaid. After a Charleston, South

Carolina, mob stole and burned hundreds of copies of an abolitionist paper from a post office in 1835, southern state, county, and local governments banned the distribution of any radical journals, severely cutting circulation for their editors. Many papers only survived for a few years and then folded, replaced by another publication in that same city or region which might itself last a year or two.

The same advanced printing technology that created the proliferation of abolitionist newspapers gave birth to a huge wave of published books and pamphlets denouncing slavery. Over 100 slave narratives, short books written by former slaves, were published from 1835 to 1860. Several anti-slavery novels, including the influential *Uncle Tom's Cabin,* appeared during that period. There were so many pamphlets published, and mailed free, by different anti-slavery groups that in 1835 it was estimated that the American Anti-Slavery Society alone was sending pamphlets of some kind to over 50,000 people each week.

The editors of many abolitionist newspapers practiced what they preached in their columns and began to work on the Underground Railroad. John Greenleaf Whittier was harboring fugitives within a few years after he started working for an abolitionist paper. The Lovejoy brothers, Elijah and Owen, Illinois publishers, were tireless underground workers as early as 1836. David Ruggles and William Still, organizers of black newspapers, ran the undergrounds in New York and Philadelphia. New York Senator William Seward, who reportedly helped finance abolitionist papers, hid slaves at his Auburn, New York, home, and so did Albany, New York newspaper editor Thurlow Weed. Joseph Poland, publisher of the *Green Mountain Freeman,* in Montpelier, Vermont, greeted passersby at his office by day and drove wagonloads of runaways to safe houses north of the capital at night. He later told friends that he also hid fugitives in the backroom of the newspaper office during the daytime.

Life was dangerous for abolitionist editors who worked on the underground. Charley Torrey, the Washington correspondent for an abolitionist paper who used journalism as a cover for his underground work, was imprisoned in Virginia and died in his cell four years later. An angry mob in Alton, Illinois, attacked the offices of editor Elijah Lovejoy twice, throwing his presses into a river. He bought new presses and continued publishing the *Observor.* On a third raid, members of the mob murdered him.

These papers had enormous influence. First, although many only lasted a few years and most had circulations of less than 5,000, collectively they reached several hundred thousand people and had readerships in every large city. The most important political, religious, and business leaders read them. The newspapers gave legitimacy to the anti-slavery movement and that legitimacy made the development and expansion of the underground possible.

Second, many of the young workers on abolitionist papers, such as Horace Greeley, became writers and editors of mainstream big city newspapers a generation later and brought their anti-slavery views to those papers.

Third, the abolitionist press kept the anti-slavery movement visible throughout the years when it was not yet politically viable, enabling the movement to expand quickly and with great general acceptance, after the passage of the Fugitive Slave Act and the Kansas-Nebraska Act in the 1850s.

Fourth, the abolitionist editors were often leaders of the first anti-slavery political parties, such as the Liberty Party and Free Soil Party. These small parties, which were all later combined to form the new and powerful Republican Party in 1855, could never have survived without the backing of the abolitionist press.

The black press was born and remained active during this time. One of the first black abolitionist papers was *Freedom's Journal*, started in 1827 by John Russwurm, the first black graduate of Maine's Bowdoin College, and his friend Samuel Cornish. Their paper was circulated throughout many southern states and was widely read in Washington prior to governmental crackdowns there in the 1830s. Ahead of the mainstream abolitionist movement, it was unable to achieve much success with subscribers or advertisers and folded in 1829. Other black abolitionist newspapers followed, however, beginning with the *Spirit of the Times,* in 1836, and the *Colored American.* Both published through the early 1840s and each had circulations of about 2,000.

By the time they folded, the abolitionist movement was beginning to build in black and white neighborhoods throughout the North. Black editors as well as white began to produce anti-slavery newspapers. Between 1840 and the beginning of the war, seventeen different black abolitionist newspapers were published. All were four to six pages in length and contained news of the anti-slavery movement and politics plus reprinted anti-slavery speeches and reprinted articles from other abolitionist newspapers. Black editors urged their readers to be proud of their color. J. McCune Smith, editor of a Rochester, New York, paper, wrote: "There is one thing our people must learn. We must learn to love, respect, and glory in our Negro nature."

Many of the black papers, like the white publications, were run by underground leaders. David Ruggles, head of the New York Vigilance Committee, served as an officer of one newspaper and William Still, head of the Philadelphia underground, was the business manager of another. The newspapers, like all abolitionist sheets, were quite public, but their black editors, like their white counterparts, had separate, secret lives as leaders of the underground.

The most successful of the black abolitionist papers was the *North Star,* published and edited by Frederick Douglass in an office near his Rochester home, where, as an underground organizer, he harbored dozens of fugitives over the years. The highly visible Douglass, who lectured throughout the North, was able to attract the best anti-slavery writers and, more importantly, received continual financial aid from wealthy anti-slavery advocates and groups. He began publishing in 1848 and soon changed the name to *Frederick Douglass's Paper.* Most of the black abolitionist sheets, though, with a much more limited market than white publications, did not do well and folded within a year or two. Many had circulations of less than 1,000 and even some big city newspapers, like those in Philadelphia, reached less than 500 readers. Their editors worked hard to raise money to keep the papers going, even receiving subsidies from wealthy white abolitionists such as Gerrit Smith.

Their overall success extended far beyond their circulations. The African Americans who did read them gained a heightened sense of self esteem they never had before. The papers also influenced the right people, substantially aiding the anti-slavery movement. Charlotte Forten, the black woman who became one of the leading abolitionists of the era, said she joined the movement because of the inspirational editorials she read in Philadelphia's black newspapers. "I am wholly indebted to the abolitionist cause for arousing me from apathy and indifference," she said.

The black and white abolitionist journals, many of whose editors were underground operators, created a groundswell of concern over slavery that grew throughout the 1830s, '40s, and '50s. Although they were always small, cult papers, their spirited columns and inspirational editorials did move hundreds of thousands of Americans to support the anti-slavery movement. Slavery finally did become a viable political issue in the late 1840s and 1850s and was finally embraced by the editors of the large big city newspapers and the great moderate middle class of Americans in the North. That could never have happened without the endless pushing and prodding of the abolitionist journals, and their underground editors, from 1831 onward.

* * *

Twelfth Street Baptist Church
150 Warren Street, Boston, Massachusetts
Open to the public

The church was one of several in Massachusetts that served as an underground station. Its freed black congregation included both Anthony Burns and Shadrach (Fred Wilkins), whose respective deportment and rescue created uproars in the country. The church's pastor was the Reverend Leonard Grimes, a freed black who served time in jail for underground activities in Washington, D.C., before moving to Boston.

Farwell Mansion
558 Massachusetts Avenue, Boston, Massachusetts
Private home

Wealthy Bostonian William Carnes built two mansions in the city. He preferred this one and left his original home vacant to live here. Slaves were hidden in the many rooms of the lavish home and, if slavehunters were seen nearby, removed to the original mansion, which had been kept in darkness for years and was a perfect hideaway. Today the mansion is headquarters for the League of Women for Community Service.

African Meeting House
8 Smith Court, Boston, Massachusetts
Open to the public

The meeting house, the center of black cultural life in Boston, was built in 1806 and it was here in 1833 that William Lloyd Garrison and others founded the New England Anti-Slavery Society. The church did not house fugitives, but members of its congregation did.

African Meeting House/Abiel Smith School
46 Joy Street, Boston, Massachusetts
Open to the public

The wood frame building housed the first school for African American children in Boston, opened in 1834. Today the building is home to the Museum of Afro-American History and contains a comprehensive exhibit on the Underground Railroad.

Faneuil Hall
Faneuil Hall Square, Boston, Massachusetts
Open to the public

Faneuil Hall was a gift to the city by a man who became wealthy in the slave trade. It first gained prominence in the 1770s when it was a public meeting hall for the Sons of Liberty and other revolutionaries who later went to war against England. It gained even more fame in the 1850s when anti-slavery meetings were held here. The surly crowd that marched on the courthouse and freed Shadrack in 1851 first met here. Dozens of the leading abolitionist speakers of the 1850s lectured in well-attended meetings here. The hall is next to Quincy Market, a large collection of outdoor and indoor shops, restaurants, and food emporiums.

John Smith House
86 Pinckney Street, Boston, Massachusetts
Private home

Smith, a freed black, moved to Boston from Richmond, Virginia, in 1848 and opened up a small barber shop. The shop became a front for the underground and a source of curiosity for clients and passersby. For no reason, black strangers would turn up at the shop but not stay for haircuts. Important Bostonians, such as U.S. Senator Charles Sumner, would also arrive for no apparent reason. Few realized that Smith was working as an underground agent, directing arriving fugitives to the homes of station-masters. Smith later served as a recruiter for black Union Army regiments in the Civil War and was elected to three terms in the Massachusetts Legislature.

Lewis Hayden House
66 Phillips Street, Boston, Massachusetts
Private home

Hayden was a former slave who escaped from Kentucky and relocated in Boston. He became an early leader in the underground and used his four-story home in the center of the city's business district as a station. He was so trusted that in 1849 the underground sent him William and Ellen Craft,

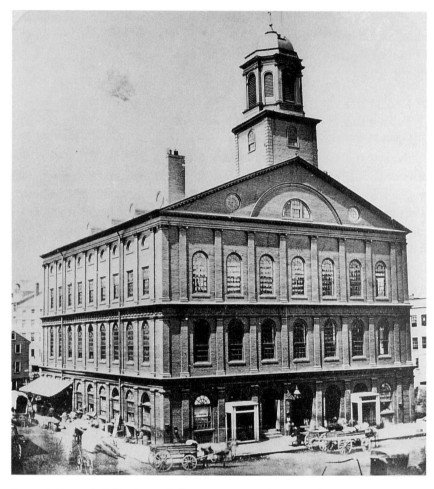

Boston's Faneuil Hall, where abolitionists met to plan several rescue attempts in the 1850s. (Courtesy of The Society for the Preservation of New England Antiquity)

the runaways who dressed as a wealthy white businessman and slave. Hayden was so determined to protect runaways (he often harbored as many as thirteen at a time), that he placed two kegs of gunpowder under the steps of his home. He greeted slavehunters looking for fugitives who knocked at his front door with a lighted candle, pointed to the gunpowder kegs, and told them he would drop the candle into them if they did not go away. Later, in 1851, Hayden was one of the organizers who rescued Shadrach from the courthouse. After the Civil War, he became involved in politics and was elected to the Massachusetts legislature in 1873. His only son died fighting for the U.S. Navy in the Civil War.

John Coburn House
2 Phillips Street, Boston, Massachusetts
Private home

Coburn was a member of the Boston Vigilance Committee, which spearheaded the abolitionist movement and ran the underground in the city. He was one of the men arrested, and acquitted, for his part in the rescue of Shadrach.

The National Park Service, in conjunction with the Museum of Afro-American History, sponsors comprehensive tours of African American heritage and Underground Railroad sites in Boston. *For further information: Bostonian Society 617-242-5655; Black Heritage Trail 617-742-5145.*

ROXBURY

William Lloyd Garrison Home
125 Highland Street, Roxbury, Massachusetts
Open to the public

Garrison was the founder and longtime editor of the first nationally distributed abolitionist newspaper, the *Liberator,* and a driving force in the national anti-slavery movement. Although asked by many to become an organizer in the underground, he refused, believing that his time could be better spent in radical journalism. *For further information: Roxbury Historical Society 617-445-7400.*

NANTUCKET ISLAND

African Baptist Church and African Meeting House
Pleasant and York Streets, Nantucket Island, Massachusetts
Open to the public

Many freed blacks worked as seamen in the prosperous whaling industry capital of Massachusetts. Whaling ships set out from Nantucket, New Bedford, and Boston for one- and two-year-long voyages in the Atlantic, Pacific, and Indian oceans to gather sperm whale oil for New England's lamps. The ships stopped at several southern ports on their way home and black seamen often smuggled runaways on board and hid them until they reached home in Nantucket. There, the runaways were sheltered at the meeting house or church until they could be sneaked aboard ships heading for New Bedford and Boston. Freed black parishioners also hid them. It was here, in 1841, that Frederick Douglass attended an anti-slavery rally and, unannounced, gave a rousing speech that so moved the organizers of the gathering that they asked him to become a regular speaker at rallies, believing that as a former slave he would be a great asset to the movement. *For further information: Nantucket Historical Society 506-228-1894.*

NEW BEDFORD

Whaling Museum
613 Pleasant Street, New Bedford, Massachusetts
Open to the public

The museum was not a sanctuary for runaways, but many of its exhibits explain the lives of sailors, many freedmen, and their exploits at sea and in New Bedford. The town itself had a number of safe houses for escaping slaves who arrived on whaling ships or commercial schooners. One of New Bedford's most prominent sea captains, Paul Cuffee, believed that slaves should be freed and returned to Africa. He liberated a dozen slaves in Georgia in 1814 and sailed to Africa with them on his vessel, *The Traveller,* leaving them in freedom in Sierra Leone. An exhibit on Cuffee is in the museum.

Johnson Home
Seventh Street, New Bedford, Massachusetts
Open to the public

Nathan Johnson was one of the most effective underground operators in New England, doing double duty sheltering fugitives who arrived by land and sea. He regularly smuggled runaways on board ships and sent them on to Canada. He spent much of his time working with the organizers of the New York Vigilance Committee, who sent hundreds of fugitives his way on land routes. One of the most charismatic was a slave named Frederick Bailey, who had fled a Maryland plantation and hid out in New York for two weeks. New York underground organizers sent him and his fiancee, Anna, to Johnson in New Bedford because the slave had worked in a ship-yard and believed he could be assimilated into the shipyard business in the busy seaport of New Bedford. Worried that Bailey might still be sought if he stayed in New Bedford, Johnson urged him to change his name. The runaway did; the name he chose was Frederick Douglass.

CONCORD

The village of Concord is one of the most storied in the United States. It was here, in this pretty little New England town, in April of 1775, that 500 minutemen opened fire on British troops in what was the first battle of the American Revolution. Later, in the nineteenth century, Concord became home to several of the most famous writers in the country, all abolitionists, including Henry David Thoreau, Louisa May Alcott, Franklin Sanborn, Nathaniel Hawthorne, and Ralph Waldo Emerson, who immortalized the battle of Concord with his poem containing the legendary line describing the volley of the minutemen as "the shot heard 'round the world." The village maintained its role in American history in the 1830s, 1840s, and 1850s as a cauldron of abolitionist activity and a popular stop on the Underground Railroad. Thoreau, Emerson, and others all harbored fugitives and helped them move northward to Canada.

Town Hall
30 Monument Street, Concord, Massachusetts

The old hall, still standing, had nothing to do with the underground, but earned a page in history during John Brown's 1859 trial for treason. Writer Henry David Thoreau was so proud of his good friend Brown's raid on Harper's Ferry, the federal arsenal in Virginia, that he left his Concord home one morning, marched across the village green, opened the door to the bell tower at Town Hall, and tolled the bell throughout the morning to celebrate the trial and Brown. Later, Thoreau, at great personal risk, harbored the five runaway slaves in Brown's army who escaped during the battle at Harper's Ferry.

Jonathan Ball Home (today the Concord Art Association)
37 Lexington Road, Concord, Massachusetts
Open to public

Ball was a local goldsmith who built a small hidden room inside a large beam and paneled chimney in his living room where he hid fugitives. Ball did not transport slaves. He left that chore to writer Henry David Thoreau, who, with a local doctor, drove slaves to nearby West Fitchburg during the night.

NEWTON

Jackson Homestead
527 Washington Street, Newton, Massachusetts
Open to the public

In letters and diaries kept by Ellen Jackson as a girl, local historians quickly identified the two-story homestead as a main station on the underground. The Jacksons built a fake produce closet in their basement between two large chimney stacks and hid slaves inside. Runaway slaves seeking shelter tossed pebbles against upstairs windows as a signal to let the Jacksons know they were outside. The Jackson women and others in the Newton area held weekly sewing circle meetings where they made new clothes for fugitives. *For further information: Newton Historical Commission 617-552-7135.*

NEWBURYPORT

Wharf Area, Newburyport, Massachusetts

None of the individual buildings in town have been recognized as underground stations yet, but there is ample documentation to show that the homes of sea captains along Federal and High Streets, near the wharf, were used to harbor fugitives. Sea captains, angered at high taxes in the early nineteenth century, often smuggled their goods off ships and into their homes via secret tunnels that ran from the wharf, up the hills, into town. These tunnels were then reportedly used generations later by the underground. Local lore has it that underground homes had certain marks on their chimneys so slaves knew where to go.

LEOMINSTER

John Drake Home, 21 Franklin Street;
Emory Stearns Schoolhouse, 51 Franklin Street,
Leominster, Massachusetts
Private homes

Drake was an example of the middle-class underground worker. Much has been written about wealthy businessmen, landowners, doctors, and lawyers in the underground, but little about middle-income Americans who aided slaves. Drake was an ardent abolitionist and one of the leading anti-slavery speakers of the era who was featured in meetings that he organized at the nearby Stearns schoolhouse. Drake was so trusted that it was to his home that the mob brought Shadrack, the slave seized from the police in the fabled 1851 Boston rescue. *For further information: Leominster Historical Commission 617-537-3684.*

WORCESTER

Liberty Farm
116 Mower Street, Worcester, Massachusetts
Private home

Stephen and Abby Foster lived at Liberty Farm, a nickname given to the home for its underground work in hiding numerous slaves fleeing from Boston. Mrs. Foster was one of the first women to publicly speak out against slavery. The Fosters gained fame in the area for refusing to pay their property taxes because women were denied the vote.

ANDOVER

William Jenkins House
89 Jenkins Road, Andover, Massachusetts
Private home

Jenkins, born in 1795, was one of several underground operators in Andover, another being Samuel Cogswell. His farmhouse, protected by thick woods, had several small rooms and underground tunnels where runaways would hide until transportation could be arranged to Canada. His gravestone reads: "William Jenkins, 1796–1878: He lived to see the fulfillment of his great desire, the abolition of slavery in America."

Harriet Beecher Stowe lived in Andover for ten years, 1852–1862, and is buried in the Phillips Academy Cemetery. *For further information: Andover Historical Society 617-475-2236.*

MILLBURY

Asa Waters Mansion and Aunt Delia's Mansion
Elm Street, Millbury, Massachusetts
Private homes

Slaves would seek the large, three-story victorian style mansions of Asa Waters and Aunt Delia, the nicknames of local women, where they were hidden in upstairs bedrooms. They usually arrived by boat on the Blackstone River and had to scale steep cliffs to reach the backyards of the homes, on opposite sides of Elm Street, and then carefully make it to rear doors of the home without attracting neighbors' attention.

FLORENCE

Ross Farm, Meadow Street;
Critchlow Factory, Pine Street, Florence, Massachusetts
Private

Austin Ross took huge chances with slaves brought to him by the underground, often keeping them in his home for months. Perhaps the biggest gamble was with William Wilson, who stayed there for 18 months and worked for Ross as a night watchman at his cotton mill. Wilson convinced Ross to loan him money, which he used to return south to rescue his young son. Emboldened by his success, Wilson then asked Ross for more money and, with his son, went south again, this time to rescue his wife and daughter. This trip was catastrophic, however. Wilson was captured and returned to slavery.

Across town, industrialist A.P. Critchlow operated a large daguerreotype factory. He employed runaways as workers, placing them amid black freedmen work crews in the factory to avoid suspicion, taught them trades, and loaned them money when they decided to leave.

LYNN

Raddin House
768 Boston Street, Lynn, Massachusetts
Private home

Several of Lynn's most successful businessmen were leaders of the underground and harbored slaves in their homes. One, William Bassett, was president of the Lynn Anti-Slavery Society. The only home from this era still standing is George Raddin's. *For further information: Lynn Historical Society 617-592-2465.*

New Hampshire

Slaves usually entered New Hampshire from northern Massachusetts. They passed from safe house to safe house through the state and then into Vermont at Strafford, Windsor, or Woodstock or, in the northern part of the state, Littleton. Many runaways traveled to Concord first, where underground workers housed them and then transported them on two separate routes to the towns of Meredith, Canterbury, Canaan, and Lyme, usually by wagons in spring and summer or on large snow sleds in winter. Safe houses were also located at Peterborough, Milford, Hancock, and Weare.

CANAAN

Furber-Harris Home
Foxhill and Back Bay Roads, Canaan, New Hampshire
Private home

The house is an excellent example of the generational links in the antislavery movement. It was home to both James Furber, an avid abolitionist, and his father-in-law, James Harris, another strident anti-slavery leader. Harris began his anti-slavery work in 1830. After his daughter married Furber the two men worked together to make their home a frequent stop on the underground. Furber also transported runaways to Lyme and other stops on the underground in New Hampshire. The home and its history are an example of the longtime presence of freed blacks in New Hampshire and other New England states. The Noyes Academy, where fourteen African-American students were enrolled, was directly across the road from the Furber-Harris home, and in 1835 a gang of townspeople raided the school and used ropes, chains, and dozens of oxen to pull it down. Conversely, the town had numerous residents proudly involved in the anti-slavery and underground movement. One of them, Tim Tilton, had "The Slave's Friend" engraved on his tombstone. *For further information: Canaan Historical Society 603-523-4202.*

PETERBOROUGH

Moses Cheney House
Upper Union Street, Peterborough, New Hampshire
Private home

The Cheney home was one of the state's key stations on the underground and exemplified family involvement in the underground movement. Deacon Moses Cheney began hiding runaways in his large, colonial-style home in 1835 and worked with others in town, including the Whitcombs, Morrisons, and Tuttles, to operate the underground. Cheney was host to Frederick Douglass on his visit there in 1840 to speak at a New England Anti-Slavery Society meeting. Cheney did not work alone. His sons were full partners in the underground operation, even helping their father transport fugitives to other towns in New Hampshire after they rested at the Cheney house. One son, Elias, became the longtime editor of the *Peterborough Transcript.* Another, Oren, was President of Bates College, where he admitted the first African-American students. He helped found Storer College, a black school at Harper's Ferry, West Virginia. *For further information: Peterborough Historical Society 603-924-3235.*

LITTLETON

Carleton House
32 Carleton Street, Littleton, New Hampshire
Private home

Edmund Carleton, a local lawyer, founded the Littleton Anti-Slavery Society in 1837 and, at about the same time, began using his home as an underground stop. His wife Mary, like so many other wives in the underground, acted as a full partner in sheltering and feeding runaways and moving them to other locations on the road to Canada. They used teams of horses and wagons to transport slaves. The Carletons never missed an opportunity to publicly denounce slavery. The lawyer became well known throughout New England when he defended, unsuccessfully, two abolitionists accused of interupting a church service with political speeches. Carleton, an avid reader, saved abolitionist newspapers; they were eventually donated to the Library of Congress as the most comprehensive collection in America. *For further information: Littleton Area Historical Society 603-444-2637.*

CANTERBURY

Chamberlain Farm
West Road, Canterbury, New Hampshire
Private home

Farmer John Chamberlain was a relative of Stephen Foster, a noted anti-slavery lecturer. He used his large farm, his home, and barns to harbor fugitives. Many members of his family were in the underground and his nephew, Mellon, who lived in Concord, often brought fugitives to his farm in wagons. *For further information: Canterbury Historical Society 603-783-9831.*

WEARE

Sawyer House
Route 77, Weare, New Hampshire
Private home

Moses Sawyer, a friend of the leading abolitionists in New England, maintained a station at his home and hid slaves in his cellar. He worked with the New Hampshire underground in transporting slaves from town to town. His cousin, Robert Brown, also operated a safe house.

CONCORD

Nathaniel White Home
144 Clinton Street, Concord, New Hampshire
Private home

Nathaniel White and his wife Armenia were leaders of the anti-slavery society in Concord and were rumored to have harbored fugitives in their home, according to family descendants. White became wealthy through his operation of railroad and stagecoach lines throughout New England and Canada. His company eventually became the American Express Company. *For further information: New Hampshire Historical Society 603-225-3381.*

LEE

Cartland Homestead, Lee, New Hampshire
Open to the public

The Cartlands moved to Lee in 1745. Their home served as a haven to fugitives throughout the 1840s and 1850s. The Cartlands, friends of poet John Greenleaf Whittier and Frederick Douglass, were Quakers and tried to shelter as many slaves as they could. Some were even put to work building stone walls near the main house and helping with the farm until they could be safely removed to Canada. The Cartlands refurbished their cellar into a large room where slaves were concealed.

JAFFREY

Amos Fortune Home
Route 124, Jaffrey, New Hampshire
Private home

Fortune had nothing to do with the underground, but he was an example of the success many freed blacks enjoyed in New Hampshire. Born in Africa in 1710, Fortune was captured by slavers and brought to the United States as a child and put into slavery. He saved enough money by selling crafts to buy his freedom at age 60. He moved from Woburn, Massachusetts, to Jaffrey and opened a tannery when he was 70. He became such a prominent citizen in the small town that although he was not an attorney, many citizens, white and black, used him as a lawyer when they had legal troubles. He helped found the Jaffrey Library and in his will left money for the local schools and a church.

MILFORD

Chase House
15 High Street, Milford, New Hampshire
Private home

Leonard Chase was an underground operator for many years and a member of an unusual group of underground leaders in Milford. Chase's business partner, Daniel Putnam, another underground worker, lived next door to Chase and slaves were hidden in both homes. Another was Tom Beach, a local newspaper editor and printer, who was jailed in 1843 following a fiery speech he gave in Newburyport, Massachusetts, at an anti-slavery rally. Another active underground group in town was the singing Hutchinson family. This large family of African-American singers toured the country to sing religious hymns at churches and public gatherings. The group also sang anti-slavery songs in their concerts, including some they wrote themselves, such as "The Bereaved Slave Mother" and "Get Off the Track." In 1862 they sang for President Lincoln at the White House.

For further information for sites in the state: New Hampshire Historical Society 603-225-3381; New Hampshire Tourism Office 603-271-2666.

Rhode Island

The underground in Rhode Island was small. Runaways usually arrived from New Bedford, Massachusetts, where they landed after voyages up the Atlantic from slaves states. They were hidden in homes at Providence or Newport and then hurried north into Massachusetts and Vermont towards

Canada. Underground leaders in Rhode Island were bold, frequently moving runaways on public railroads, such as the Providence and Worcester Railroad. Slaves were placed on cars in Central Falls, Rhode Island, usually in the evening, and taken off when the train pulled into Worcester. They sometimes traveled in baggage cars and sometimes, using fake passes, as freedmen in passenger cars.

PROVIDENCE

Moses Brown Property/Dodge House
10 Thomas Street, Providence, Rhode Island
Private home

The saga of Moses Brown, whose family founded Brown University, is one of the most inspiring in the story of the anti-slavery movement. He was a nephew of sea captains James and Obadiah Brown, who made a fortune in the slave trade from 1740s to the 1780s, using their New England-based ships to transport slaves from Africa to the southern colonies. Disgusted with the slave trade, Moses and two of his three brothers, Nicholas and Joseph, refused to have anything to do with the transportation or sale of slaves, although a fourth brother, John, continued in that business. Moses and his brothers got out of the slave trade around 1800 and invested heavily in ships to participate in the growing whaling industry. The Browns not only made money through whaling voyages and the sale of sperm oil for lamps, but were one of the first families to see the possibilities for extended businesses in a single industry. They invested in the whaling ships of other companies, reaping large profits, built factories to manufacture candles for the oil their ships were bringing home and then, moving into retail, opened up stores to sell oil, candles, and other products. By the 1820s, Moses Brown had become one of the wealthiest men in America and began giving away his money to Brown University and to fund other philanthropic interests.

During those years, Moses Brown secretly became involved in the anti-slavery movement and the underground railroad. His mansion at Humbolt and Wayland Avenues, built in 1786 but no longer standing (the Seril Dodge House now stands on the property), was a haven for runaways who arrived in the nearby seaport of New Bedford. In 1819, Brown began to help freed blacks publicly, buying a large lot in Providence for a group of African Americans. He reportedly gave away thousands of dollars to runaway slaves to help them get to Canada. It is uncertain whether any runaways were hidden on his numerous ships. *For further information: Rhode Island Historical Society 401-331-8575.*

WESTERLY

Charles Perry House
4 Margin Street, Westerly, Rhode Island
Private home

Perry, one of the wealthiest men in Rhode Island, did not harbor slaves in his house, but built and maintained a group of stone huts with sod and tree branches for roofs a few miles from his home in a densely wooded area. Runaways would live there for a period of a few days to a few weeks until Perry and others could move them to another stop on the underground. Perry was a very public abolitionist and was derided by several townspeople who did not support his anti-slavery views. He once escorted Frederick Douglass to an anti-slavery meeting in Westerly and, as Douglass spoke, was pelted with eggs and had a pail of water dumped on him by a man in the gallery. *For further information: Westerly Historical Society 401-377-2602.*

PAWTUCKET

Daggett Home
Slater Park, Route 1A, Pawtucket, Rhode Island
Open to the public

The Daggetts owned slaves from the early 1700s through the 1800s. The present home was constructed in 1685 and remodeled in 1790. A secret attic, entered via a hidden door, was similar to many hideaways on the underground and was used by the Daggets to hide from Indians still in the Rhode Island area in the late 1600s.

NEWPORT

Touro Synagogue
72 Touro Street, Newport, Rhode Island
Open to the public

Ironically, Touro Synagogue, one of the oldest synagogues in America, and a stop on the underground, was built by slaves. According to oral histories, members of the congregation hid runaway slaves within the synagogue, bringing the fugitives food and clothing and arranging for them to move out of Newport to another safe house on the underground. Newport was one of the New England seaports with a busy slave trading business in the eighteenth century. A slave auction block stood at the corners of Long Wharf and Washington Streets. It was also home to one of the area's first anti-slavery groups. It was not uncommon to see slaves walking down a gangplank from one of the large ships while abolitionists, standing on top of boxes, lectured against the evils of slavery.

Isaac Rice Homestead
54 William Street, Newport, Rhode Island
Private Home

Isaac Rice was a black freedman who worked as a gardener for the wealthy in Newport in the 1830s, '40s, and '50s. He became friendly with many slave servants of rich southern families who vacationed in the fashionable resort. Rice earned enough money to build a small home and from there ran an underground station, helping as many runaways as he could, including Frederick Douglass. *For further information: Newport Historical Society 401-846-0813.*

CENTRAL FALLS

Elizabeth Buffum Chace House
Hunt and Broad Streets, Central Falls, Rhode Island
Private home

Elizabeth Chace had her first encounter with slavehunters as a child, when she and other children linked their arms together to form a barricade to prevent slavecatchers from chasing her grandfather as he attempted an escape with several other runaways. Later, as an adult, she and her husband became active in the underground and hid many slaves in their two-story wood frame home, often forging papers for runways to use as they boarded public trains and rode to Worcester. *For further information: Historic Central Falls 401-723-5354.*

For further information on sites in the state: Rhode Island Historical Society 401-331-8575; Rhode Island Office of Tourism 401-222-2601.

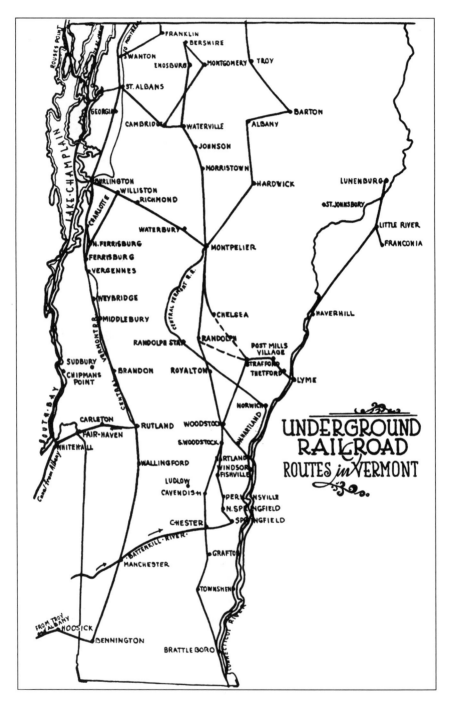

This map of Vermont shows how underground leaders devised the fastest routes to take slaves through the state to Canada. (Courtesy of the Ohio Historical Society)

Vermont

The Green Mountain State was one of the jumping-off points to the final destination of the railroad—Canada. It enjoyed heavy traffic because it was easily accessible from Albany, New York, different towns in New Hampshire, and the Connecticut River valley which ran from Canada through lower Vermont and into Massachusetts. Fugitives followed the Albany line to Bennington and were taken northward toward Burlington and then Canada. Others came into the state through Massachusetts to Brattleboro and moved northward from there. Still others, smaller in number, entered from Lyme or Littleton, New Hampshire.

There were two trunk lines to the railroad in Vermont. The western line started at Bennington, where fugitives stayed with Dr. Samuel Wilcox and other abolitionist families and then traveled north to Charlotte, Brandon, Fair Haven, Manchester, Castleton, and Burlington. Slaves were moved to St. Albans and finally to Canada. Some of the operators along this route were Daniel Roberts in Manchester, D.E. Nicholson in Wallingford, and Erastus and Harley Higley in Castleton. They were aided by a number of local ministers and newspaper editors. Wallingford was the setting for John Trowbridge's best selling 1857 anti-slavery novel *Neighbor Jackwood–A Domestic Crisis,* which told the story of the Underground Railroad in that area, using pseudonyms for operators. Many of the towns on this route had their own anti-slavery groups, which often numbered one hundred residents in their memberships.

The eastern line started in Brattleboro and went northward to Chester, Townshend, Windsor, Woodstock, Montpelier, and Hardwick. Fugitives often stayed with Willard Frost in Brattleboro, who then moved them north to the homes of W.R. and Oscar Shafter in Townshend, Oscamel Hutchinson in Chester, and Colonel Jonathan Miller and newspaper editor Joseph Poland in Montpelier. Miller fought in the Greek Revolution in the 1820s and later attended the world anti-slavery convention in London in 1840. Fearful that slavecatchers would descend on Montpelier because it was the state capital, Poland and Miller created three highly secretive routes out of Montpelier, taking fugitives in different directions; the routes eventually brought them to Canada after stops at various homes and farms.

BURLINGTON

The Reverend Joshua Young House
Willard and College Streets, Burlington, Vermont
Private home

Rev. Young was typical of the abolitionist ministers throughout the New England area who publicly preached against slavery from their pulpits and secretly hid slaves in their homes and on their property while working with others in the Underground Railroad to help fugitives escape to northern cities of Canada. Young was an 1845 graduate of Bowdoin College who then studied theology at Harvard. While living in Boston he witnessed the escape of a slave, Shadrack, and became an ardent abolitionist and member of the Underground Railroad, harboring fugitives at his home there. His arrival as a minister at the Unitarian Church, in Burlington, in the early 1850s, began a decade of anti-slavery activity.

The highlight of his years in Burlington was a passionate anti-slavery speech he gave following the deportation of fugitive slave Anthony Burns from Boston in 1854. In it, he told his parishioners that the rights of man were protected by God, not laws, and that "there is a power superior to Congress, a law higher than any human constitution" and that this "God of might" had to settle the slavery question, not legislators. The speech was published in Burlington newspapers and clearly marked him as an abolitionist.

Young and his wife, who was just as involved in the underground as her husband, did not want to hide runaways in their home because they feared slavecatchers would find them. They turned their barn into a comfortable hideaway for slaves and, for over a decade, would hide from one to six at a time, bringing them food and clothing. Young also worked with dozens of others in Burlington, including several professors at the University of Vermont, to organize the underground station there and frequently arranged transportation to Canada for slaves in his care, or those hiding with neighbors.

Like many, Young paid dearly for his activities. He attended the funeral of John Brown in North Elba, New York, in 1859, where he delivered a sermon. This speech enraged some of his most prominent Burlington parishioners, who also suspected him of hiding slaves, and they withdrew from the church. Church leaders then forced Young to resign. He later preached in the Massachusetts towns of Hingham, Fall River, and Groton.

The Reverend John Wheeler House
(now University of Vermont History Department)
Main and South Prospect Streets, Burlington, Vermont
Private

Organizations formed to raise money to ship freed slaves to Liberia, in Africa, known as Colonization Societies, were quite popular throughout the 1850s. One of the largest was in Vermont and its president was the Rev. John Wheeler. He moved to New England after spending years in Charleston, South Carolina, where he conducted religious services for slaves. In addition to his public work as head of the society, which eventually did ship over 500 former slaves to Africa, Wheeler secretly worked as a member of Burlington's closely knit Underground Railroad, harboring fugitives and aiding in their escape to Canada. Wheeler became president of the University of Vermont. The University later purchased his home.

The Samuel Wires House
118 South Willard Street, Burlington, Vermont
Private home

Samuel Wires was an insurance agent in Burlington who lived across the street from Rev. Young. His wife and family objected to hiding slaves in their home, so Wires told other operators in the state to send slaves to his office on College Street. Slaves arrived there, often starving or shivering from harsh New England winters. Wires, who had keys to nearby stores for just such evenings, hurried through Burlington to obtain food and clothing for the fugitives, whom he put up in his office until morning. He then contacted Young or Lucius Bigelow, one of Burlington's most prominent residents, who often hid slaves in his spacious three-story home. When there was little pressure from marauding slave catchers, Bigelow paid for train tickets to send runaways to Canada. If slavecatchers were in the Burlington area, Bigelow and his friend Wires sneaked slaves out of the rear of Bigelow's home, hid them in wagons or carriages, and drove them to train stations where they were hidden inside baggage cars on freight trains. *For further information: Chittenden County Historical Society 802-655-2138.*

WEST WINDSOR

Bezaleel Bridge Home
Sheddsville Cemetery Road, West Windsor, Vermont
Private home

From 1848 to 1863, Bezaleel Bridge Jr. owned this two-story home, perched on top of a small hill and, according to oral histories, hid slaves in a false closet he built on the side of the main chimney on the first floor. Others in the area transported runaways, staying at his farmhouse, to other underground stops north of West Windsor. *For further information: West Windsor Historical Society 802-484-7474.*

BENNINGTON

First Congregational Church
Monument Avenue, Bennington, Vermont
Open to the public

There are no known records of underground activity at the church, but it has a prominent place in the anti-slavery movement as the home of one of the nation's few African-American pastors of a white congregation, the Reverend Lemuel Haynes. The flinty Haynes, born in 1753 in Connecticut as a freedman, joined a Massachusetts militia unit of the Continental Army when the American Revolution began and fought with distinction in several battles, including Benedict Arnold's Hudson Valley (New York) campaign and in the attack on Fort Ticonderoga. Haynes became a minister in 1785 and remained in the pulpit for nearly fifty years, delivering his last sermon when he was eighty. He worked at other churches in Vermont in addition to his years as pastor in Bennington and was acclaimed as one of the area's most energetic preachers and a leader in the Second Great Awakening religious movement.

Rev. Haynes' work in the Underground was hard to define. He rarely preached about slavery in public, did not harbor fugitives, and lived in the years before the Underground Railroad was organized. He was, however, a close friend and political advisor to Vermont Governor Richard Skinner, a fierce anti-slavery politician, Joseph Burr, a heavy contributor to the American Colonization Society, and Stephen Bradley, who introduced one of several bills to outlaw slavery in the United States.

FERRISBURG

Rowland Robinson Home
Route 7, Ferrisburg, Vermont
Museum open to the public

Robinson, a devout Quaker, was born here in 1796 and in 1835 helped form the Vermont Anti-Slavery Society. In 1843 he organized the much-publicized anti-slavery convention held in Ferrisburg and enjoyed the friendship of abolitionist leaders around the nation.

Robinson lived in a large two-story, wood frame house, entered through a handsome portico at the front. He converted a small bedroom on the eastern end of his home into a hideaway reachable via a false door, for fugitives. Servants and members of the family brought food and clothing to runaways up a back staircase. Slaves normally stayed with Robinson for a few nights and then were driven by him or his friends to another depot several miles north. Robinson was known to drive slaves as far as 35 miles to another safe house, sometimes during snowstorms. He also drove many to his brother-in-law's farm in a secluded rural area of Vermont, where the runaways stayed for up to three months before slipping into Canada. Robinson's activities in the underground were well known and slavecatchers constantly watched his house. Several times slavecatchers, accompanied by sheriffs, burst into his home looking for fugitives but never discovered the secret bedroom.

WOODSTOCK

Titus Hutchinson House
26 Elm Street, Woodstock, Vermont
Currently a business office

Hutchinson was a former Chief Justice of the Vermont Supreme Court when he became involved in the anti-slavery movement in 1841. The Vermont chapter of the brand new, anti-slavery Liberty Party, a national organization, nominated Hutchinson for governor in 1841. The poorly organized party did not do well anywhere in the state and Hutchinson received only 3,039 votes. However, he won ten times as many votes as the party's presidential candidate, James Birney, and his success on the state level, plus the growing state anti-slavery society, helped make the anti-slavery movement in Vermont permanent.

Hutchinson worked as a lawyer by day but by night he and others in the railroad constructed a makeshift tunnel that connected his cellar to the banks of the nearby Kedron River. Runaways sailed up the river, hidden in rowboats, and entered the tunnel on the river bank. *For further information: Woodstock Historical Society 802-457-1822.*

For further information on sites in the state: Vermont Historical Society 802-828-2291; Vermont Office of Tourism 802-828-3237.

Maine

Most runaways reached Maine by sea. The state had a busy shipping industry from the 1820s through the Civil War and entrepreneurs there enjoyed a healthy business with southern states. Abolitionist sea captains from Maine secretly loaded as many fugitives as they could on to their vessels in southern ports such as Charleston and Savannah and took them to Portland, a coastal town, or to a variety of towns along the Kennebec and Penobscot Rivers. There, underground leaders met the ships at local wharves and quickly whisked the slaves to safe houses. The underground moved the runaways north along the Penobscot and then by land to New Brunswick, Canada. The Underground Railroad was first publicly uncovered there in 1837 when, in a bitter political dispute, the governor of Maine turned down a formal request by the governor of Georgia to extradite a runaway who arrived on the *Boston,* one of the many commercial ships that carried cargo—and fugitives—back from southern ports.

AUGUSTA

Nason House
12 Summer Street, Augusta, Maine
Private home

The two-story Nason home in Augusta is tucked neatly into a grove of trees. In it, the owners built a room to harbor fugitives behind a large bookcase. The entire bookcase could be pulled out, revealing a fake panel that looked like the original wall. Removing the fake panel revealed the secret chamber. Slaves in the secret room could move down into the cellar and then out a rear exit. Reul Williams, an underground leader, lived in a fourteen-room mansion across the street. He, too, harbored fugitives.

BRUNSWICK

Harriet Beecher Stowe House (today an inn)
63 Federal Street, Brunswick, Maine
Open to the public

The author lived in several homes during her life. It was here, while her husband taught at nearby Bowdoin College, that Stowe wrote most of *Uncle Tom's Cabin,* a compilation of horror stories, told to her by numerous abolitionists, concerning slavery. She lived here with her husband for several years and then moved to Cincinnati and, later, Hartford, Connecticut. *For further information: Penebscot Historical Society 207-729-6606.*

VASSALBORO

Farwell Mansion
4 Riverside Drive, Vassalboro, Maine
Private home

The Farwell home is a lovely two-story, white colonial home, with five imposing columns on the front porch supporting its roof. It was built in 1842 by Captain Ebenezer Farwell, who made his fortune in the slave trade and was killed on a trip to Africa to buy slaves. Israel Weeks, an abolitionist, then purchased the home. Weeks and members of his family built a tunnel from the middle of their cellar to a point some fifty yards into their back yard. Runaways entered the tunnel entrance, concealed by underbrush, and then hurried into the home, where they were fed and clothed.

GARDINER

Episcopal Parish House
83 Dresden Avenue, Gardiner, Maine
Private home

The rather unimposing two-story parish house, whose first floor contains large, ceiling-to-floor windows, contained a huge cellar where fugitives were hidden. A local minister built two secret rooms in the cellar to conceal runaways. There was also a room big enough to hold two people built in the attic and fugitives entered it via a pull-down staircase. Parishioners who supported the ministers who hid the slaves frequently sought writs for trespassing against any strangers they saw walking near the church.

LAMB HOUSE

220 Main Avenue, Gardiner, Maine
Private home

The Lamb home, just seventy yards from the Kennebec River, was part of the underground for more than a decade. Slaves were hidden in a basement storage room or in a large room built into the attic (that area today contains two large bedrooms). Runaways arrived and departed concealed on boats sailing on the Kennebec.

ROBBINSTON

Brewer House (bed and breakfast inn)
Route 1, Gardiner, Maine
Open to the public

Captain John Brewer and his wife Henrietta built their large, white, two-story home, with its front and back porches supported by white columns, in 1828. The captain and his children began harboring slaves there in the early 1830s. Slaves would arrive by boat on the nearby Penobscot River under the cover of darkness. They were hidden in the bedroom of the home and then, after a few days' rest, sent by boat farther up the river and eventually into Canada.

BLUE HILL

Downeast Arcady Inn
Main Street, Gardiner, Maine
Open to the public

The main building of the home, now a bed and breakfast inn, was built in 1834. According to local historians, the home, near Penobscot Bay, was connected by a tunnel to nearby woods. A turret tower on one corner of the home contains a false room, big enough to hide at least two people (still standing today).

For further information on sites in the state: Brewer Historical Society 207-989-7825; Maine Historical Society 207-774-1822; Maine Office of Tourism 207-623-0363.

* * *

Harriet Tubman and the Endless Crusade

Excepting John Brown, of sacred memory, I know of no one who has willingly encountered more perils and hardships to serve our enslaved people than you have.

—Frederick Douglass to Harriet Tubman

Harriet Tubman, one of eleven children, was born into slavery in 1820 on the Brodas Plantation in Bucktown, Maryland. She was of medium build and average height and strength. A very religious woman, she dearly loved the members of her family, particularly her parents. She labored like others on her plantation, obedient to her masters, until she was a full-grown woman of 29. There was nothing in her appearance or background to suggest that this ordinary looking woman would become one of the greatest heroines of the underground movement and one of the most venerated women in United States history.

Tubman was fed up with slavery by the time she reached her twenty-ninth birthday. One morning another slave on the plantation told her he overheard the owner talking about selling Harriet and several of her brothers. Harriet escaped that night. Traveling on foot, she wandered through forests and forded streams for several days until she finally crossed over the border into free Pennsylvania. She was ecstatic and she wrote later, "I looked at my hands to see if I was the same person. There was such a glory over everything. The sun came up like gold through the trees and I felt like I was in heaven."

After some help from the underground, she made it to Philadelphia and its Vigilance Committee, but turned down offers

Harriet Tubman was one of the boldest rescuers in the underground. She made nineteen raids into Southern states and brought three hundred African Americans out of slavery. Runaways called her "Moses." (Courtesy of the Harriet Tubman Home)

to be hurried on to Canada. She had other plans. Vigilance Committee leader William Still found her a job as a domestic in Philadelphia and she had reasonable protection against slavehunters within the 20,000 member free black community there. She saved her money and ten months later, in 1850, around the time the Fugitive Slave Act was passed, daringly returned to Maryland, to Baltimore, where her sister worked as a slave. One quiet evening she helped her sister and her two children slip away from their home and led them back to Philadelphia. Buoyed by her success, she decided on another rescue mission a few months later. And then another. And another.

By the time the Civil War began, Harriet Tubman, risking her life on each trip, made nineteen different raids into southern plantations, mostly in Maryland and Delaware, and rescued approximately three hundred slaves, including her mother and father and all the members of her family. She brought many out of the states through the southern Pennsylvania and Delaware underground routes, using most of the same safe houses again and again. Many of her trips were accomplished through funds raised in northern towns for that purpose and she was supplied with food, clothing, and wagons from countless underground operators. Slavers in Maryland and Delaware were alerted to her activities and there were rewards posted for her capture as well as any of the runaways in her care. It became so dangerous for Tubman that she always traveled with a loaded pistol.

The daring raider was successful for several reasons. She was deeply religious and believed that God watched over her and would never permit her capture or the capture of those under her care. "I never met any person, of any color, who had more confidence in the voice of God, as spoken to her soul. She said she never ventured only when God sent her. Her faith in the Supreme Power was truly great," said Delaware abolitionist leader Thomas Garrett.

She was a tough disciplinarian who would not permit anyone she rescued to slow up the caravan or quit on her when the trip became hard. She would pull out her pistol, aim it directly at the head of a slave who wanted to stop and warn him or her, "Dead niggers tell no tales. You go or die." They went.

Tubman was well organized and a careful planner who paid great attention to details. She also had a large network of friends and acquaintances in Maryland and Delaware who both looked out for and worked for her. As an example, she paid a freed black man to follow the men who nailed up posters offering rewards for her and her charges and to tear them down. She always began her rescues on Saturday nights so that her party could be far along the underground route by Monday, when the owners of the stolen slaves could run ads for them in southern newspapers. She kept her groups together and moved them as quickly as possible. She carried opiate-type drugs to quiet babies if they started to make too much noise that could give away their presence. If fearful of capture, the shrewd Tubman sometimes had her party board trains heading south, not north, back into the slave states, because hunters would never expect such a daring maneuver.

Her exploits were heralded throughout the abolitionist communities of the northern states. John Brown called her "General Tubman" and said she was "one of the bravest persons on this continent." Senator William Seward said of her that "a nobler, higher spirit, or truer, seldom dwells in human form." Abolitionist Samuel May said "she deserves to be placed first on the list of American heroines."

During the mid- and late 1850s, Tubman became friendly with most of the abolitionist leaders and top politicians in the North. She frequently lectured to abolitionist groups, wrote for anti-slavery newspapers, and lived for weeks with different abolitionist leaders in the United States and Canada. She participated in several rescues, such as the much heralded one in Troy, New York, and raised money for the underground. During the Civil War, she served as a spy for the Union Army in the Carolinas and helped liberate hundreds of slaves on plantations in South Carolina when the Union Army invaded the area in 1861 and 1862.

Tubman was lauded for her exploits before, during, and after the Civil War. As a token of appreciation, William Seward sold her a home near his Auburn, New York, mansion, for a minimal amount of money and Harriet lived there with her parents. The bold underground emancipator died there on March 10, 1913, at the age of 93, and moments after she passed away, a crowd of friends waiting outside the home sang "Swing Low, Sweet Chariot."

* * *

Pennsylvania

Only Ohio had more intricate underground routes and more traffic than Pennsylvania. The state had two main entry points: at Philadelphia and at the lower border along the Maryland line. Many fugitives made it to Philadelphia from the eastern shore of Maryland or through Delaware. Others arrived through Chester, Lancaster, and Delaware Counties and towns such as Chambersburg and Gettysburg on the state's Maryland border and then headed northeast to Philadelphia. Others came on ships from southern ports. The Philadelphia Vigilance Committee, headed by two African Americans, Robert Purvis and William Still, then sent the run-aways through New Jersey to New York or, on Pennsylvania routes, up through the eastern part of the state to Elmira and Olean, in New York. The eastern routes took runaways to safe houses in the communities of Towanda, Estella, Huntersville, Muncy, Norristown, Quakertown, Phoenixville, Reading, Lansdale, Pine Forge, Williamsport, Lewisburg, Columbia, Milroy, and Coatsville.

The second main entry to the state came at small western towns such as Fishertown, Bedford, Shippensburg and, in the far west, Mt. Morris and Uniontown. Slaves making it to Uniontown were sent on a trek to Pittsburgh and then to Lake Erie and Canada. Slaves entering the central border of the state in the Bedford and Chambersburg area followed underground routes to Harrisburg, often stopping in safe houses in Carlisle and Gettysburg. Others followed a route through Pleasantville, Gistown, and Altoona to Indiana, and then to Pittsburgh. From Pittsburgh the line took slaves directly north to the Erie area, where there were safe houses in Franklin, Meadville, Townville, Cambridge Springs, Albion, Girard, Branchville, Union City, and Waterford. Runaways then either made their way north to Niagara Falls or Lake Erie ports or sailed across Lake Erie into Canada, hidden on boats.

PHILADELPHIA

Johnson House
6300 Germantown Avenue, Philadelphia, Pennsylvania
Private home

When the Johnson family first used their three-story stone home as a refuge for slaves, they were merely adding to the historic luster of the home, built in 1765. The house still has bullet holes from the battle of Germantown, a key conflict of the American Revolution, which raged around the Johnson home in October, 1777. Later, the Johnsons, who were Quakers, willingly hid any slaves sent to them by the Philadelphia Vigilance Committee. Slaves went directly to the home at night or were hidden in nearby mills by day and sneaked through the town to the Johnson house after dinner. Runaways were hidden in third-floor bedrooms that had dormer windows overlooking the street. They were sheltered and fed and, after one or two nights, moved on by wagons to Quaker villages in Norristown or Plymouth Meeting. A close friend of the Johnsons was Louisa May Alcott's father, Bronson Alcott, the principal of a nearby school who was fired for admitting African-American students and who was rumored to be working in the Philadelphia underground with the Johnsons.

Frances Ellen Watkins Harper House
27 Bainbridge Street, Philadelphia, Pennsylvania
Private home

Born a free woman, the black poet Frances Ellen Watkins Harper was not an activist in the Philadelphia underground but reportedly harbored slaves from time to time. She was best known as an ardent anti-slavery speaker. Born in Maryland, she fled that slave state 1853 and moved to Philadelphia, where the local community supported her writing. Her most famous poem was "Bury Me in a Free Land."

Campbell African Methodist Episcopal Church
167 Kinsey Street, Philadelphia, Pennsylvania
Open to the public

The church was founded in 1817 and in 1838 established the African Colored School in one of its rooms. Several members of the church worked on the underground and often finalized arrangements for transporting runaways in casual meetings after church services.

Mother Bethel African Methodist Episcopal Church
419 Sixth Street, Philadelphia, Pennsylvania
Open to the public

The first Mother Bethel church was established in 1794 by pastor Richard Allen, who in 1830 organized the African American Convention in Philadelphia. The second church, built on the same site in 1805, was an underground station for fifty-five years and hundreds of slaves were hidden in its rooms by a succession of pastors including Allen, Morris Brown, Edward Waters, William Quinn, Willis Nazrey, and Daniel Payne.

Anna Preston Home
State and Rose Hill Roads, West Grove, Philadelphia, Pennsylvania
Private home

Preston, a graduate of the Women's Medical College of Philadelphia and a Quaker, frequently hid slaves in her home and then drove them to a nearby Quaker community in Oxford, sometimes dressing slaves in Quaker clothing to avoid detection.

Hosanna A.U.M.P. Church
At Lincoln University, Route 1, two miles from Oxford (a Philadelphia suburb), Chester, Pennsylvania
Open to the public

The tiny brick church with a single, narrow, double-door entrance and single, thin chimney was founded in 1829 by members of the freed black community in the area. Black abolitionist leaders such as Harriet Tubman and Frederick Douglass lectured there. Fugitives were hidden inside the church or at the homes of members. Several dozen young black men from the Oxford area volunteered to fight with the 54th Massachusetts Volunteers, the all-black regiment celebrated in the movie *Glory*. Seventeen of them are buried in the Hosanna Church cemetery.

Cox Home
Route 1, Kennett Square, Pennsylvania
Tours by permission

John and Hannah Cox, Quakers, were so prominent in the underground and abolitionist movement that John Greenleaf Whittier wrote a poem about them on their fiftieth wedding anniversary, "Golden Wedding at Longwood," which celebrated their underground work. Their 500-acre estate is now known as DuPoint Pierce Park Estate.

Longwood Meeting House
Route 1, Kennett Square, Pennsylvania
Open to the public

The Quakers in the Philadelphia area were often divided in their feelings about the increasingly violent anti-slavery movement in the 1850s. Several dozen radical anti-slavery Quakers split off from the main church and formed the Longwood Meeting House in 1854. Noted black and white abolitionists, such as Sojourner Truth, Susan B. Anthony, and William Lloyd Garrison lectured there. Runaways were hidden inside the church for a night or two and then at the homes of members. Most went undetected, despite distinct proslavery feelings by many in the Philadelphia area. The church today is one of the best preserved of the hundreds of underground sites in America. It serves as headquarters for the Brandywine tourist information center and visitors can take organized tours of the house and its grounds and see an exhibit about the underground. *For further information: Historical Society of Pennsylvania 215-545-0391; Philadelphia Visitors and Convention Center 215-636-3300.*

LUMBERVILLE

Sunnyside/Lewis Sisters Home
Old Kimberton Road, Lumberville, Pennsylvania
Private home

The large home and farm were owned by the three Lewis sisters, area social lions in public and a trio of the most active underground operators in private. The sisters hid slaves in barns on their property or in the rooms of their expansive house. Several slave marriages were performed at the estate. Slavecatchers sometimes raided Sunnyside looking for fugitives. The sisters inevitably charmed the hunters, offering them snacks and tea, and told them to look wherever they wanted, just as long as they did not go into their "ladies private bedrooms." The hunters agreed and never found any slaves, who were, of course, hidden in their bedrooms. The sisters were

as bold as they were gracious, and took on the dangerous task of hiding
William Parker, the runaway who was at the center of the much-publicized
1851 Christiana riot in the southern part of Pennsylvania where a slavecatcher was killed. Parker was rushed to Sunnyside in the middle of the
night and kept there for several days until the underground could move
him into New York and then Canada.

DOWNINGTON

Thomas Home/Downington Public Library
330 East Lancaster Avenue, Downington, Pennsylvania
Open to the public

Zebulon Thomas was a farmer who built two separate farmhouses on
opposite sides of a local road. He spent months digging a tunnel that ran
under the road so he could harbor runaways in one of the houses and move
them quickly to the other if he was visited by slavecatchers. Although one
of his charges, a young girl, was kidnapped by slavecatchers, the rest hid
there in safety until they could be moved. The small stone home, built in
1800, now serves as Downington's Public Library. *For further information:
Downington Historical Society 215-269-6009.*

LIONVILLE

Vickers Tavern
Gordon Drive, Lionville, Pennsylvania
Open to the public

John Vickers had a crawl space underneath the first floor of his home in
which he hid most of the slaves in his care. He also owned a pottery shed
where he harbored others. He even hid slaves in his pottery kiln if it was
cool. Today, the Vickers home is a tavern. The owner proudly shows off
the secret trap door that led to the crawl space where the runaways hid.

PHOENIXVILLE

Schuykill Friends Meetinghouse
Route 23 and White Horse Road, Phoenixville, Pennsylvania
Open to the public

Schuykill was a Quaker meeting house that also served as a station on
the underground. It gained some notoriety when Henry "Box" Brown, the
runaway whose friends shipped him to Philadelphia in a wooden box,
demonstrated how he was shipped and ultimately emerged from the crate.

WILLOW GROVE

Kirk Homestead
200 Kirk Road, Willow Grove, Pennsylvania
Private home

William Kirk arrived in Willow Grove in 1841, became a Quaker, then an avid abolitionist in 1846. His home had two cellars—one for storing goods and a second, larger, cave-like area used for harboring fugitives.

BUCKINGHAM

Mount Gilead A.M.E. Church
Holicong Road, Buckingham, Pennsylvania
Open to the public during services

The church, which sits on top of a mountain, was one of the final stops on the underground road in Pennsylvania before runaways crossed the Delaware River and traveled into New Jersey. The first church was built in 1835 and the present structure in 1852. The church's first minister was Ben Jones, a runaway slave nearly killed in a kidnapping attempt. The interior of the church can only be viewed during services, which are infrequent.

FLEETWOOD

Kirbyville Inn
Rich Maiden Road, Fleetwood, Pennsylvania
Open to the public

Like many underground site proprietors, the recent owners of the Kirbyville Inn had no idea they operated an old underground station until the inn underwent renovations. Workers discovered a secret attic and some artifacts that indicated fugitives stayed there. The attic was built so that passersby and neighbors could not see runaways through the two windows in the roof. It is unknown how many years the inn served as an underground stop.

BIRDSBORO

Hopewell Furnace National Historical Site
Route 345 (south of town), Birdsboro, Pennsylvania
Open to the public

African Americans first arrived at Hopewell in the 1750s to become workers at the Hopewell Furnace, which was one of the country's busiest ironworks. The furnaces at first produced standard iron products, such as carriage frames, pots, and utensils, but from 1775 until 1781 black workers at the company turned it into an arsenal for the Continental Army, producing thousands of cannon balls and several dozen large cannons, some of which were used at the siege at Yorktown, which brought the war to an end. The ironworks returned to commercial business at the conclusion of the Revolution and the black community in the area grew. The community used their homes and the thick woods near the ironworks to hide runaways throughout the 1840s and 1850s. The African Episcopal Methodist Church there opened in 1856 and also served as a hideaway. *For further information: Pennsylvania German Society 215-582-1441.*

READING

Bethel A.M.E. Church
119 North Tenth Street, Reading, Pennsylvania
Open to the public

The church was the religious and social center of life for the more than 200 blacks living in the Reading area in the 1840s and 1850s. Members of the congregation hid some slaves in the church at night or took them to their homes. There were so many runaways hidden in Reading that by the mid-1850s local newspapers frequently carried ads offering rewards of from one to five dollars for fugitives. Preachers at the church worked with the countywide underground to send runaways to other towns. Reading was a major rail center and many fugitives were hidden on freight and baggage cars and forwarded to either Elmira or Philadelphia, particularly on lines owned by the Reading Railroad. *For further information: Historical Society of Berks County 215-375-4335.*

DOUGLAS TOWNSHIP

Pine Forge
Pine Forge Road, Douglas Township, Pennsylvania
Open to the public

When Thomas Rutter began his ironworks in the area in the early 1700s, white colonists were still worried about Indian raids, which were infrequent but a very real concern. To protect himself and his family, he built Pine Forge, an estate with a huge manor house connected to large underground tunnels. He and his family planned to hide in the tunnels if attacked by Indians (there are no records of attacks). More than one hundred years later Rutter's descendants, strong anti-slavery advocates, used those same tunnels to harbor runaways. Today it is a Seventh Day Adventist school.

MERCERSBURG

South Fayette Street (downtown area), Mercersburg, Pennsylvania
Private homes

Mercersburg is only a few miles from the border of Maryland, a slave state, and many runaways made their homes here in the 1820s and 1830s, often with fake papers indicating they were freedmen. The town's black population grew throughout the nineteenth century until it was about 20 percent African American in the early 1850s. Some former slave families fled the area after the Fugitive Slave Act was passed, fearful of kidnapping, but others stayed. Thirty-three men from Mercersburg fought with the 54th Massachusetts Volunteers, the all-black U.S. Army regiment. *For further information: Livesay Historical Society 717-328-3810.*

MUNCY

McCarty-Wertman House
34 North Main Street, Muncy, Pennsylvania
Open to the public as an inn

The home was built during the American Revolution and served as an underground station late in the 1850s. The two-story wood frame structure housed from one to five slaves in a cellar that was closely guarded by members of the family. Today it is a country inn. *For further information: Muncy Historical Society 717-546-3431.*

SMITHPORT

Medbury Home
604 East Main Street, Smithport, Pennsylvania
Private home

The home is located on an old Indian trail that connects New York, upper Pennsylvania, and eastern Ohio. Families who lived in the home hid slaves in the large cellar and then sent them north to either Olean or Elmira, just over the New York State line, where they were eventually taken to Niagara Falls and Canada. *For further information: McKean County Historical Society 814-887-5142.*

UPPER DARBY

Sellars Hall (rectory of St. Alice's Church)
150 Hampton Road, Upper Darby, Pennsylvania
Private residence

Sellars Hall was the 1850s home of John Sellars II, who was an underground activist along with his son-in-law, Abraham Pennock, who also lived in town. Pennock, a friend of John Greenleaf Whittier, James Russell Lowell, and other abolitionists, was the publisher of a local abolitionist newspaper.

LIMA

Honeycomb A.M.E. Church
166 Barren Road, Lima, Pennsylvania
Open to the public

Delaware County was home to several hundred African Americans in the 1840s. The church was built in 1852 and soon afterward became a shelter for runaways traveling the underground from Delaware to Philadelphia.

PLYMOUTH MEETING

Abolition Hall
Germantown Pike and Butler Pike, Plymouth Meeting, Pennsylvania
Open to the public

Plymouth Meeting was a long-established Quaker settlement by the time the underground movement began in Pennsylvania. The anti-slavery feelings of most Quakers in Pennsylvania were well known, but until the late 1850s the Friends here were secretive about their work on the underground and not particularly public in their anti-slavery feelings. They became far more open after passage of the Fugitive Slave Act and the Kansas-Nebraska Act. The Friends in the tiny village built Abolition Hall in 1858 as a meeting place for anti-slavery advocates and as a refuge for runaways. Several Quakers hid runaways sent to them by black underground operator Dan Ross of Norristown. The Hall later became the art studio of Thomas Hovenden, who painted "John Brown's Last Moment" there.

MAULSBY HOUSE

Butler Pike, Plymouth Meeting, Pennsylvania
Private home

The Maulsby home, built in the 1720s, is one of the oldest in Pennsylvania. The large stone house was used to harbor fugitives, probably from the mid-1820s until the Civil War. Pro-slavery residents of the county suspected its residents of being members of the underground and constantly threatened to burn down the house if they ever found slaves there. Underground operators in the area, who acknowledged the heated feelings of some area residents, had to be extremely careful in moving slaves in and out of the home. Thanks to the shrewd operations of the Maulsbys, and later the family of artist Tom Hovenden, the local pro-slavery residents never detected anyone.

HARRISBURG

Thomas Morris Chester Site
Market Square and Third Street, Harrisburg, Pennsylvania

An historical marker notes the site of the home of Thomas Morris Chester. The anti-slavery advocate was an attorney and abolitionist pamphleteer before the war and a correspondent during it, one of the few African Americans to work as a journalist for mainstream newspapers. He later moved to England and worked as an attorney. He and his family were leaders in the Harrisburg underground along with Dr. William Rutherford, the McClintock sisters, and Joseph Bustill.

Several underground operators worked in Harrisburg because the Pennsylvania state capital was a major eastern railroad hub. Operators put slaves on the baggage or freight cars, or sometimes on passenger cars with fake papers, and moved them north to Canada. A favorite train was the Northern Central Railroad, which took fugitives out of Pennsylvania to Elmira, New York. *For further information: Historical Society of Dauphin County 717-233-3462; Harrisburg Convention and Visitors Center 717-231-7788.*

CHRISTIANA

Resistance Monument
High Street, Christiana, Pennsylvania

The monument commemorates the resistance of local farmers and underground workers to a raid by Maryland slaveholder Edward Gorsuch in September, 1851, to recover his runaway, William Parker. Gorsuch was killed and his son wounded in a gunfight that began a decade of opposition to the newly enacted Fugitive Slave Act.

COLUMBIA

Wright Mansion
Second and Cherry Streets, Columbia, Pennsylvania
Private home

William Wright was one of America's first underground operators, reportedly harboring fugitives as early as 1804. He sent them on to the home of his sister, Hannah Gibbons, or two African-American underground workers, Stephen Smith and William Whipper.

GETTYSBURG

Dobbin House
89 Steinwehr Avenue, Gettysburg, Pennsylvania
Open to the public as a restaurant

Dr. Alexander Dobbin built this large, two-story stone house on his farm in 1776. Sometime in the 1830s or 1840s his son Matthew, then living in the house, constructed a secret room between two floors, reached by sliding wooden pantry doors, where he hid slaves sent to him by the Underground Railroad. Matt Dobbin, a staunch anti-slavery advocate, once led five others from Gettysburg, all armed, on a raid to a nearby town to free captured runaways (the slavehunters had left before Dobbin and his men arrived). The major battle in the war, which eventually brought about freedom for all slaves, was fought in Gettysburg and Dobbin House was hit with dozens of stray bullets during the three-day battle (the bullet holes are all still visible). Today, the owners of Dobbin House, one of Gettysburg's largest restaurants, proudly displays the secret room to their patrons. *For further information: Adams County Historical Society 717-334-4723.*

BELLEFONTE

Linn House
100 North Allegheny Street, Bellefonte, Pennsylvania
Private home

Bellefonte was a small African-American community prior to the Civil War. The Linn home, with a secret third-floor room, was a stop on the underground, as was the local A.M.E. Church. Later, the community was home to William Mills, grandfather of the Mills Brothers, the fabled 1940s and 1950s singing group.

MILROY

Milroy Presbyterian Church
Lower Main Street, Milroy, Pennsylvania
Open to the public

The Dobbins family of Gettysburg, Pennsylvania, built a small, secret room for runaways between the first and second floors of their home. The house is a restaurant today and diners marvel at the hiding space. There are also hundreds of bullet holes in the restaurant, all fired during the Battle of Gettysburg in July, 1863. (Courtesy of Dobbins House)

Reverend James Nourse, pastor of the church, started an underground station there and served as protector to many slaves, including Charles Ball, who wrote his autobiography in 1836.

POTTSVILLE

Gillingham House
622 Mahantango Street, Pottsville, Pennsylvania
Private home

Quaker James Gillingham, his wife, and children ran this station on the underground. They kept runaways overnight in their spacious, two-story red brick home but also let some stay as long as several weeks, keeping them busy with household chores. The fugitives who worked in Gillingham's yard tried to keep out of sight but, if neighbors spotted them, one of the children would ask the neighbors to keep quiet. They did. Gillingham ran the underground with two African Americans, John Lee and Nicholas Biddle. *For further information: Historical Society of Schuykill County 717-622-7540.*

BEAVER FALLS

Geneva College, Beaver Falls, Pennsylvania
Open to the public

The college served as a major station on the underground when it was located in Northwood, Ohio. Faculty and students hid fugitives in a string of caves in the hills surrounding Northwood prior to the Civil War. The school was moved to its present Beaver Falls campus in 1880 where it maintains a large, interesting exhibit of the college's underground work in Northwood.

NEW RICHMOND TOWNSHIP

John Brown's Tannery Museum
Township Road, New Richmond Township, Pennsylvania
Open to the public

John Brown, who lived in Ohio, New York, Kansas, Maryland, and Pennsylvania during his lifetime, established a commercial tannery in this tiny village near Lake Erie. Brown employed fifteen to twenty men making leather goods from 1825 to 1835. This was one of the first sites where Brown worked with the underground. He hid runaways in a false cellar under the building that housed a barn and his tannery. It is unknown how many slaves he sheltered over the years or if his workers aided him in his underground work. Brown, hung by the federal government in 1859, ran the government's post office in Richmond Township while he lived there. His first wife is buried nearby. Today, the tannery has been recreated as a museum.

ERIE

Commodore Perry House
Second and French Streets, Erie, Pennsylvania
Private home (being developed as an operating tavern)

The seaport of Erie was one of the country's major underground terminals because fugitives found it relatively easy to board passenger and cargo ships that would take them across the lake and to freedom in Canada. Erie and the surrounding towns of Cambridge Springs, Girard, Union City, Waterford, Branchville, and Albion all had underground houses.

The Perry home was first owned by Admiral Oliver Perry, the hero of the war of 1812. The home was later remodeled for use in the underground. A secret basement was home to slaves while they stayed there. To depart, they walked through false doors built into the sides of stone fireplaces in the large, wood frame home. Behind the fireplaces were tunnels built from stone that took the slaves to the shore of the bay, where they could board boats.

Fugitives arriving at Erie took two routes. One, by land, brought them through towns in far western New York state near the lake and eventually to Niagara Falls, where they crossed on the suspension bridge. A second, sea route, carried them across Lake Erie to ports in Canada. They usually crossed on small cargo ships, where friendly sea captains could hide them. *For further information: Erie County Historical Society 814-454-1813.*

BROWNSVILLE

Nemacolin Castle
Front Street and Second Avenue, Brownsville, Pennsylvania
Open to the public as a museum

Jacob Bowman, a trader, moved to this tiny village near the Monongahela River in Fayette County in 1786 and built a stone home, which he used as a trading post. The house was enlarged in 1847 and turned into an underground station by the Bowman family. The house had many rooms in which to hide slaves and a special "lookout room" where Bowman and his wife and children could peer out over the surrounding area to watch for slavehunters. Fugitives were taken from the Bowman home to the small black community at Belle Vernon, where they stayed a few days and then moved on. The home was later named the Nemacolin Castle and is open to the public today as a museum.

NEW CASTLE

White Home
305 North Jefferson Street, New Castle, Pennsylvania
Private home

Joseph White built this home in 1840 and began to shelter runaways shortly afterward. He constructed a Dutch oven and a large fireplace, local historians said, in order to warm up fugitives finishing their travel in the middle of the night. It is an indication that White, and so many others, often housed large groups of runaways traveling together. The two-story brick house is owned by St. Paul's Lutheran Church. *For further information: Lawrence County Historical Society 724-658-4022.*

WASHINGTON

LeMoyne House
49 East Maiden Street, Washington, Pennsylvania
Open to the public

The first LeMoyne in America was Dr. Julius LeMoyne, a longtime political activist who stormed the Bastille in the French Revolution. He moved to Washington in 1812 and built this home. His son, Dr. Frances Julius LeMoyne, became an avid abolitionist, formed an abolitionist society in Washington, and once ran for President on an abolitionist ticket. He and his family housed an underground station in their home, harboring anywhere from two to two dozen fugitives at one time in a large bedroom on the third floor converted for that purpose. LeMoyne built the first crematorium in America and served on the board of nearby Washington College. The wealthy LeMoyne also donated large sums of money to anti-slavery causes and educational institutions. His $20,000 contribution was the seed money for the LeMoyne Normal School in Memphis, Tennessee, today LeMoyne-Owen College. It was one of the South's first black colleges, founded in 1862, just after the Union Army occupied the city. *For further information: Washington County Historical Society 412-225-6740.*

WILLIAMSPORT

Long Reach Plantation
2887 South Reach Road, Williamsport, Pennsylvania
Open to the public as a restaurant

Williamsport was critical to the operation of the underground because of its location on the Pennsylvania Canal and easy traveling distance to Elmira, over the New York state line. One of the leaders there was businessman Thomas Updegraff, who owned a large merchandising store in town and lived in an eighteenth-century home on the canal. Updegraff hid slaves and sent them to other destinations via wagons or canal boats. The building was restored in 1986 and turned into a country inn.

PENNSDALE

The House of Many Stairs
Lower Main Street, Pennsdale, Pennsylvania
Private home

The "House of Many Stairs" was a Pennsdale, Pennsylvania, underground station with seven sets of staircases built so that runaways in hiding could flee if slavecatchers approached the home. (Courtesy of the Lycoming County Historical Society)

What was known in the 1850s as Bull's Tavern was nicknamed the House of Many Stairs because it had seven different staircases, all difficult to climb and all designed to make it easy for runaways to flee and difficult for pursuers to conquer. There were small hideaways built into the house at the top of some staircases. It is unknown if the proprietor, Edward Morris, built the staircases for that purpose since the building served as a stagecoach stop and inn and the stairs may have been constructed for room access. Morris was an underground leader, however, and found it easy to use the very busy tavern and stage stop as a cover for his operations. *For further information on the Williamsport/Pennsdale area: Lycoming County Historical Society 717-326-3326.*

For further information on sites in the state: Historical Society of Pennsylvania 215-545-0391; Pennsylvania Office of Tourism 717-787-5453.

New Jersey

There were two main underground routes through New Jersey, which served as a corridor state for runaways headed somewhere else. The first was a combination of sea routes from the slave state of Delaware across Delaware Bay to the Salem and Greenwich area of South Jersey. Slaves crossed the bay in boats with a combination of green and yellow lights on their bows and were met near shore by other boats with the same identifying lights. At Greenwich, runaways disembarked at a tiny community of Quakers and freed blacks. At Salem, runaways found the home of Abigail Goodwin, who spent most of her adult life aiding fugitives. From the Goodwin home runaways were moved north through Woodbury, Westville, Gloucester City, Medford, and Mt. Holly to the Camden area. Fugitives then moved either west into Philadelphia, where they were sent north toward Canada through Pennsylvania, or to New York, where they continued through New England or directly north through New York State and to Canada. A second line ran across central and northern New Jersey from the Trenton area through Hopewell, Princeton, Bordentown, New Brunswick, and Perth Amboy. Slavecatchers often lurked at the Raritan River crossing at New Brunswick and underground workers had to be vigilant. Other runaways picked up the route at the port of Perth Amboy, a few miles inland from the Atlantic, where merchant vessels carrying slave stowaways would dock and captains quietly turned over their fugitives over to the underground, whose workers would spirit them on to Rahway, Jersey City, and then by ferry to New York.

LAWNSIDE

> Mount Pisgah A.M.E. Church
> Moudly and Warrick Roads, Lawnside, New Jersey
> *Open to the public*

Lawnside, originally named Free Haven, was a small community of freed blacks in a thickly wooded area of Camden County, close to Philadelphia. Some of the residents who resided there in the 1850s were former slaves who escaped from Maryland. Among the families who resided there were the Stills. William Still became one of the leaders of the Vigilance Committee in Philadelphia and one of the most successful of all underground officials. Most of his seventeen brothers and sisters lived parts of their lives in Lawnside. Several of the family men fought for the Union Army in the Civil War. The church was there before the Stills. Erected in 1792, it is one of the oldest Methodist churches in New Jersey and from about 1830 to 1861 served as a station on the underground, maintained by the Stills and others in the community.

PETER MOTT HOUSE

Gloucester Road and White Horse Pike, Lawnside, New Jersey
Private home

Peter Mott's wood frame home in Lawnside was built in 1845 and quickly became a key stop on the underground for fugitives on the line from Philadelphia to New York. Mott was a former slave who moved to New Jersey from Delaware. The small home had a secret room behind locked double doors over a cellar where slaves were hidden. Mott fed and clothed runaways and then moved them along to Mt. Holly and Mt. Laurel. The house was saved from destruction by local residents in 1990 and placed on the National Register of Historic Places.

SALEM

Goodwin House
47 West Market Street, Salem, New Jersey
Private home

Slaves began fleeing Delaware and finding their way to Salem, one of New Jersey's southernmost towns, in the 1790s. They began to arrive in much larger numbers after the New Jersey legislature passed a gradual emancipation act in 1804. The Goodwin sisters, Abigail and Elizabeth, both Quakers, began their work on the underground in 1836. They organized a local sewing circle to make clothes for the fugitives they hid. The sisters, who lived modestly, regularly sent their own money to the Philadelphia Vigilance Committee to aid other runaways.

Abigail wrote of her contributions: "Thee will find enclosed five dollars, a little for so many to share it, but better than nothing. Oh, that people, rich people, would remember them instead of spending so much on themselves and those who are not called rich might if there was only a willing mind give too of their abundance." *For further information: Salem County Historical Society 609-935-5004.*

LUMBERTON

D.B. Cole House
Creek Road, Lumberton, New Jersey
Open to the public by appointment

Cole devised one of the most unique hiding places in the entire underground system behind his farmhouse. In case anyone was watching, he brought slaves into his carriage house, fifty yards from his own home, and then quickly out its back entrance to an old well. Runaways climbed down into the well on a long rope and dropped softly into the middle of a large room at the bottom that had a twenty-foot high ceiling. There, far below the ground, they were safe. Today, the Cole home is a tenant farmhouse on a larger farm and can be seen from the roadway.

MANNINGTON

Tide Mill Farm
100 Tide Mill Road, Mannington, New Jersey
Open to the public

Like many underground sites, the farmhouse of Quaker George Abbotts was not a known station until the mid-1980s, when, during remodeling, residents discovered a secret room under the floor of nutmeg a room in the house. Abbotts apparently hid slaves in the secret room and ventilated it with a twenty-foot long air vent that extended underneath his backyard. Slaves reached the farmhouse in the swampy area by walking and crawling on top of logs they pushed through the knee-deep water.

MT. HOLLY

Ashurst Mansion
Ashurst Lane and Garden Street, Mt. Holly, New Jersey
Private law office

The mansion, which had several safe houses, was one of the finest buildings in Mt. Holly. The family sheltered slaves and fed them and, when it was safe, transported them to other stops in New Jersey with their own wagons and teams of horses. *For further information: National Society of the Colonial Daughters of America 609-267-1054.*

PRINCETON

Witherspoon Presbyterian Church
124 Witherspoon Street, Princeton, New Jersey
Open to the public

The church, constructed in 1840 at the height of the Second Great Awakening in New Jersey, served as a center for religious and social activities for freed blacks in the Princeton area. Runaways were hidden inside the church and at nearby homes in Princeton. William Robeson, a former slave who moved to New Jersey at age fifteen after escaping from a plantation in North Carolina, became pastor of the church in the early twentieth century. His grandson was the gifted Paul Robeson, who became an all-American football star at Rutgers University and was one of the first blacks to play in the National Football League. Following an injury, he turned to the stage and became a world-famous actor, singer, and political activist. *For further information: Historical Society of Princeton 609-921-6748.*

HADDONFIELD

Edgewater
Mill Road, Haddonfield, New Jersey
Private home

Thomas and Josiah Evans lived in this three-story building, which was erected in 1748. The Evans operated an underground station there in the 1850s. They hid slaves in their attic by day and transported them to Mt. Holly at night. Despite their caution, Josiah Evans was stopped with a slave, Joshua Sadler, as he was driving to Mt. Holly. Faced with arrest and the return of the slave to his plantation, Evans simply paid several hundred dollars for the runaway's freedom. Sadler settled in the area and later started a school for African-American children.

Underground stations have always been difficult to document. The National Park Service, however, lists two other reported sites in the state: the Jesse Chew House, in Sewell, and the Meyers Building, in Marlton. Other sites were believed to have been located in Jersey City, Perth Amboy, New Brunswick, Princeton, Lambertville, Burlington, Swedesboro, and Evesham. *For further information: Historical Society of Haddonfield 609-429-2462.*

New York

New York City, along with Philadelphia and Boston, served as both a destination and transportation hub for the underground, much like a modern major city airport where passengers switch planes to fly somewhere else. Runaways arrived in New York City via boat from southern states or overland on the Philadelphia–New Jersey–New York underground. They either remained in the city, where there was a large and protective freed black community, or moved on. There were two routes out. The first went northeast into New England. Runaways were taken by wagons through lower Westchester County to the New England underground line, which began at Stamford, Connecticut, and then took fugitives to Boston.

A second route out of New York went directly north to Albany. Runaways usually went on steamboats, hidden somewhere on board, or traveled on public railroads using fake papers. They then headed northwest to Ithaca and Syracuse, in the middle of the state, Rochester, and then to Niagara Falls and Canada. Others went to Albany and then traveled northeast to Lake Placid and Troy, and from there into Vermont and, using the efficient Vermont underground, to Canada.

There were small routes in the western area of the state connected to the eastern Pennsylvania line. On one, fugitives moved north out of Philadelphia to Elmira, New York, and then through Tompkins County, with safehouses in Ithaca, then to Syracuse, Rochester, and Niagara Falls. Others followed routes to Olean or Jamestown, where they were sheltered, and then picked up a trail that took them to Warsaw, Pearl Creek, Wyoming, and other villages and eventually to Niagara Falls. Some fugitives went from Elmira to Peterboro, the much-publicized farm community established by wealthy abolitionist Gerrit Smith. Runaways could stay there, protected by the influential Smith, and become farmers or move on, transported by Smith's men and wagons.

The New York City Vigilance Committee, headed by David Ruggles, a grocer, had substantial financial support from the Tappan brothers, Arthur and Lewis, and deep commitments from city ministers and their congregations. Sympathetic dock workers often helped fugitives sneak off ships or, if not involved in the work of the underground, merely looked the other way when they saw them scurrying down a gangplank. Underground organizations were strong throughout the state, particularly in the Albany, Syracuse, and Rochester areas. Powerful businessmen and political figures, such as U.S. Senator William Seward, aided the underground privately and publicly protected its members.

NEW YORK CITY

Isaac Hopper Home
110 Second Avenue (Manhattan), New York, New York
Open to the public

Isaac Hopper, a Quaker, began aiding runaways in Philadelphia with his family when he was nine years old. By the time he was a teenager, in the 1790s, he was a worker on the underground. He moved to New York City in 1829 and opened a store on Pearl Street where fugitives met him and were sent to safe houses throughout the city or hidden in the rear of the store.

Bridge Street African Methodist Episcopal Wesleyan Church
273 Stuyvesant Avenue, Brooklyn, New York
Open to the public

Brooklyn's African-American community was already thriving during the American Revolution. The present church property was used for outdoor religious services for a mixed white and black community as early as 1766 and the first church structure was erected in 1794. The white and black congregation split later and in 1828 the current Wesleyan Church was constructed for the black community. It soon became a major stop on the underground as its successful middle class black community members gave support in shelter, food, and money for fugitives who chose to travel on to Canada.

Plymouth of the Pilgrims Church
75 Hicks Street, Brooklyn, New York
Open to the public

The fiery Henry Ward Beecher, brother of Harriet Beecher Stowe, was the pastor of this large, 2,500-seat church that drew parishioners from throughout New York, many of whom traveled over 90 minutes and took ferries to get there for his passionate sermons. Newspapers reported that thousands jammed the aisles and stood outside the church to listen to Beecher. The minister, an animated speaker, preached against slavery for years. His sermons were often accompanied by theatrical displays, such as mock slave auctions. Like many other abolitionist preachers, violence

drifted throughout his sermons and he bragged that a gun was a more powerful moral agent than a bible. The church reportedly served as an underground station, but there are few records because its operations had to be
extremely secretive since Beecher attracted so much public attention. The
church did have several tunnels beneath it, making it a likely place for
slaves to be hidden. It was a magnet for the great orators of the Civil War
era. In addition to Beecher, others who spoke there included Horace Greeley, Ralph Waldo Emerson, Wendell Phillips, Senator Charles Sumner, and
Clara Barton. Later, its guest lecturers included Booker T. Washington and
Martin Luther King Jr.

Siloam Presbyterian Church
260 Jefferson Avenue, Brooklyn, New York
Open to the public

Members of the church sometimes hid slaves in the church itself, usually
for a night or two, or sheltered them in their Brooklyn homes until arrangements could be made to move them out of the city. Members of the congregation also donated money to the New York Vigilance Committee to
assist other runaways.

Mother Zion African Methodist Episcopal Church
140 137th Street, New York, New York
Open to the public

Mother Zion, originally built on Leonard Street in 1800, was the first
African-American church in New York State. Its most prominent pastor,
the Reverend James Varick, lectured against slavery for years and the
church's rooms and basement were used to harbor fugitives. It was nicknamed "Freedom church." Later, it became the founding church in the
A.M.E. Conference of Churches. The church was later moved to its current
location in Harlem, where one of its pastors was Reverend Benjamin Robeson, brother of singer and activist Paul Robeson.

*For further information: New York Historical Society 212-873-3400; New
York City Convention and Visitors Center 212-484-1200.*

TROY

National City Bank Building
State and First Streets, Troy, New York
Open to the public

Troy and nearby Albany were major switching stations on the railroad where travelers from New York City would go northwest to Syracuse, Rochester, and Canada or northeast through Vermont to Canada. On April 27, 1860, fugitive slave Charles Nalle was captured by slavehunters in Troy and brought to the United States Commissioner's office in this building. An angry crowd gathered outside to protest the seizure. The commissioner ruled that Nalle had to be taken back to his plantation in Virginia and ordered a team of guards to escort him to a boat on the Hudson a few hundred yards away. Outside, a small band of angry abolitionists, white and black, led by Harriet Tubman, rushed toward the guards. Tubman grabbed one of Nalle's manacled arms and would not let go.

The guards managed to get Nalle onto a ferry boat to take him to a larger ship, despite Tubman hanging on to him, but the growing crowd followed them onto the boat as Tubman's group battled guards as it moved down the river. One of the abolitionists, a freed black man, was killed and several others knocked down and severely wounded. The guards were either beaten up and driven off or held back as Tubman, still holding Nalle, pulled the man off the boat. With the help of others, they rushed him to a nearby wagon, which took him out of Troy and to freedom in Canada. A plaque on a wall of the bank commemorates the rescue. *For further information: Rensselaer County Historical Society 518-272-7232.*

AUBURN

William Seward Home
33 South Street, Auburn, New York
Open to the public as a museum

William Henry Seward was not only the leading radical, anti-slavery politician in the country in the 1850s, but a worker on the underground who hid slaves in his home as well as a publisher who helped produce abolitionist newspapers and books (Frederick Douglass' autobiography was printed in his home). Seward was one of the most successful public figures in America. He served two terms as governor of New York and later two terms in the U.S. Senate. He left the Whig Party and helped form the New York State Republican Party in 1855. The New Yorker gained international fame for a speech in which he denounced all proslavery laws and said that there was a "higher law" than those passed by Congress—god's law. Seward was the runner-up to Abraham Lincoln at the 1860 Republican Convention and became Lincoln's Secretary of State. He was attacked and nearly murdered as part of the plot

The Historic Seward House
Auburn, New York

U.S. Senator and later Secretary of State William Seward was the leader of the radical wing of the Republican Party in the 1850s. Hundreds of slaves were hidden in the rear, second-story bedrooms of his home in Auburn, New York. (Courtesy of the William Seward House)

to assassinate Lincoln and other cabinet officers in 1865. Seward recovered and continued in office, becoming most famous for the United States' purchase of Alaska in 1867, dubbed "Seward's Folly" by the press.

Seward was very vocal in his support of the Underground Railroad and was severely criticized for it by southern politicians. He told crowds that he loathed the Fugitive Slave Act and openly urged them to defy it, telling one group in Ohio to "extend a cordial welcome to the fugitive who lays his weary limbs at your door, and defend him as you would your household Gods." A wealthy man, Seward put up thousands of dollars to bail abolitionists out of jail. He was the man who made bond for the rescuers of the fabled "Jerry" in Syracuse. He also posted bail for a newspaper editor charged with aiding fugitives.

Seward and his wife frequently entertained visitors, usually New York state politicians, at their large, two-story home. He used the constant coming and going of people and carriages as a cover for his underground operations. The Sewards hid slaves in the upstairs rooms of the rear wing of their home while people were in the house. When the home was empty of guests, the Sewards invited the runaways to spend time with them downstairs and all dined together.

Seward bought several acres of land near his home in Auburn and, as previously noted, sold it to Harriet Tubman for a minimal sum in recognition of her services.

Harriet Tubman Home
180 South Street, Troy, New York
Open to the public as a museum

Tubman moved into this home she purchased from William Seward after the Civil War. She bought it for her parents, whom she liberated from their Maryland plantation, and lived in it with them most of her post-slavery life. The activist was buried with full military honors in Auburn's Fort Hill Cemetery, March 15, 1913. *For further information: Cayuga County Historical Society 315-253-8051.*

SYRACUSE

Jermain Loguen Grave
Oakwood Cemetery, Syracuse, New York

Loguen was a slave who escaped from his Tennessee plantation and made it safely to Canada. He became a minister there and returned to the United States, risking imprisonment, to found churches in several New York cities before settling in Syracuse. Loguen established underground stations at his church and his home and harbored hundreds of runaways over the years. He also supervised one of the country's largest city underground organizations in Syracuse, one that extended out into several villages surrounding the town. Syracuse had a large freed black community, a number of abolitionist ministers, and its own successful abolitionist newspaper. *For further information: Onondaga Historical Society 315-428-1862.*

PETERBORO

Peterboro Area Museum and Gerrit Smith exhibit
Main Street, Peterboro, New York
Open to the public

Gerrit Smith was the son of Peter Smith, who became wealthy in the fur trade and real estate businesses. Gerrit was a humanitarian who spent all of his adult life in the anti-slavery cause. He was one of the East Coast's most active supporters of freed blacks, arranging for dozens to serve as tenant farmers on his vast estate in central New York. He was one of the most successful operators of the Underground Railroad, hiding runaways in his barn and a secret room beneath his kitchen. He donated large sums of bail money for jailed abolitionists and slave rescuers and contributed to the legal defense in many of the well-known rescue trials. Smith, the cousin of women's activist Elizabeth Cady Stanton, took dangerous risks. The biggest was paying for the guns John Brown used in his attack on Harper's Ferry. Following Brown's arrest and hanging, Smith shrewdly had himself committed to a local insane asylum and his lawyers offered reports from doctors as proof that whatever help Smith gave to Brown was done when he was mentally unsound. Smith was never charged in the Harper's Ferry raid.

The mansion itself burned down in 1936, but there is a small museum concerning Smith's life and the lives of African Americans who settled in the area after the Civil War.

JAMESTOWN

Catherine Harris House
1610 Spring Street, Jamestown, New York
Private home

Catherine Harris was a longtime underground activist whose home was one of the first stops for runaways traveling the Atlantic lines through eastern Pennsylvania and into New York State. Jamestown, home to several underground operators, was a small but fiery abolitionist community. *For further information: Fenton Historical Society 716-483-7521.*

ITHACA

St. James African Methodist Episcopal Zion Church
116 Cleveland Avenue, Ithaca, New York
Open to the public

The church was built before the Civil War for the growing African-American population of Ithaca, home to Cornell University and a major stop on the underground. The pastor during the 1850s, Reverend Samuel Perry, hid slaves in the basement of the church. Members of the church housed runaways in their homes and barns. *For further information: Tompkins County Historical Society 607-273-8284.*

ROCHESTER

Susan B. Anthony House
17 Madison Street, Rochester, New York
Open to the public

Whether the home of America's leading women's activist actually served as a station on the underground remains a mystery, but it is well documented that Harriet Tubman and other underground operators and well-known abolitionists visited there often. Anthony fully supported the abolitionist cause and her brother Merritt was a member of John Brown's army in Kansas. The home is a National Historic Landmark.

Frederick Douglass Monument
Central Avenue and St. Paul Street in Highland Park,
Rochester, New York

Douglass lived in Rochester for many years and published the *North Star*, his abolitionist newspaper, in an office there. He harbored hundreds of fugitives over the years, sometimes sheltering as many as thirteen at a time. Many hid in his home and at his newspaper office. The home burned down, but in 1898 Rochester officials erected this monument, which was dedicated by then Governor Theodore Roosevelt. *For further information: Rochester Historical Society 716-271-2705; Rochester Visitors and Convention Center 716-546-3070.*

Spring House Restaurant
3001 Monroe Street, Rochester, New York
Open to the public

The four-story Spring House Hotel, built in the 1840s, was one of many hotels that lined the Erie Canal, connecting the Hudson River to Buffalo. Renovations over the years disclosed many hidden rooms in the basement where runaways were hidden. Many fugitives moved in and out of these safe houses as they traveled the length of the canal to Buffalo and then to Canada.

BUFFALO

Michigan Avenue Baptist Church
511 Michigan Avenue, Buffalo, New York
Open to the public

The church was a station for many traveling along Lake Erie toward Niagara Falls. One of its members was former slave William Wells Brown, who became a nationally prominent anti-slavery lecturer in 1847 at the urging of William Lloyd Garrison. Brown wrote hundreds of newspaper columns for abolitionist newspapers and became America's first African-American novelist. He became a doctor after the Civil War. *For further information: Buffalo and Erie County Historical Society 716-873-9612.*

LEWISTON

The village of Lewiston was already etched into American history when the underground movement adopted it in the 1840s. The town was burned to the ground in the British assault on Fort Niagara during the War of 1812. Local residents rebuilt the entire town in two years and it later became a busy stop for business travelers when a long suspension bridge was built between it and Canada in 1850. The bridge also became the escape route out of the United States for runaways (all that's left of the historic bridge today are two of its large granite columns, located in Art Park on River Road). Underground operators throughout the Lewiston area harbored fugitives and a plaque located in the First Presbyterian Church, on Cayuga Street, commemorates their work. *For further information: Lewiston Historical Society 716-754-4212.*

Amos Tyron Home
4772 Lower River Road, Lewiston, New York
Private home

Reverend Amos Tyron's home was a productive station for the underground because it was built on a sloping piece of ground. The house had two stories of living space and, because of the slope of the ground, had four separate and different-sized cellars below where slaves were hidden. Tyron aided runaways in crossing the Niagara River at night.

Riverside Inn
115 S. Water Street, Lewiston, New York
Open to the public

The inn, an historic building next to Niagara Falls, became a favorite restaurant for Lewiston residents. Its busy traffic of customers offered a perfect front for the protection of fugitives, who were hidden in its cellar and spirited across the suspension bridge at night.

Niagara Frontier Bible Church
Mohawk and River Roads, Lewiston, New York
Open to the public

Slaves were hidden in the church until boat transportation could be arranged for them to cross the Niagara River upstream from the falls where it was often calm. Sometimes, in particularly bad winters, the river would freeze over and tiny parties of up to ten slaves, their life's belongings in sacks slung over their shoulders, arms tight against their coats to ward off chilling winds, could be seen walking slowly across the frozen ice bridges of the river. *For further information: Lewiston Historical Society 716-754-4214.*

For further information on sites in the state: New York Historical Society 212-873-3400; New York Visitors and Convention Center 518-474-4116.

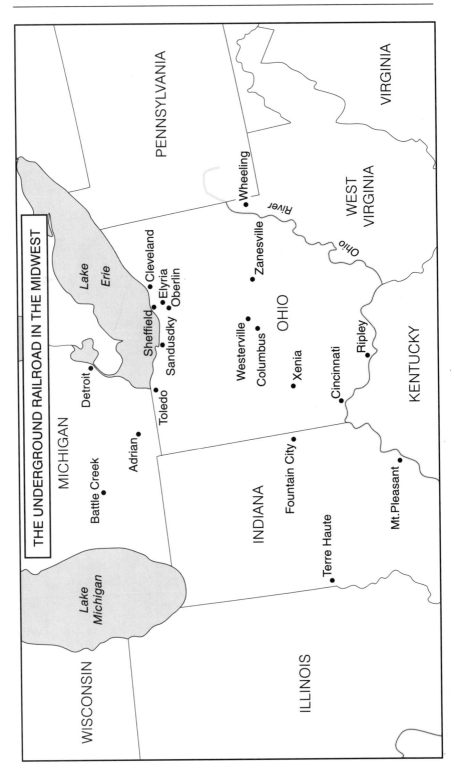

THE UNDERGROUND RAILROAD IN THE MIDWEST

* * *

Levi Coffin: "President of the Underground"

Levi Coffin watched, as always, for activity in the thick woods near his two-story brick home on the outskirts of Newport, Indiana. Suddenly, just after darkness fell, he noticed branches of trees near his home moving slowly and shadowy figures moving about behind them. There, between some trees, was yet another small group of frightened runaway slaves looking for freedom—and for Levi Coffin.

A devout Quaker, Coffin was perhaps the most successful underground leader in America, nicknamed the "president of the Underground Railroad" by many. He began aiding runaway slaves as a teenager in North Carolina, one of the few in that slave state to offer assistance, and left the state because of his deep opposition to slavery. He and his wife moved to the Quaker village of Newport (now Fountain City), Indiana, in 1826 to establish a mercantile store there and, secretly, to open a safe house for fugitives he knew were starting to flee Kentucky's large plantations with regularity and cross the Ohio into Indiana. Coffin's underground depot was working within a year of his arrival in Newport, where many of his former friends from North Carolina had settled and where other Quakers from northern states had moved. Many residents in the town were opposed to slavery and these friends, including local police and judges, formed a net that protected Coffin and his underground work.

Newport was a perfect geographic terminal for the underground because of its position on a direct route north from Ohio River crossing points in Madison and Jeffersonville. The Quaker businessman, whose store was successful enough to permit him to branch out into other small businesses in the area, such as a mill

185

Underground Railroad leader Levi Coffin lived in Fountain City, Indiana, and Cincinnati, Ohio. He managed to protect over two thousand fugitives during thirty-four years' work on the Underground Railroad. (Courtesy of the Levi Coffin House)

which produced linseed oil, quickly established several escape routes from Newport to thwart the slavehunters from Kentucky who roamed through the area. These routes wound through small farms and communities in the central Indiana area and took runaways north to Decatur and Fort Wayne.

The underground leader's work cannot be placed in the category of any other except perhaps John Rankin and John Parker of Ohio and the leaders of the Philadelphia and Boston undergrounds. Coffin not only harbored fugitives, but arranged for wagon transportation for them to other safe houses, often driving up to twelve of them himself. He developed a large network of assistants throughout the area and within an hour could dispatch a rider to reroute fugitives on the run if slavehunters were spotted in the area. He had friends in every small Quaker village throughout Indiana, and runaways sought by slavehunters would be taken there and hidden for weeks until the danger had passed. Coffin gave fugitives new clothes, fed them, and brought in doctors to care for them.

Coffin was shrewd, too, and understood local politics. He was such a prominent businessman that he was soon asked to join the boards of local businesses, including the biggest bank in Newport. He was a close personal friend of the mayors, councilmen, and newspaper editors in the area. Some of his closest business confidants were the best lawyers in the southern Indiana area and through them he would loudly announce that anyone who tried to meddle with his "work" would be arrested and undergo both criminal and civil prosecution and wind up paying him thousands of dollars in settlements.

His public image and legal threats enabled him not only to ward off slavehunters, but to conduct his underground work more publicly than anyone else in the northern states. His work became so acceptable and so safe that he frequently kept slaves in his home for two to three weeks, putting them to work on odd jobs, until he could transport them (although on several occasions he was threatened by slavehunters and had to send runaways on their way prematurely). In his years in Indiana, he managed to harbor nearly one thousand slaves.

Coffin, a good businessman, decided to move to Cincinnati, one of the busiest port towns in the country, in 1847. He took his family to Ohio and became the leader of the underground in Cincinnati as soon as he arrived. Coffin followed the same pattern he used so successfully in Indiana, becoming quite prominent through his business connections and befriending lawyers whom he would use to threaten any slavehunters. Protected through his rough persona and legal friends, he freely ran the underground again, once more caring for about one thousand fugitives in thirteen years in the Queen City, often moving a dozen or more at night out of his brick home to other sites on the Ohio underground toward Canada.

Coffin's work on behalf of slaves did not end with the start of the Civil War. In 1863, he helped organize the Freedmen's Bureau, the federal office that aided freed slaves and built schools for their children. He toured Europe in 1864 and 1867 to raise money for the Western Freedmen's Aid Commission, which he ran in Ohio. He was one of the guest speakers at the huge Cincinnati rally of blacks and whites to celebrate ratification of the Fifteenth Amendment which gave blacks the vote, in Indiana. Later, long after the war ended, he and his family took a long awaited vacation in Canada and wherever he went he was surrounded by thankful slaves whom he liberated.

* * *

Indiana

Directly across the Ohio River from Kentucky, the free state of Indiana was, along with Ohio, a popular crossing point for runaway slaves. The routes into and through Indiana were dangerous, though, because many residents of the lower part of the state did not see slavery as the evil as did many other northerners. They offered no aid to escaping slaves and had no compassion for abolitionists. Slavehunters from Kentucky crossed the Ohio frequently and searched for slaves throughout the state, particularly after the passage of the Fugitive Slave Act in 1850. Underground workers had to be particularly careful because of the danger that surrounded them.

According to underground maps of 1848, not made public until 1896, escaping slaves entered Indiana at seven towns on the Ohio: Rockport and Evansville in the southwest corner of the state, Leavenworth, Marvin's Landing, New Albany (across the Ohio from Louisville), or upriver at Madison or Lawrenceburg. Some made it into the state by land on a route that began in Cincinnati, Ohio. The banks along the Ohio at many of these crossing sites were steep, but heavily wooded and provided protective cover. The land ran uphill from the river for miles so the journey to the first safe house was a wearying one. Once within the borders of the state, slaves looked for known underground safe houses within a few miles of the river; from there they went north on three main routes.

The eastern route ran close to the Ohio Border. Runaways on this route made their way to Richmond, halfway up the state, and then north to underground homes in Fountain City, Winchester, Portland, Decatur, Fort Wayne, and Auburn. The central line of the railroad began in the New Albany area and ran up the middle of the state to Indianapolis and Loganport and then north to Plymouth, South Bend, and into Michigan, at Battle Creek, where the underground spirited fugitives across the state to Detroit. The western line, which hugged the banks of the Wabash River, took runaways to safe houses in Vincennes, Terre Haute, Lafayette, Rensselaer, and then South Bend and into Michigan. Some escaping slaves were taken to small villages along the southern shore of Lake Michigan and secretly boarded cargo-laden barges that carried them to points in Michigan where they picked up other underground roads. There are only a few sites still standing that served as underground stations, but local and county historical associations in Indiana claim that the state had more than thirty safe houses during the 1850s. More sites are under investigation.

FOUNTAIN CITY

Levi Coffin House
Route 27, Fountain City, Indiana
Open to the public

Levi Coffin moved to this two-story, brick, federal-style home in 1826 and lived in it for twenty years before departing for Cincinnati in 1847. Slaves were hidden inside the various rooms of the house and in nearby outbuildings. Coffin, who ran a mercantile business in Fountain City, then

Levi Coffin's two-story brick home in Fountain City, Indiana, was the major switching station for the underground in the state. (Courtesy of the Levi Coffin House)

named Newport, was the leader of the underground in Indiana. A successful businessman and civic leader, he dealt with enough public officials, ministers, newspaper editors, businessmen, and traders to let people in neighboring states know that his home was a well-guarded safe house. Slaves came to him from Kentucky and Ohio and, in his twenty years in the small town, he reportedly sheltered close to 1,000 fugitives.

The home itself has had an interesting life. The Coffins never returned after leaving in 1847 and various owners lived in it until 1910, when an entrepreneur turned the home into a hotel and added a wing. It was placed on the National Register of Historic Landmarks in 1966 and purchased by the state of Indiana in 1967. By the early 1970s, the hotel wing was removed and the home was restored to appear as it did in the early

1840s. The home is open to the public and tours are offered by a well-organized staff of volunteers. Thousands of schoolchildren tour the home annually.

TERRE HAUTE

Allen Chapel, African American Methodist Episcopal Church
1411 South Sixth Street, Terre Haute, Indiana
Open to the public

The current church rests on the site of the original building, which was a major underground stop in the 1840s and 1850s. Members of the church congregation kept supplies of food and clothing in the church for the fugitives, who arrived frequently, sometimes as many as six or seven in a wagon driven by an underground worker from Vincennes. A pastor during the 1850s, the Rev. Hiram Revels, later became one of the nation's first African-American U.S. senators during the Reconstruction period. Today, the church maintains a museum of the underground work of the church and others in the Terre Haute area. *For further information: Vigo County Historical Society 812-235-9717.*

CARTHAGE

Mt. Pleasant Beech African Methodist Episcopal Church
Main Street, Carthage, Indiana
Open to the public

The church was founded on land first farmed by a group of freed blacks who left North Carolina and arrived in Terre Haute in 1828, when the entire area was still raw frontier. They established an A.M.E. church on the site in 1832 and in 1840 the church hosted the state's first African Methodist Episcopal Conference. Two of the leading black underground operators in the state, Bishop Morris Brown and Reverend Paul Quinn, visited the church frequently in the 1840s, aiding locals in establishing a safe house for runaways. From the 1840s until the outbreak of the Civil War, hundreds of fugitives found temporary protection within the walls of the church.

For further information on sites in the state: Indiana Office of Tourism 317-232-8860.

Ohio

* * *

Two Neighbors

The two most prominent underground leaders in the state of Ohio were neighbors in Ripley, Ohio, who between them claim to have rescued and protected over 2,500 runaways. Ripley was a small town overlooking the Ohio River. Like Oberlin and Xenia in the state, it was a community full of many passionate underground workers who frequently risked their lives and fortunes in the anti-slavery movement. The small town had 300 public members in its anti-slavery society. Runaways knew exactly where Ripley was and how to find its underground leaders, white minister John Rankin and black foundry owner John Parker.

The tombstone above the graves of John and Jean Rankin appropriately reads "freedom's heroes." Perhaps no other family in America (the Rankins had thirteen children who helped them in their underground work) had so much influence in the underground movement. Rankin was born in a slave state, Tennessee, in 1793, the son of a blacksmith. He hated slavery and, after ordination as a minister, moved to Ripley in 1822. He plunged into the anti-slavery cause, writing a series of editorials for a local newspaper against the institution. In 1828 he built his home on a bluff overlooking the river and called it "Liberty Hill." The home, with a barn, soon became a haven for runaways, who looked for a lamp on his porch as a sign that there was no danger.

For thirty-three years, Rankin preached against slavery. He founded the Free Presbyterian Church of America in 1845 and was the first president of the Ripley

Rev. John Rankin of Ripley, Ohio, claimed to have saved over two thousand slaves in his thirty-three years of work in the underground. (Courtesy of the Ohio Historical Society)

Rankin lived in this small home on top of a steep bluff overlooking the
Ohio River. A long series of stairs connected the front door to the
riverbank and runaways who climbed them later remarked it was like
"climbing to heaven." Six of Rankin's sons fought for the Union Army in
the Civil War. (Courtesy of the Ohio Historical Society)

Anti-Slavery Society. He wrote articles against the institution and hid
runaways in his home and barn, sometimes as many as twelve at a
time. His sons helped him transport fugitives with their wagons and
horses when darkness fell. Rankin organized others in southern and
central Ohio and by the early 1840s ran a network of routes and safe
houses that covered nearly 150 miles of Ohio. He scoffed at reports
that southern slaveowners posted a $2,500 bounty for his capture,
dead or alive. The minister was greatly saddened by the Civil War, in
which six of his sons fought for the Union Army. He believed that
Congress should have simply paid southerners to free the slaves.

He remained active in social movements and moved to Ironton,
Ohio, in 1873 and died there in 1886 at the age of ninety-three. His
granddaughter Jeannette, who moved to Colorado, became the first
woman to be elected to the U.S. Congress.

His counterpart in town was former slave and foundry worker
John Parker, a big, burly man who became one of the more
successful businessmen in Ohio after the war. Parker was born a
slave in Kentucky but was sold as a teenager to a doctor in Mobile,
Alabama. The doctor hired him out to a local foundry where he
earned money for himself and his owner. The resourceful Parker

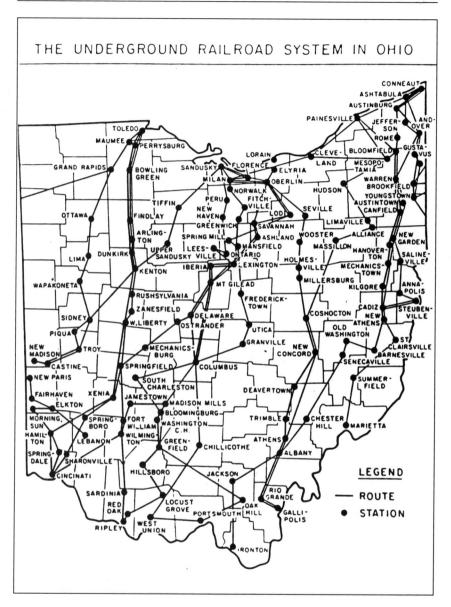

THE UNDERGROUND RAILROAD SYSTEM IN OHIO

LEGEND

— ROUTE

● STATION

This map of actual underground routes in Ohio shows has extensive the railroad was, with over two hundred safe houses. (Courtesy of the Ohio Historical Society)

talked a Mobile woman into buying him from the doctor for $1,800, about twice the market rate for young male slaves. He then entered into an agreement with her to use his foundry earnings to buy his freedom for $2,000. Working day and night, he earned the money in eighteen months and was freed in 1845.

Parker moved into the black community of Ripley and went to work at a foundry there. He met several escaped slaves from Kentucky who told him that many runaways had neither the resources to navigate their way out of the state nor the money to buy boats or pay boatmen to take them across the Ohio. One night, spurred on by a friend, Parker crossed the Ohio, found a group of fearful slaves on the run, and guided them to Ripley. He was encouraged by his foray and repeated it a month later. He then began to engage in rescue full time, riding deep into Kentucky to bring out slaves—individually, in families, and in groups of a dozen or more. He kept a record of his rescues and when the Civil War ended estimated that he rescued 440 men, women, and children. He turned them all over to the underground in Ripley, which transported them to Canada.

The thrifty Parker began saving his money as soon as he arrived in Ripley and after the war purchased his own iron foundry. He secured a number of federal patents for his imaginative ways of processing steel and became a well-to-do citizen of Ripley.

Ohio was the most heavily traveled underground road in the North, since it had over 200 underground homes. It abutted what was then Virginia and Kentucky, two large slaves states, and only the waters of the Ohio River parted them. A natural boundary, the Ohio was quite narrow at some points, sometimes just fifty yards wide, particularly near Wheeling, Virginia (now West Virginia), and easy to cross. The river also froze over in winter, enabling runaways to walk to freedom. Popular crossing points were in Washington County, in the southeast portion of the state, Ripley, and Cincinnati. From there, slaves moved north on dozens of different, intricately laid-out routes through just about every county in the state. The most popular routes ran to the port cities of Cleveland and Lorain in the northeastern part of the state, and Sandusky and Toledo in the northwestern part, all bordering on Lake Erie. Runaways were then concealed on schooners crossing the lake to Canada. A popular land route took fugitives through the north central part of Ohio, with Oberlin a major stop, to Toledo and then northwest into Michigan, where they cross the Detroit River in to Canada.

* * *

Bishop William Hanby, head of the Westerville, Ohio, underground, lived in this house with his family and hid slaves in a barn at the rear (no longer standing). The barn and a leather goods store run by the Bishop's sons was burned down in the 1870s in a fight between drinkers and the Bishop's temperance group. (Photo by Author)

WESTERVILLE

Hanby House
160 West Main Street, Westerville, Ohio
Open to the public in summer

One of Ohio's staunchest opponents of slavery was Bishop William Hanby of the United Brethren Church. In the 1850s he lived with his two sons in this modest, two-story wood frame home ten miles from Columbus. The boys ran a leather goods business in a building behind the house. Runaways hid in a barn next to the leather goods business and, after dark, dined with the Bishop and his wife and joined the entire family in lengthy evening prayers.

Hanby's work in the anti-slavery movement was efficient—none of his temporary boarders were ever caught—but the good bishop found nothing but trouble for his work in the temperance movement which swept through Ohio in the 1870s. Hanby and his followers were opposed to the sale or consumption of alcohol and protested the opening of Westerville's first saloon. The owner refused to close down and a few weeks later the saloon was mysteriously blown up and destroyed. Later, the same fate befell a second saloon operator who opened a tavern and watched it burn to the ground. No one was ever arrested. Several months later, late at night, someone burned down Hanby's barn and his sons' leather goods building. No arrests were made. However, Hanby and his followers did succeed. No other bars were opened and to this day most of Westerville is dry. *For further information: 614-891-6289.*

COLUMBUS

Kelton House
586 East Town Street, Columbus, Ohio
Open to the public

Musty, faded photographs and a long-ago romance unlocked the secrets of the Underground Railroad at the home of Fernando Kelton. His ornate, two-story home in the refurbished Town Street neighborhood of Ohio's capital was a popular stop on the state's underground line for many years. Runaways were hidden in servants' quarters upstairs at the rear of the building. Kelton was a wealthy businessman and such a prominent figure in the city that he was named one of the honorary pallbearers when President Lincoln's casket was paraded through Columbus after his assassination.

The Keltons housed, clothed, and fed their escaped slaves and sent them on their way after a few days, usually by wagons north to Oberlin. It is unknown how many slaves stopped off at the Keltons. Descendants of the family lived in the home for years and in the 1970s the house was willed to the Columbus Junior League, which began to restore it as a public museum. While the contractors were working on the museum, Ruth Lawrence, an African-American woman, was rummaging through an old trunk in her attic across town. She came upon a group of remarkably well-preserved pictures of someone's nineteenth-century wedding. She knew that Columbus was a segregated city through the 1960s and was surprised at all the white people in the photos. She showed the pictures to her husband, James, who, for the first time, told her the story of a lost little slavegirl.

The girl was his grandmother, Martha. It seems that she arrived at the Kelton home all by herself one night in 1852 when she was ten. The orphan girl, who escaped from a Virginia plantation with others, seemed too fragile to send to Canada all alone. She was asked to stay with the Keltons. They obtained fake papers that showed she was a freed black. Ten years later, after the start of the Civil War, Martha began to date James Lawrence, an engaging, freed black man in Columbus. The pair fell in love and wanted to marry. The Keltons were thrilled and hosted the wedding in the parlor of their home, with whites and blacks in attendance, and photographed by a beaming Fernando Kelton. One hundred and ten years later, the photos resurfaced.

"We tell the love story in our tour of the home and everybody finds it fascinating," said Georgeanne Reuter, director of Kelton House. "It gives a very human touch to a very horrible war." Fernando Kelton's son Oscar was killed in the Civil War. *For further information: 614-464-2022.*

MOUNT PLEASANT

Benjamin Lundy Home
Union and Third Streets, Mount Pleasant, Ohio
Open to the public

Lundy was a leading abolitionist who bragged that he had traveled more than 25,000 miles speaking out against slavery. He was the editor of one of the nation's first abolitionist newspapers, the *Genius of Universal Emancipation*, and published numerous anti-slavery books as well. William Lloyd Garrison was his protégée. There is much speculation that he used this home as an underground stop, but no real documentation.

CLEVELAND

The city of Cleveland was a major port before the Civil War and grew rapidly during it when large deposits of oil were discovered in Pennsylvania in 1863. Cleveland expanded as a transportation (boat and rail) center when thousands of barrels of oil a day were sent there for national shipping. Large oil-related businesses, such as John D. Rockefeller's Standard Oil, had headquarters in the city. Runaways found it rather easy to move in and out of Cleveland because of its size and busy wharf area at the foot of Superior Street. Dozens of friendly captains hid slaves on their schooners and dropped them off when they crossed Lake Erie and reached Canada. Slaves arrived in Cleveland via wagons, boats on the Cuyahoga River, and railroads using forged passes. Local historians know of underground sites in the city, but none have been restored. Cleveland is home to the Harriet Tubman Museum, housed on the campus of Case Western Reserve University. The museum is one of the largest dedicated to Tubman and her work, with more than 5,000 artifacts and documents.

WILBERFORCE

Afro-American Museum and Cultural Center
1350 Brush Row Road, Wilberforce, Ohio

The town, named after William Wilberforce, the British politician who helped end slavery in the British Empire, is home to the national Afro-American Museum and Cultural Center, which has an extensive collection of books, diaries, letters, and photos of African-American history. There were several underground stops in the town, such as the home of Rev. Daniel Payne, Wilberforce University's first president, but none are open to the public. *For further information: 513-376-4944.*

XENIA

Xenia, which is next door to Wilberforce, was a much more active underground stop and the city does have a number of underground sites still standing, although none are open to the public.

The Reverend Samuel Wilson House
204 E. Market Street, Xenia, Ohio

The Reverend Samuel Wilson House gained notoriety in the early 1830s when it was used for an anti-slavery convention, held despite a jeering mob gathered outside. Wilson and his wife, who gave birth to nine children, were leaders in the anti-slavery movement and the Liberty Party for many years. Slaves were hidden in bedrooms.

The David Monroe House
246 E. Market Street, Xenia, Ohio

The David Monroe House was home to Xenia's leading abolitionist, who emigrated from Scotland in 1818. He was one of the leaders of the anti-slavery movement and hid slaves in a false basement under his barn, which was rumored to have been connected to his home via a tunnel. His sons ran a leather goods store in another part of town and hid slaves in their basement.

Davis House
559 E. Market Street, Xenia, Ohio

There was a false cellar under the Davis House where runaways were hidden.

Colonel Charles Young House
1120 Route 42, Xenia, Ohio

Colonel Charles Young was the third black graduate of West Point (1889) and lived in the house from 1912 until 1956. The home was built in 1859 by Laura Smith, a former slave. It is unclear how many tunnels were connected to the basement of the home, but local historians say that a crack, still visible in the middle of the highway in front of the house, sits over one of them. The home was bought by the Omega Psi Phi fraternity at Wilberforce University in 1983 and turned into a seventeen-room fraternity house. The national office of the fraternity is trying to raise funds to buy Young's furniture and restore the house to a museum.

The Hilltop Road House
1351 Hilltop Road, Xenia, Ohio

The Hilltop Road House was built in the 1850s as a residential home and contained a false basement, filled with bales of hay, for hiding. The false basement was discovered when the home was renovated in the 1960s.

The Nosker Residence
550 Route 68, Xenia, Ohio

The Nosker Residence was uncovered as an underground site in the 1950s, when the owners tried to dig a well in the front yard and, instead, drilled right into a long-hidden cave connected by a tunnel to the basement of the home. Later, another owner, trying to plant a garden, fell into a second tunnel. The home was built in the 1790s, but it is uncertain when it became an underground stop. *For further information: Greene County Convention and Visitors Center 937-429-9100.*

WELLINGTON

David Webster Home
Route 18, Wellington, Ohio
Private home

Wellington is ten miles south of Oberlin. Webster and his son harbored fugitives in their home and, late at night, used one of their wagons to transport them to the neighboring town. Webster and his wife built an oversized, twelve-foot-wide fireplace and within it constructed a small, hand-operated elevator that took fugitives down into the basement, where they hid if slavehunters were in the area. None of the hundreds of fugitives who stopped at the Webster place were ever detected.

HUNTINGTON

Ansel Clarke House
Route 58, Huntington, Ohio
Private home

Clarke, a congregational minister, made the most of the runaways who stayed with him for several days before the underground moved them north. Local lore has it that Clarke invented Ohio's first shower: He cut a hole in the ceiling of his bathroom and asked the fugitives staying with him to dump large buckets of water over his head while he soaped his body.

SHEFFIELD ON THE LAKE

Burrell Homestead
2792 E. River Road, Sheffield on the Lake, Ohio
Private home

Robbins Burrell lived in this home in Sheffield, Ohio. His brother Jabezz, who struck it rich in the California Gold Rush of 1849, lived in nearby Oberlin and sent him runaways in wagons. Burrell hid them for a day or two in his barn and then sent them to a cousin, Aaron Root, who hid them on schooners bound for Canada. (Photo by Author)

Robbins Burrell moved into this home in the 1840s just before his brother Jabez left for California in the Gold Rush of 1849, where he struck it rich. Upon Jabez's return in 1851, the two brothers and a cousin, Aaron Root, who owned a shipyard on nearby Lake Erie, began a carefully planned underground operation that lasted twenty years. Jabez sent runaways by wagon ten miles to Robbins' two-story, red brick home, which sat on a 740 acre homestead. Runaways hid in Robbins' barn and at night were taken by boat on the nearby Black River to Root's shipyard. There, they were hidden on Root's schooners bound for Canadian ports.

The Burrell homestead itself was one of the larger homes in the area. Slaves not in the barn often slept in the wide hallways upstairs (the Burrells had twelve children who slept in three bedrooms). Susan Brewer, a friend of the family, has lived there for three years. "We keep reading diaries and letters that pop up and we learn more and more about the history of the house and the underground," she said. "It kind of makes this home a very special place."

ELYRIA

John Monteith House
218 East Avenue, Elyria, Ohio
Open to the public

John Monteith, the first President of the University of Michigan, moved to Elyria, Ohio, and started a girls' high school. By day he was a teacher and by night an underground leader. His home, which was used as the school, was one of the most elegant in the area. (Photo by Author)

This wooden door in the cellar led to a fifty-yard-long underground tunnel that connected Monteith's home to the Black River, where slaves took rowboats to Lorain and to schooners which carried them to Canada. (Photo by Author)

John Monteith, the first president of the University of Michigan, arrived in Elyria, 30 miles west of Cleveland, in 1832 when he was named principal of the area's first high school. He left that job after a few years and founded one of the Midwest's first girls' academies. By 1840, Monteith was a leader in the northern Ohio underground. He built a three-story high wood frame home for his family near the Black River. Runaways arrived at his home by wagon at night and lived with the family. If slavehunters were in the area, they hid in the basement or in three-foot-deep, eight-foot-high closets Monteith had built into his walls. They usually left via a secret tunnel that connected the basement to the river bank, a heavily wooded area about seventy yards away. The Elyria Woman's Club took over the building in 1954 and renovated it (the tunnel entrance was discovered during construction). The club began giving public tours of the home in 1995.

"It is an example of the way in which the underground used the rivers and lakes in this part of the country," said Charlotte Norris of the Woman's Club. "Monteith was never caught, but people were very suspicious of him and he often had to flee anti-slavery meetings when spotted by locals."

Kanisha House
142 Cleveland Street, Elyria, Ohio
Open to the public

This dumbwaiter in a fake fireplace in the Kanisha House in
Elyria, Ohio, carried slaves up to a hidden room. Once concealed
they slid a door across the opening, giving the structure the
appearance of a chimney. (Photo by Author)

The small, two-story blue wood frame house on Elyria's busy business
street was built in the late 1840s as a stagecoach stop on the road to Cleveland and was used for a time by the Pony Express riders. Joshua Myers
lived in the building while it was a stage stop and began working for the
Ohio underground. For added protection, Myers built a thirty-yard-long
tunnel that ran from his basement to an open field behind the building.
He also built a secret room between the second and third floors where
fugitives could hide if slavecatchers were in Elyria, which was often. The
compartment was entered via a dumbwaiter built into a stone-walled tri-

angle in the basement. When the dumbwaiter went up, the wall looked like an ordinary fireplace.

Over the years, the building has served as a family residence, tavern, and brothel. It was purchased by the First Community Interfaith Institute in 1982 when its leaders heard of its underground history. It has been restored, slowly, since the early 1990s. "Anyone who comes here to the Institute and hears the story gets an immediate feeling of hope," said Gerald Johnson, director of the Institute.

* * *

A Town Rescues a Runaway

Runaway slave James Price arrived in Oberlin in 1856 and liked the town. Instead of moving on to Canada, he stayed in Oberlin with false papers. Two years later, on September 13, 1858, four slavecatchers with a writ for his apprehension spotted him walking along a road that connected Oberlin to the neighboring town, Wellington. Price, who felt safe after two years, had no fear of the men, dressed as farmers, and walked toward them when they waved to him. They convinced Price that he could earn good money as a day laborer for a farmer in Wellington, who had sent them out to find workers. He agreed and was then grabbed from behind and shoved into their wagon.

The men planned to take Price to a judge in Wellington with their writ but as they drove south two Oberlin men saw them and presumed that Price had been kidnapped. They rode as fast as they could into Oberlin, galloping through the streets to alert leaders of the underground. Within the hour, more than one hundred men and women from the town descended on the American Hotel, in Wellington, where the slavehunters held Price. The mob was not the usual abolitionist elite—the wealthy and powerful—but a mix of white and black men and women, teenagers and men who worked in a broad range of professions, from lawyers and doctors to ditch diggers and farmers. There were dozens of Oberlin college professors and students in the crowd. They stormed the hotel, shoving aside the slavehunters, and rescued Price. As the crowd held the slavehunters at bay, Price was put into a wagon and hustled out of the area and taken to Canada.

Local police then arrested thirty-nine men in the crowd and charged them with violating the federal Fugitive Slave Act of 1850.

The most famous rescue of slaves captured by slavehunters took place in Oberlin, Ohio, in 1859. Thirty-nine men were arrested from the crowd of more than two hundred. They posed for this picture in the yard of the Cuyahoga County Jail, in Cleveland, where they were incarcerated for three months and, during that time, published their own newspaper and gave speeches. (Courtesy of the Oberlin College Archives)

The men were jailed in Cleveland to await trial. At the same time, an anti-slavery grand jury in Lorain County indicted the slavecatchers for violating Ohio's personal liberty laws.

The thirty-nine Oberlinites in jail then startled the country by refusing to meet the modest bail set for them and opted to remain in prison—hopeful that their incarceration would lead to nationwide protests. They were right. The Oberlin rescue was important news throughout Ohio and the northern states. Its wide mix of people gave a more credible face to the abolitionist movement. Torchlight rallies were held throughout Ohio and more than two thousand

The Oberlin rescuers stormed the American Hotel (left) in
Wellington to free runaway John Price, apprehended by
slavecatchers earlier in the day, and sent him to Canada.
(Courtesy of the Oberlin College Archives)

citizens marched thirty miles to Cleveland for a mass demon-
stration.

Abolitionist groups around the country held protest meetings,
signed petitions, and staged rallies for the Oberlin rescuers. Parades
were held in their honor. Abolitionist newspapers heralded their
acts of bravery. Several prisoners gave moving speeches from their
jail cells to crowds gathered in the prison yard. In letters, prisoners
urged the wives of voters to withhold sexual favors from their
husbands until they voted Republican. The prisoners gained even
more national notoriety when they began to publish their own
newspaper, the *Rescuer*, from their cells.

The federal government did bring two of the men to trial. Both
were found guilty and given short jail terms, but as the weeks
passed, federal officials in Ohio and in Washington began to realize

that the arrests had backfired. The abolitionists and underground leaders in the Cleveland jail were winning more public relations points in their cells than the federal government could ever win in court. Finally, after three months, federal prosecutors agreed to drop all charges against the Oberlin rescuers in return for the Lorain County prosecutor's dropping of charges against the slavehunters.

The Oberlin underground leaders were released and triumphantly returned to Oberlin, where they rode in buggies and wagons in a torchlight parade through town to First Church, across the street from the college. All along the parade route were bonfires, bands, and people singing. A two-hour-long church service to honor them ended with the more than 3,000 people jammed inside the church and on the lawn outside singing *La Marseillaise*.

Many of the homes of underground leaders and rescue leaders of Oberlin are still standing and kept in pristine condition by their current owners. Any tour of the town should begin at the First Church and the Underground Railroad monument and then continue through the tree-lined streets of the tiny town that made such a huge impact on American politics.

* * *

OBERLIN

The First Church
Main Street and Lorain, Oberlin, Ohio
Open to the public

The First Church served as a house of worship each Sunday morning and as the meeting hall for the abolitionist movement at various nights of the week. Underground leaders, all members of the church, milled about on the large, shady lawn after Sunday services and discussed ways to transport runaways hiding in local homes. The handsomely designed brick church has a semi-circular balcony that overlooks a pulpit and organ. A memorial was held here for the three Oberlin citizens killed by U.S. Army troops in John Brown's Raid on Harper's Ferry.

The Underground Railroad Monument
South Professor Street (in front of Talcott Hall), Oberlin, Ohio

The Underground Railroad Monument was designed by an Oberlin student, Cameron Armstrong. It is a replica of a twenty-foot-long section of

Oberlin was one of the busiest underground stations in the Midwest. Its heritage is commemorated by this monument, designed by an Oberlin College student, and the "healing garden" surrounding it. The monument's railroad ties point to heaven . . . and North. (Photo by Author)

railroad track cemented into the ground at a forty-five-degree angle, pointing up toward heaven and north toward Canada. It was unveiled in 1977. In 1998, the college added a "healing garden," which has herbs similar to those used for food by slaves on the run.

The Bardwell House
181 East Lorain, Oberlin, Ohio
Private home

The Bardwell House was home to the missionaries the Reverend John Bardwell and his wife Cornelia. They moved there in 1846 and for fifteen years hid slaves in secret rooms beneath the eaves of their roof.

The Langston House
207 East College Street, Oberlin, Ohio
Private home

The Langston House was the home of Oberlin's most renowned citizen, James Langston. He was the first black graduate of Oberlin College and returned there as a professor in the 1850s. He used his home to shelter runaways and was a member of the anti-slavery society. During the Civil War he was the driving force in the organization of the 127th Colored Regiment from Ohio. At the end of the war, Langston became Ohio's first black attorney and later was the first black lawyer to argue a case before the U.S. Supreme Court. He served eleven years on the Oberlin Board of Education in the postwar years and became President of the Equal Rights League, the forerunner of the National Association for the Advancement of Colored People (NAACP). He moved to Virginia, set up a law practice, and was elected to Congress, the state's first black lawmaker. He later served as Minister to Haiti and President of Howard University. His grandson was Langston Hughes, the acclaimed poet.

The Oberlin Railroad Quilt
Senior Center, 90 East College Street, Oberlin, Ohio
Open to the public

The Oberlin Railroad Quilt was designed and sewn by Oberlin Citizens to portray different events in town that were connected to the anti-slavery movement, the rescues, and the underground activities of the residents.

Martin Luther King Jr. Park
East Vine Street, Oberlin, Ohio

There are three monuments in the Martin Luther King Jr. Park. One commemorates the Oberlin rescue, one the three Oberlin men who fought with John Brown at Harper's Ferry and were killed, and one the legacy of Dr. King.

Wilson Evans Home; Chauncey Wack Home
East Vine Street, Oberlin, Ohio
Private homes

Across from the park are the homes of Oberlin's pre-Civil War odd couple—Wilson Evans and Chauncey Wack. The two-story red brick home of Evans, an undertaker and prominent abolitionist, served as an underground station. Evans took part in the Oberlin rescue and his brother-in-law, Lewis Leary, was one of the three killed at Harper's Ferry. Next door, fifty yards away, stands the quiet looking two-story wood frame home of Wack, who hated the abolitionists and Evans so much that he not only spoke out publicly against the anti-slavery movement but testified against those arrested in the rescue.

Wilson Evans, who lived in the home on the right, and Chauncey Wack, who lived in the home to the left, were the odd couple of Oberlin, Ohio. Evans was a leader in the underground and an ardent abolitionist. Wack hated his neighbor and the abolitionists so much that he testified against them at the Oberlin rescue hearings. The men were neighbors for more than twenty years. (Photo by Author)

General Miles Shurtleff Monument
South Professor and Morgan Streets, Oberlin, Ohio

The heroic statue of General Miles Shurtleff stands in a small park at the intersection of South Professor and Morgan Streets. Shurtleff, an Oberlin professor, left the safe groves of academia when the Civil War broke out and led a regiment of troops. He was captured and spent a year in a Confederate prison camp. Told he could go home upon his release, the weak and sickly Shurtleff refused and took over command of the 8th Colored Regiment and fought on until the end of the war. The statue of the General points North—to freedom.

James Monroe House; Little Red Schoolhouse; Frank Jewett House
73 South Professor Street, Oberlin, Ohio
Open to the public

The home of James Monroe, the town's most vocal abolitionist and underground leader, was moved to a small park where it now stands next to the Little Red Schoolhouse and the Frank Jewett House. Monroe was a professor and state legislator and an underground leader so bold that he told others to send him notes describing runaways as "slaves," not coded

Monroe's home in Oberlin was modest from the outside, but it was elegant inside, with servants' quarters attached in a rear wing. (Photo by Author)

notes about "parcels." He ran his underground station for more than ten years and during the war was a leader in efforts to win the vote for freed slaves. The Little Red Schoolhouse, built in 1836, was the town's first public school and was one of the first racially integrated schools in America. The Jewett House had nothing to do with the underground, but much to do with American life. Jewett was a chemistry professor and for years told his students that all of life would be easier if someone would just invent a lighter type of metal for construction. Sitting in a back row one semester was Charles Martin Hall, who went on to invent aluminum and helped found the Alcoa Aluminum Company.

Westwood Cemetery, Oberlin, Ohio

The most touching reminder of the abolitionist movement and Underground Railroad can be found in a monument in the center of Westwood Cemetery, on the south side of Oberlin. It is there that little Lee Dobbins was buried in 1853. The four-year-old boy, quite ill, arrived in Oberlin after several weeks on the run from his Virginia plantation with his adoptive mother. His own mother died in slavery and he was taken in by her friend. His adoptive mother was not only on the run from slavery and her owner, but also the man she was forced to marry, a black overseer, who frequently

In Memory Of

THE FUGITIVE SLAVES WHOSE JOURNEY
TO FREEDOM BROUGHT THEM TO OBERLIN.

SHIELDED BY AN ALMIGHTY ARM,
THY GRIEFS AND SUFFERINGS NOW ARE O'ER,
BEYOND THE REACH OF TYRANT'S HARM,
FREED SPIRIT, REST FOREVER MORE!

LONE LITTLE WANDERER, NOW NO MORE
'MID STRANGER HEARTS TO SEEK FOR LOVE,
THOU'ST GAINED THY HOME, THY NATIVE SHORE
AND BOUNDLESS LOVE THY BLISS WILL PROVE.

THY FATHER CALLED THEE, SUFFERING ONE,
HE KNEW AND FELT THY UNTOLD GRIEF,
TO HIM COMPLEXIONS ALL ARE ONE,
HE DIED ALIKE FOR THEIR RELIEF.

LEE HOWARD DOBBINS
AGED 4 YRS.
DIED IN OBERLIN,
A FUGITIVE SLAVE ORPHAN
MARCH 26, 1853

Lee Dobbins, aged four, died in Oberlin during flight
from Virginia to Canada. The little boy was buried in
Westwood Cemetery following a funeral which
attracted more than two thousand townspeople.
(Photo by Author)

beat her. The child was too sick to travel by the time he made it to Oberlin with his mother, who was also ill. Underground leaders urged the mother to continue on to Canada and leave the boy behind so that local doctors and nurses could care for him. Their care did little good; he died a month later. Lee, in his four weeks in bed, became a symbol of the antislavery movement to the townspeople. His funeral, held at First Church, drew more than 2,000 mourners, so many that the crowd spilled out of the church and on to the lawn. They prayed for the little boy and then followed his casket in a long, sad funeral procession to Westwood.

For further information on sites in Sheffield, Elyria, and Oberlin: Lorain County Visitor's Office 216-245-5282. The office has self-guided tour booklets that can be obtained by writing the Office at 611 Broadway, Lorain, Ohio 44052.

AKRON

John Brown's Home
514 Diagonal Road, Akron, Ohio
Open to the public

This was one of the fiery abolitionist's many homes, having lived here during the 1840s. The home was turned into a museum and many artifacts and photos tied to Brown's life and career are on display. There is a monument to Brown in nearby Perkins Park. *For further information: Summit County Historical Society 216-535-1120.*

JEFFERSON

Joshua Giddings Office
112 North Chestnut Street, Jefferson, Ohio
Open to the public

Joshua Giddings was an influential U.S. Congressman and one of the leaders of the anti-slavery movement in Ohio. He led a group of more than 2,000 protesters to Cleveland in 1858 to protest the arrest of Oberlin citizens in the rescue of runaway John Price. Giddings harbored fugitives in his home and law office. One, Charlie Garlick, remained after emancipation and lived in a backroom at the office for years. *For further information: Ashtabula Chamber of Commerce 440-998-6998.*

ASHTABULA

The Hubbard House
"Mother Hubbard's Cupboard"
1603 Walnut Boulevard, Ashtabula, Ohio

Abolitionist William Hubbard built this large two-story home on the shores of Lake Erie and, during construction, had a tunnel dug to connect the basement of the house to a bluff overlooking the lake. Slaves stayed at Hubbard's home for several days while he made arrangements to have ship captains take them across the lake to Canada. The fugitives left through the tunnel at night, waded out to a waiting rowboat, and were taken to schooners. *For further information: Ashtabula Chamber of Commerce 440-998-6998.*

CINCINNATI

The Queen City was a major depot for the underground. Runaways crossed the Ohio River near Cincinnati, especially when it froze over to form an ice bridge, or made it to the town via wagons driven by underground workers. Levi Coffin ran a large and productive Cincinnati underground that protected thousands of slaves over the years. However, there are no public sites in the town proper because of constant construction and renovations in the city.

Harriet Beecher Stowe House
2950 Gilbert Avenue, Cincinnati, Ohio
Open to the public

The writer lived in the city in the late 1840s and early 1850s. She hid fugitives in her two-story, white clapboard home that sat on top of a hill. It was in Cincinnati, too, where she met underground leaders such as John Rankin, of Ripley, who told her intriguing stories about runaways that helped her compose *Uncle Tom's Cabin* (Eliza in the novel was a real runaway saved by Rankin after she jumped from one ice floe to another to cross the Ohio in a storm). Stowe also traveled in and out of Kentucky and witnessed several slave auctions, events that hardened her opposition to slavery. *For further information: 513-632-5120.*

WEST LIBERTY

Pioneer Home
10245 Township Road 47, West Liberty, Ohio
Open to the public/ antique shop

Pioneer Home was built by Judge Benjamin Piatt. He would not break the law by protecting runaways, so he adroitly had his wife do it. She invented a careful flag signal system so that slaves knew if the Judge was home. A flag up meant he was gone and they could enter for food, protection, and a trip to another station. If it was down they either passed on to another station or waited until he left and the flag went up again. *For further information: 513-465-4801.*

PAINESVILLE

Rider's Inn
192 Mentor Avenue, Painesville, Ohio
Open to the public as an inn

Rider's Inn was built in 1812 as a stagecoach stop. It later became a private residence where fugitives were hidden. The home served as a hospital for Union Army soldiers wounded during the Civil War. *For further information: 440-354-8200.*

ZANESVILLE

Stone Academy
435 Putnam Avenue, Zanesville, Ohio
Open to the public/museum

The building was erected in 1809 to house the state legislature before Columbus became the capital. It later became a school for boys and served as many years as the Putnam Female Seminary.

MARIETTA

Washington County, in the southeast part of the state, was one of the most active in the underground, with more than twenty-five established safe houses. Today, a travel office, Marietta Tours, offers trips to as many as fifteen of the existing sites (tours can be shorter and include fewer sites). The trip, which can be two days long, extends throughout the county and includes homes, offices, and barns. It also includes a restored plantation in West Virginia. *For information: 740-374-2233.*

SPRINGBORO

Located 38 miles north of the Ohio River near Dayton, Springboro, along with Ripley, Xenia, and Oberlin, was a major hub of the underground in the state. It was home to a large Quaker population and a population devoted to the protection of runaways for more than forty years. The town contained several dozen active safe houses, many connected to each other by underground tunnels, sometimes as high as eight feet. Visitors can take a self-guided walking tour (brochures are available at town hall) of the underground sites. The tour includes some stores that were residential homes in the 1840s and 1850s. Stops include the Ke-We Ice Cream Parlor, Booth's Gifts, Jonathan Wright House, Joseph Stanton House (now Sally's Quilts), and Brenda's Flowers. *For further information: Springboro Historical Society 513-748-0916.*

* * *

Runaways: Charlie

A slave named Charlie (last name unknown) fled his plantation in Loudoun County, Virginia, in 1856 on the night he learned he was going to be sold to another owner and fled on foot to Wheeling, West Virginia, the next morning. Starving, he sneaked into the City Hotel just as it opened and begged for bread. The landlord, who used his hotel as an underground station, looked at him suspiciously. "You're a runaway," he said. Charlie denied it, but the landlord knew better and told him he would help him but that he had to be careful because slavehunters were always in Wheeling. He sent Charlie to the nearby farm of a friend and his wife who hid runaways; the couple fed and clothed the fugitive.

Later that day, slavehunters rode up to the home and said they suspected a runaway slave was hiding somewhere in Wheeling and wanted to search the house and nearby barn. The man and his wife had sent Charlie up a ladder to a secret room in the attic, completely sealed off from view. They denied seeing any runaways. The slavecatchers looked through their home, barn, and outbuildings and, finding no one, moved on. As soon as Charlie came down, the farmer and a friend took him to the barn, where they saddled up three horses and rode off. The two farmers rode with Charlie all the way to the Ohio River, where they put him in a boat they kept hidden under logs and bushes. They told him where to go on the other side of the river, in Ohio, and that people there would move him through the state to Detroit. Paddling as fast as he could, Charlie made his way across the river as the two farmers, watching the area for pursuers, waited. Then they tugged on the reins of their horses, turned them around, and trotted back toward Wheeling while Charlie landed in Ohio.

* * *

Michigan

* * *

Battleground in Detroit

Henry Thornton and his wife Rutha fled slavery in Kentucky the night before the Fourth of July in 1831 and made their way through Ohio to Detroit, where they were welcomed by the free black community there. Two years later, after someone from their hometown spotted them, slavecatchers with proper legal papers had the Thorntons apprehended and taken to court, where a local judge ruled they had to be returned to their owners in Louisville the following Monday.

Late Sunday morning, tearful friends of Rutha's, Mrs. George French and Mrs. Madison Lightfoot, visited the woman for a final time at the large, two-story jail on Fort Street. While jailers were not looking, Mrs. French exchanged clothes with Rutha and a few moments later, "Mrs. French" (Rutha) calmly walked out of the building with Mrs. Lightfoot. Moving casually but steadily, the two women traveled several blocks and then, out of sight, Rutha was helped into a carriage that took her to the wharf where she was smuggled across the Detroit River into Canada.

The next morning, guards began to escort Henry Thornton to the wharf at Randolph Street where he was scheduled to board a steamer that would take him to Ohio. The runaway was then going to be transported back to Kentucky. A large mob of freed blacks, many armed with clubs, knives and swords, blocked them. The sheriff ordered the mob three times to disperse, but they would not. As the sheriff turned around to return to his office after his third plea, he knew he was in trouble. There, in front of him, was Thornton, pointing a gun someone had given him at the head of his guard. Other guards then charged toward Thornton as the sheriff rushed through the crowd. Blacks began to swing clubs and a riot began. The sheriff was knocked unconscious and dozens of others were injured. Friends hustled Thornton away in the melee and drove him north of town in a cart. Told that his wife was already safe, he was taken across the river to Canada.

Detroit was transformed into an armed camp. Police roamed through the black community looking for Thornton. Patrols were posted at dozens of street intersections. Riders traveled throughout the outskirts of the city, questioning residents about Thornton's escape. Thirty freed blacks were arrested that day and served sentences varying from three days in jail to six months' probation, with street cleaning in lieu of jail. On the Canadian side, trouble followed Thornton. Authorities in Sandwich, fearful of legal problems with Detroit authorities, arrested the Thorntons and held them until the Canadian government could decide what to do with them.

The Thornton case quickly became a legal and political controversy. Canada had welcomed slaves for decades, and its government had just passed an act officially prohibiting the return of fugitive slaves to another country. The Thornton case was the first to test the new law when the governor of Michigan, then still a territory, demanded extradition. Debate over the demand raged in the Canadian parliament for weeks. In Detroit, a mob of blacks attacked the jail again in mid-July and set it on fire. A week later the jail's stables were torched. More police were hired to protect government buildings, boat traffic between Detroit and Canada was temporarily halted, and a 9 P.M. curfew for blacks was established in town. U.S. Secretary of War Lewis Cass sent a regiment of U.S. Army troops to the city to restore order.

As Canadians debated the case, a special commission in Detroit, appointed to study the rescue and riot, issued a report that laid all blame for the disturbance on the black mob, found Thornton guilty of violating the 1793 Fugitive Slave Act, and demanded extradition. Pressure mounted in Canada as anti-slavery forces insisted that Canada protect the Thorntons. Southern politicians put pressure on Canadian politicians through their Canadian business partners. Finally, after two months of raging debate and enormous political pressure, Robert Jameson, Canada's Attorney General, recommended to the government that since the Thorntons had not broken any Canadian laws in their flight they should remain in Canada. The executive council agreed and the Thorntons stayed in Canada. That ruling in 1833 set a precedent that would remain in force until the Civil War and protected tens of thousands of American fugitive slaves who reached Canadian soil.

There were two main routes that took runaways into Michigan and to Detroit, the main entry point to Canada, just across the Detroit River. The first route came into Michigan along the shores of Lake Erie through the Ohio towns of Toledo and Sandusky. A second route entered the southern parts of the state from three feeder lines from Indiana and then split into three routes, two running east/west and one running north/south. The underground used New Buffalo, a small town just a few miles north of South Bend, Indiana, as a switching station to send some slaves north and some east. Runaways who went north traveled the length of the Michigan peninsula, along Lake Michigan, and stayed at safe houses in the communities of St. Joseph, Benton Harbor, Grand Haven, Muskegon, Manistee, Traverse City, and Mackinac City and then crossed over into Canada. Some of the fugitives changed direction at Grand Haven and took a line that ran directly east to Detroit through underground havens at Grand Rapids, Ionia, Lansing, and Brighton.

Other runaways turned east at New Buffalo and took either of two lines to Detroit. The first, the more southern route, which hugged the Indiana border, went through Mottville, Coldwater, Hillsdale, Morenci, Adrian (the home of women's underground leader Laura Haviland), Saline, Ann Arbor, Ypsilanti, and Detroit. Another eastern line took runaways on an underground route from New Buffalo through Niles, Cassopolis, Schoolcraft, Battle Creek, Marshall, Albion, Parma, Jackson, Dexter, and then to Ann Arbor, Ypsilanti, and Detroit.

* * *

DETROIT

By the 1850s, Detroit had developed into a bustling urban center and commercial hub and one of the fastest growing cities in America. The city has a long history, dating back to its days as Fort Detroit, a key fur trading post in the 1700s. It became a French fort, but was captured by the British in the French and Indian War. The development of Detroit was slow until the 1830s, when Lake Erie shipping became prosperous and railroad lines began to extend into midwestern cities such as Detroit and Chicago. The city exploded in growth throughout the 1840s and 1850s and, at the same time, was home to a large community of freed blacks and abolitionists. The city is located on the narrow Detroit River, directly across from Windsor, Ontario, in Canada. Runaways sought out Detroit because it was an easy crossing point and had a well-organized Underground Railroad. The underground proved so successful that one morning in 1859 the *Detroit Daily Advertiser* reported the crossing of a dozen fugitives who had arrived via the underground from Missouri ("all the way from Missouri" is how the impressed writer put it).

Slaves who arrived in Detroit were housed in several black churches and in the homes and barns of underground members. A large wharf at West Jefferson Street is where most runaways crossed over into Canada in ferries or, late at night, in rowboats. Slavehunters began to frequent Detroit as early as 1831, but had little luck kidnapping runaways because of the efficiency of the underground there. It is impossible to determine how many fugitives traveled through safe houses in Detroit to freedom in Canada, but since it was a major point of entry, the number probably totaled over twenty thousand people.

There are several sites in Detroit that can be visited. Civic organizations and historical societies have also erected numerous markers to note a former underground site. The Detroit African-American Museum, on Frederick Douglass Boulevard, has an underground exhibit.

Elmwood Cemetery
1200 Elmwood, Detroit, Michigan
Open to the public

Some of Detroit's outstanding African Americans from the Civil War era are buried in Elmwood, the city's oldest cemetery, opened in 1846. These include underground leaders George DeBaptiste and William Lambert. Fourteen soldiers from the 1st Michigan Colored Regiment, one of the many black units who fought in the Civil War, are also buried here. A marker citing the heroism of the regiment can be found in front of the Duffield School, the site where the soldiers trained before fighting in campaigns in South Carolina, Georgia, and Florida.

Second Baptist Church
Monroe and Beaubien Streets, Detroit, Michigan
Open to the public

The church, one of the oldest African-American churches in America, was founded in 1836 by thirteen former slaves who settled in Detroit and separated from the First Baptist Church. The church leaders harbored slaves within its walls throughout the 1840s and 1850s or asked church members to shelter runaways in their homes. The church also entered a secret alliance with Baptist churches in Canada to spirit slaves out of the country. Reverend William Monroe, who was the pastor in the 1840s, ran a school for African-American children in the church basement.

Underground Railroad River Crossing Site
Downtown, river area at West Jefferson Street, Detroit, Michigan
Open to the public

The main entry point to Canada across the Detroit River was near West Jefferson and Sixth Street. Nearby was the Seymour Finney home and barn. Finney arrived in Detroit in 1834 and was one of the underground leaders there for twenty-six years. Runaways hid in his barn and were then put in boats to cross the river at night.

For further information: Detroit Historical Society 313-833-7934; Detroit Visitors and Convention Bureau 313-202-1800.

BATTLE CREEK

The city was one of the key underground sites in the country, but time has claimed most of the safe houses. Recently, government agencies and private corporations have joined forces to bring back the history of the underground in the area through a variety of statues, sculptures, and school programs.

Underground Railroad Sculpture
South of Linear Park, Battle Creek, Michigan
Open to the public

In 1993, local leaders unveiled this twenty-eight-foot-long, fourteen-foot-high, seven ton sculpture by artist Ed Dwight (funded by the Kellogg Foundation). The monument has two sides. One side depicts Harriet Tubman leading a family of slaves out of a forest and toward a river. The other shows Battle Creek underground leader Erastus Hussey and his wife ushering runaways into their cellar for protection. Hussey, Battle Creek's mayor and state senator, was one of Michigan's most prominent citizens and was also the editor of the *Liberty Press*, an abolitionist publication.

Sojourner Truth Gravesite
Oakhill Cemetery, Battle Creek, Michigan
Open to the public

Sojourner Truth was born Isabella Baumfree and freed from slavery under New York legislation passed in 1828. She adopted her new name (a traveler for truth) when she rose up during a New York church service to give the first of hundreds of inspiring anti-slavery speeches. Truth visited many large cities and small towns from 1840 to 1860, dressed in plain clothes and a large, white turban, speaking out against slavery. She was most famous for her "Aren't I a Woman?" speech, reprinted often, in which she humanized slavery for listeners and rallied women, black and white, to the anti-slavery cause. She moved to Battle Creek in 1856 and died there in 1883, at the age of 105, and was buried in Oakhill. *For further information: Historical Society of Battle Creek 616-965-2613.*

ADRIAN

Laura Smith Haviland Statue
City Hall, Main Street, Adrian, Michigan
Open to the public

Laura Haviland, a Quaker who moved from Canada to Adrian, became one of the most active underground leaders in the country, harboring hundreds of fugitives in her home and running the underground organization in Adrian. She also worked closely with underground leaders who sent her runaways from Indiana. The hard-working woman, who dressed plainly and usually had a nondescript bonnet on her head, was nicknamed "Auntie Laura" and remembered fondly by runaways who eventually made it to Canada. She and a friend, Elizabeth Chandler, founded the first anti-slavery society in Michigan.

Haviland was one of the most inventive and hard-working underground organizers in America. She ran an efficient underground station in her home, making certain there was always enough food for individuals and groups who came her way. She kept in close touch with leaders throughout Michigan and Indiana so that the underground was run efficiently; it was never difficult to find horses or wagons at a moment's notice with Haviland around. She was also a risktaker and frequently traveled into Indiana to assist in helping groups of people move on the underground. She enjoyed assuming various roles, dressing up as a nurse, schoolteacher, and farmer, sometimes looking like a man, in order to move runaways through the state.

Like many men and women in the underground, Haviland was a polished public speaker who could motivate crowds. In one of her most rousing speeches, she called the United States "the land of whips and chains"; said of freedom in America that "the liberty bell cracked and refused to ring because it knew that men, women, and children were being bought and sold like pigs and sheep."

Haviland was a fast talker and loved to engage in discussions with slave-hunters who traveled through the Michigan area posing as men interested in buying cattle. Under this guise they casually questioned farmers and townspeople about runaways. One man knocked on Haviland's door one morning and she immediately knew what he was up to and invited him in. She was so glib and convincing about her ignorance of the underground while displaying her knowledge of beef that at the end of an hour she actually sold him twelve head of her cattle. Her activities were well known and in the mid-1850s it was reported that slavehunters posted a $3,000 bounty for her murder or capture.

Haviland and her brother started the Raisin Institute, a school for black and white children in the Adrian area; and she also founded the Michigan Girls Training School in the town.

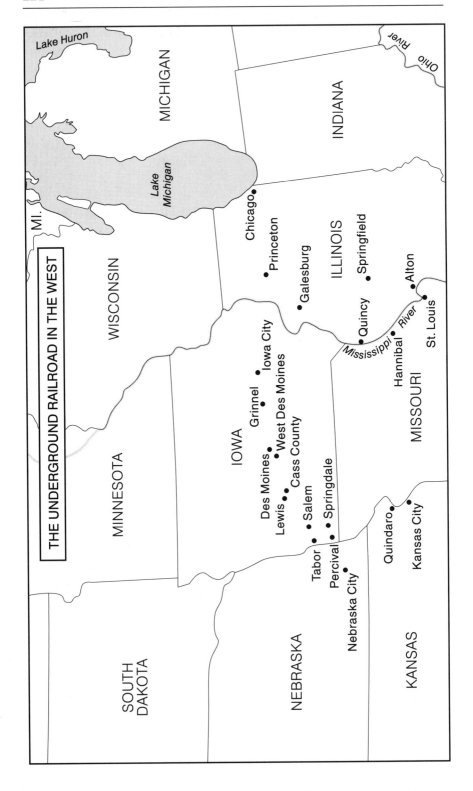

THE UNDERGROUND RAILROAD IN THE WEST

* * *

John Brown's Terrible Swift Sword

I, John Brown, am now quite certain that the crimes of this guilty land will never be purged away; but with blood. I had as I now think vainly flattered myself that without very bloodshed it might be done.

—John Brown, December 2, 1859

John Brown, a tall, thin muscular man with a wide, granite-like face, full and flowing beard and fierce eyes, was not a Kansan. He moved there from North Elba, New York, in 1855 specifically to begin an Underground Railroad in Kansas. He was convinced that the newly passed Kansas-Nebraska Act would make the Kansas territory free soil and that its legislature would outlaw slavery and offer a safe haven for slaves fleeing the nearby slave state of Missouri and other southern states. He also arrived in Kansas driving a wagon full of weapons, a sure sign that he was looking for trouble.

Brown was first exposed to slavery at the age of twelve, when he saw southern U.S. Army officers with their slaves near his home in Ohio, where he grew up. His disgust with slavery led him to study theology, but he never became a minister. Brown spent his adult life in several businesses, including tanneries, land surveying, and sheep raising, but most failed. In 1842 he wound up as a small farmer in North Elba on land given to freed blacks and abolitionists by millionaire abolitionist leader Gerrit Smith. Brown became a strident abolitionist during his time in North Elba. In 1854, after passage of the Kansas-Nebraska Act, five of Brown's sons (he had twenty children with two wives) moved to Kansas and invited him to join them. His sons were not there to farm. In their letter asking

No one man inspired as much admiration in the North and hatred in the South as John Brown, an underground leader in Kansas whose attack on a federal arsenal at Harper's Ferry, Virginia, in 1859, set off a chain reaction of events that led to the Civil War. (Courtesy of the Society for the Preservation of New England Antiquity)

him to move, the sons told him to bring guns and ammunition. Wrote one: "We need them more than we do bread."

It was in Kansas where Brown became world renowned as a violent abolitionist. By the time he arrived, Kansas was in turmoil and newspapers referred to the territory as "bloody Kansas." Pro- and anti-slavery forces each sponsored their own political organizations and each elected their own state legislatures. Up to 5,000 proslavery Missourians moved into Kansas to vote illegally whenever there was an election. It was such a political volcano that the new governor had to be named from outside the state. Soon after Brown's arrival, an army of 800 proslavery men attacked the town of Lawrence, tore apart the two newspaper offices, burned down the hotel, sacked the office of the governor and looted dozens of stores. Shortly afterward, other proslavers murdered several farmers with well-known anti-slavery views. John Brown then decided that the war against slavery had started.

On May 25, 1856, Brown and his sons, and a small group of men, raided a farm in Pottawatomie, whose owners had slaves, and murdered five men. Within a few weeks, Brown had a small army of thirty men who attacked and captured a group of twenty-two proslavery men after a pitched battle at a fresh water spring called Black Jack. He let the men leave in exchange for the release of free soil men captured earlier by other proslavery forces. Brown's notoriety grew after the murders and the battle at Black Jack and, by the summer of 1856, he had assembled an armed militia of more than 150 men.

It is unclear exactly what Brown and his men did that summer since they operated secretly. Various forces battled each other throughout Kansas in the summer of 1856 and a political peace was unattainable. Missourians rode in and out of the state on raids. Armed free soil brigades battled proslavery brigades. Secret armies trained and attacked farms.

Between 1856 and 1859, in addition to his military operations, John Brown and his men apparently traveled extensively through Kansas, Nebraska, and Iowa, establishing dozens of underground stations for runaway slaves. Records in all three states show constant connections to Brown and his men. He believed the strong support he received from abolitionists in all three states meant that others in those states were ready for a national war against slavery. He was certain it was time for a rebellion to free the slaves, wherever they were.

To do that, he needed money. Brown returned East and on a winter and spring sojourn through Massachusetts, Connecticut, and New York raised an undisclosed amount of cash for his "war"— rumored to be as much as $10,000—from several leading abolitionists and anti-slavery groups. The true story of his fund-raising is murky. It appears that he convinced abolitionist groups that the money was to defend Kansas against attacks by Missourians, not for offensive attacks by Brown's army. It also appears that he stretched the truth concerning his battles to make himself appear as the constant victim and never the aggressor. The money he raised eventually funded his attack on Harper's Ferry in 1859, which failed and resulted in his capture and execution. Brown's financial backing by leading abolitionist groups was never forgiven by the South. Many southerners later charged that the real start of the Civil War was the attack on Harper's Ferry, not Fort Sumter, and placed the blame for the war squarely on the abolitionists.

Knowing he had a large crowd and a group of reporters at his hanging, Brown handed his jailers a final statement predicting bloodshed over slavery and walked proudly, head held high, to the gallows. His execution was seen as the final act of collaboration between the federal government and southern slaveholders and cemented opposition to slavery among hundreds of thousands of previous moderates throughout the northern states. Within months of his death an old marching song was given new lyrics and became known as "John Brown's Body." The lyrics were later changed by Julia Ward Howe and the song became "The Battle Hymn of the Republic."

* * *

Nebraska

Nebraska and its sister state Kansas were caught up in the slave furor in 1854, when Congress passed the Kansas-Nebraska Act, permitting each state to decide whether it would allow slavery within its borders. The bloody confrontations were centered in Kansas, not Nebraska, so anti-slavery residents in Nebraska were able to establish a small underground railroad, called the "Jim Lane Trail," which ran through Nebraska City, Peru, Falls City, and Nemaha City. Stops included barns, cabins, and tunnels. Runaways stayed in Nebraska for a few days and then moved into Iowa and northwest toward Canada.

NEBRASKA CITY

John Brown's Cave; Mayhew Cabin
20th Street and 4th Corso, Nebraska City, Nebraska
Open to the public

John Kagi, his father, and brother-in-law Allen Mayhew, were three of the underground leaders in Nebraska. Kagi was a close associate of John Brown and would aid him in the famous raid on Harper's Ferry in 1859, where Kagi was killed. In mid-1851, the men built two cabins near a deep ravine on their land. They told neighbors they needed a large cellar because they were members of a new "vegetarian society" and needed it to store the vegetables they were growing. The men dug a three-chambered cellar, or cave, its ceilings and walls supported by thick wooden beams, beneath the two homes. The cave, about forty-five-feet long and fifteen-feet wide, was large enough to house three dozen fugitives. It was entered through a trap door in Mayhew's twelve-foot-by-sixteen-foot cabin. The exit into the ravine allowed runaways a quick way to flee if they were discovered. The exit was covered with brush, and a hollow log connecting the ravine to the cave provided fresh air.

Several Kagi brothers lived in the area and their wives made clothing for the runaway slaves. Mrs. Mayhew baked corn bread and helped with medical needs. The railroad stop was used from the mid-1850s until the start of the Civil War.

Since the town was on the Missouri River, it was a key stop on the Underground Railroad that John Brown put together in the West. No records were kept on the number of fugitives who hid in the caves, but years after the war local residents told reporters that they had seen wagons carrying as many as thirteen slaves driving toward the Mayhew cabins. Others claimed to have seen as many as a dozen runaways leaving the cabin and crossing the Missouri on a ferry.

Today, the cave and the Mayhew cabin are a museum that anchors an historic district. Included in the district is the refurbished Otoe Railroad Station, a museum where turn of the century Nebraska City's Main Street has been recreated; an exhibit of early steam engines, buggies, and wagons; and the A.M.E. Church, one of the first black churches in Nebraska.

For further information on sites in the state: Otoe County Historical Society 402-873-7198; Nebraska Historical Society 800-833-NSHS; Nebraska Office of Tourism 402-471-3791.

Kansas

Strife-torn Kansas had one underground line in the eastern part of the state that began at Mound City and ran north through Osawatomie, Topeka, Holton, Lawrence, and Oskaloosa. Runaways on that route were then moved north into Nebraska, where they usually stopped at Nebraska City and then crossed the Missouri River into Iowa and continued their journey. The Osawatomie station was run by John Brown and members of his family.

OSAWATOMIE

John Brown Memorial Park
U.S. Route 169, Osawatomie, Kansas
Open to the public

The small park commemorates Brown's residence in Osawatomie with a restored cabin where he reportedly lived. There is also a bronze statue of Brown in town, unveiled in 1935, the 135th anniversary of his birth. On May 25, 1856, Brown and his men used Osawatomie as headquarters for their raid on the Osawatomie area and murdered five slaveholders there in the continuing "Bloody Kansas" battles that ripped the state apart in the 1850s. The attack by Brown and his army was one of the turning points in the national debate concerning slavery, proving to southerners that abolitionists would take up arms to dismantle slavery and proving to northerners that southerners would never give up their venerated institution. *For further information: Osawatomie Historical Society 913-755-3532.*

BALDWIN

Robert Hall Pearson Park; Black Jack Spring
Route 56, Baldwin, Kansas
Open to the public

The park is the site of the "Black Jack" confrontation between a unit of the Missouri Militia and John Brown's Army in 1856. Brown's men surprised the militia and defeated the force of 29 men, killing four in a bloody skirmish. Brown's army captured the survivors and released them shortly thereafter. Today the area is part of a large recreational park. *For further information: Santa Fe Trail Historical Society 913-594-5495.*

KANSAS CITY

Quindaro Underground Site, Kansas City, Kansas
Open to the public

Quindaro was a town built by John Brown and other abolitionists to offer a safe haven to runaways fleeing the slave state of Missouri. The town grew to more than 100 acres and contained saloons, residential homes, churches, hotels and had its own stagecoach stop. Several residents in town harbored fugitives. The town lost its charter in 1862 and eventually fell into disrepair. Recently, a preservation group has begun efforts to restore the village.

For further information on sites in the state: Kansas State Historical Society 913-272-8681; Kansas Office of Tourism 785-296-2009.

Missouri

Missouri was always a battleground for the slavery and anti-slavery forces. The state, with slaves and freed blacks, proslavery advocates and abolitionists, was admitted to the Union as a slave state in the Missouri Compromise of 1820. Underground leaders were fearful of Missourians and kept most of their safehouses in river towns such as Kansas City, Joplin, Hannibal, Potosi, and St. Louis. John Brown was also influential in the running of the Missouri underground. His legendary raid into Missouri in 1859, in which he freed a dozen slaves and transported them along railroad lines into Canada, angered the pro-slavery forces in the state.

HANNIBAL

Mark Twain Museum
208 Hill Street, Hannibal, Missouri
Open to the public

The riverfront town was the home of author Mark Twain (real name Samuel Clemens), whose novel *Huckleberry Finn* chronicled the adventures of a young white boy aiding a runaway slave. Twain was a keen observer of the slavery debates in Hannibal. The town, nicknamed "Little Dixie," served as a base of operations for slavecatchers. The full activity of underground work in the town was never fully disclosed, but several residents reportedly hid runaways in their homes. Others were hidden in a network of caves that riddled the Hannibal area (such as the one in which Tom Sawyer and Becky Thatcher found themselves in Twain's *Tom Sawyer*). Twain's father served as a juror in the much-publicized 1841 case of three abolitionists—George Thompson, John Burr, and Alan Work—who were sentenced to prison for trying to free slaves in the Hannibal area. Twain was six years old at the time and attended the trial to see his father. The trial not only made an impact on the young boy, but gave him ideas that later surfaced in his books. One of his early works was a story about the trial, *A Scrap of Curious History*. *For further information: 573-221-9010.*

ST. LOUIS

Old Courthouse
11 North Fourth Street and Broadway, St. Louis, Missouri
Open to the public

For years, the front steps of the Old Courthouse were used as an ad hoc slave auction block for regularly scheduled slave sales in St. Louis, with little notice outside the river city, until 1854. That was when the eight-year-long litigation involving slave Dred Scott's battle to win legal freedom from his master finally reached the courts in Missouri. Scott, a slave to an army officer, lived for four years in free states with the officer. The officer then brought Scott and his wife back into Missouri, where Scott sued, charging that four years' residence in free states made him a free man. His owner charged that since he was once a slave, he was always a slave. The owner also said that as property Scott had no standing to sue.

The slave lost his first case, but, surprisingly, won in a second trial in a Missouri county court in 1850. The case was appealed to the Missouri State Supreme Court, which found for the owner. It was moved into the federal courts in 1854, but a federal circuit court in St. Louis (the Old Courthouse) upheld the state court's finding and kept Scott in slavery. Scott's lawyer, a Vermont man who had moved to St. Louis, then took the case to the U.S. Supreme Court, which ruled against Scott. In its decision, written by Chief Justice Roger Taney, the court declared slaves were property, not people, and that Scott's master had the right to keep him in bondage even though he had resided for several years in free states. The decision infuriated many northerners, moderates as well as radicals, and convinced them, following the Kansas-Nebraska Act and Anthony Burns trial in Boston, that the federal government was firmly in the grips of proslavery forces and had to be toppled in upcoming elections in 1858 and 1860.

For further information on sites in the state: Missouri Historical Society 314-746-4500; St. Louis Convention and Visitors' Bureau 314-421-1023; Missouri Office of Tourism 573-751-4133.

* * *

Runaways: William Wells Brown

William Wells Brown of Missouri spent months planning a complicated escape with his mother and sisters in the spring of 1833. The group made it across the Mississippi River into Illinois and believed they were safe, but after two days they were hunted down by slavecatchers who surrounded them, tied them up, and brought them back to Missouri. Brown was returned to his owner, but his elderly mother was sold to a slavetrader who planned to take her to New Orleans for sale to a cotton planter. The trader kept her and other slaves chained to each other in the hot, crowded cell of a large steamer docked in St. Louis. Her son William was allowed to visit his mother one last time. He wrote in 1839:

"On seeing me, she immediately dropped her head to her bosom. She moved not, neither did she weep. I approached, threw my hands around her neck, kissed her, and fell upon my knees, begging her forgiveness. She finally raised her head, looked me in the face and said, 'My dear son, you are not to blame for my being here.

You have done nothing more nor less than your duty [led escape attempt]. Do not, I pray you, weep for me. I cannot last long upon a cotton plantation. I feel that my heavenly master will soon call me home and then I shall be out of the hands of the slaveholders.'"

* * *

Iowa

John Brown's underground trail out of Kansas and Nebraska emptied into Percival, a small town in Iowa that was located at the juncture of the corners of Kansas, Nebraska, Missouri, and Iowa. Brown stopped there with the twelve slaves he freed in Missouri on his fabled 1,500-mile trek to Canada. From Percival, the underground road went east into Illinois on two lines. The southern line, which ran along the Iowa-Missouri border, included safe houses in Salem, Cincinnati, Bloomfield, and Croton. The northern line, which cut across the center of Iowa, included among its many stops safe houses in Tabor, Lewis, Stuart, Redfield, Adel, Des Moines, and Grinnell. The line was picked up again close to the Mississippi River at Iowa City and included the towns of West Liberty, Muscatine, Tipton, De Witt, Low Moor, and Clinton. The homes in these towns were frequented by Brown and his men, sometimes to harbor runaways, sometimes to raise money, and sometimes to buy or procure arms for his battles. The underground operated in Iowa as early as the 1840s. As in other areas, the leaders of the underground included prominent politicians, such as Josiah Grinnell, and ministers, such as John Todd. Other underground leaders in the state included James Townsend, John Painter, Moses Varney, John Safely, Sam Yule, and Jonathan Casebeer.

SALEM

Lewelling Quaker House
401 South Main Street, Salem, Iowa
Open to the public

The home is an example of the local influence of some of the leaders in Iowa's smaller communities. Henderson Lewelling was a Quaker who built a large stone house in 1840, complete with a secretive underground tunnel where dozens of runaways hid from slavecatchers. The town's justice of the peace, Nelson Gibbs, another member of the underground, made a front room of the house his office and courtroom. One of the reasons he chose the home was evident in 1848. A gang of slavehunters raided Salem looking for runaways and found them in the Lewelling house. They insisted in removing the slaves but Gibbs rode to the home and, invoking his powers as local justice, immediately held a trial concerning the case. Naturally, he ruled in favor of Lewelling and ordered the slavehunters out of town.

SPRINGDALE

William Maxon; John Brown Marker
Country Road X-40, Springdale, Iowa

Three miles north of town stands a marker honoring Brown and local underground leader William Maxon. It is on the site of Maxon's farmhouse that served as an underground depot where many slaves were hid in the late 1850s and where Brown recruited men for his 1859 raid on Harper's Ferry. "Let some poor slave mother whom I have striven to free with her children from gallows stair put up a prayer for me . . ." reads the quote from Brown on the marker. Several citizens donated three-foot-long spikes to Brown's brigade for the trip to Harper's Ferry and the Quaker congregation gathered at the Friends Meetinghouse there to pray for them. *For further information: Cedar County Historical Society 319-886-2740.*

GRINNELL

Josiah Grinnell House
1125 Broad Street, Grinnell, Iowa
Museum: Open to the public

Young Josiah Grinnell, thirty-four years old when he helped found the Republican Party in Iowa in 1855, was already one of the state's most powerful politicians when he first met John Brown. Grinnell was just as fierce as Brown in his hatred of slavery and by the time the two met was already a major figure in the Iowa underground. He sectioned off a large room in his home, which he called "the liberty room," where slaves were housed, clothed, and fed. He worked with a network of underground leaders in the state to move slaves across Iowa and either to the free community of Chicago, Illinois or on to Canada. In 1858, he hid John Brown and the dozen runaways Brown freed from two Kansas farms during a trek to Canada. "They were the darkest, saddest specimens of humanity I have ever seen, glad to camp on the floor, while the veteran (Brown) was a night guard, with his dog and a miniature arsenal ready for us on one alarm," said Grinnell of the visit by Brown, his men, and the dozen fugitives in his care.

Grinnell continued his work in the underground through the beginning of the Civil War. A staunch supporter of President Lincoln, Grinnell was elected to Congress in 1863 and served two terms. He returned to Iowa and founded Grinnell College, serving as a trustee for thirty years. The town was later named after him. *For further information: Poweshiek County Historical Society 515-623-5188.*

WEST DES MOINES

Jordan House
2001 Fuller Road, West Des Moines, Iowa
Museum: Open to the public

James Jordan, the first white settler in West Des Moines, built this impressive, sixteen-room Victorian style home in 1848. Jordan used the many rooms in his home to harbor fugitives and worked with other underground leaders in the well-organized railroad in that state. Today the home also houses a railway museum, a museum of local community history, and an Underground Railroad Museum. *For further information: Polk County Historical Society 515-255-6657.*

TABOR

Todd House
705 Park Street, Tabor, Iowa
Open to the public by appointment

The home, a low-slung, one-story farmhouse built out of oak, walnut, and cottonwood trees on an adobe basement, was the home of Reverend John Todd, pastor of the Tabor Congregational Church for thirty years.

Todd became friendly with John Brown, who with his men visited Tabor and the Todds many times. The 2,000 rifles purchased for the battle to free Kansas were stored there. Todd hid some runaways in his home and others in a barn behind it. Tabor was home to several members of the underground movement and abolitionists who supported Brown in his Kansas wars. Some townspeople disliked Brown and, fearing retribution by proslavery forces, once held a public meeting to denounce him. *For further information: Fremont County Historical Society 712-374-2719.*

LEWIS

Hitchcock House
Hitchcock Park, West of town, Lewis, Iowa
Open to the public

The house was one of the many underground stations in Iowa in the 1850s. A local historical association recently restored the house as it appeared in the 1850s, with exhibits in the home as it looked as an underground stop. Country music events are also held at the home. *For further information: Cass County Historical Society 712-243-1460.*

KEOSAUQUA

The Pearson House
County Road and Dodge Street, Keosauqua, Iowa
Open to the public in summer

Benjamin Pearson built this home in the 1840s and it quickly became a popular stop on the underground line because of its twin cellars, built to harbor runaways. Pearson built one cellar with an outside entrance and a second cellar with a concealed interior trap door entrance. He constructed the double cellars so that he could hide slaves in the basement, entered via the trap door, but still have a basement that could be reached from the outside. The clever architectural ruse worked; neighbors or slavehunters believed the cellar could only be entered from the outside and none of the many fugitives hidden in the Pearson home were ever detected. *For further information: Van Buren County Historical Society 319-293-3766.*

For further information on sites in the state: Iowa State Historical Society 515-281-5111; Iowa Office of Tourism 515-281-3100.

Illinois

The geography of Illinois made it valuable territory for the underground. The state is wedged between the slave states of Missouri and Kentucky and its southern tip is just eighty miles from the border of Arkansas and Tennessee, two more slave states. Illinois also has the Ohio and Mississippi Rivers as its boundaries, making river crossings an easy escape for slaves traveling the underground. The two major underground routes in the state began at river towns. One started at Alton, directly across the Mississippi from St. Louis. Alton was home to the Illinois Anti-Slavery Society, founded there in 1837, and abolitionist newspaper publisher Elijah Lovejoy, who was murdered by a proslavery mob in 1837 following a series of anti-slavery editorials.

Two major underground routes began at Quincy, across the Mississippi from Hannibal, which then went northeast toward Chicago and the large free black community there. One route included stops at Galesburg, Toulon, Princeton, Aurora, Elgin, and Byron. A second major route began at Quincy and then moved to the Dillion, Delavan area in mid-state. Another was comprised of safehouses at Ottawa, Peru, and Magnolia. One major route picked up at Jacksonville and Griggsville and then connected to a line that began at Dillion and Springfield. Several smaller lines ran nearby. One line ran through Hancock, McDonough, and Fulton Counties and included stations in Mendon, Round Prairie, Plymouth, Roseville, Canton, and Farmington. A line through Ogle County included safe houses at Sugar Grove and Buffalo Grove. Another started in Sparta, in the far southern part of the state, and ran north through Springfield, Delavan, Dillon, Elm Grove, Tremont, Deacon Street, Groveland, Morton, Washington, Metromora, Crow Creek, Work Ford, and Greenville and hooked up with the Quincy/Dillion line.

PRINCETON

Lovejoy Homestead
State Route 61, Princeton, Illinois
Open to the public by appointment

Owen Lovejoy was a fierce and admired abolitionist minister. He and his wife harbored slaves in their two-story white clapboard home in Princeton as early as 1837, when a slave named C. Reign Beau arrived one night seeking shelter. Lovejoy kept up his underground activities through the 1840s, despite an indictment in 1843 (he was acquitted at trial by a friendly jury). He began to travel throughout the state to preach against slavery in the mid-1840s and by the time the Kansas-Nebraska Act was passed in 1854 he was one of the state's leading abolitionists. Lovejoy was a political confidant of Abraham Lincoln and, with Lincoln and others, helped found the new Republican Party in Illinois in 1856. Lovejoy later served in Congress and was one of the strongest supporters of the Emancipation Proclamation. *For further information: Bureau County Historical Society 815-875-2184.*

ALTON

Rock House
Clawson and College Streets, Alton, Illinois
Private home

The home to the Reverend Elijah Lovely, it was one of several underground stops in Alton, an abolitionist center. The state's anti-slavery association was created in a meeting inside the house.

Elijah Lovejoy Monument and Grave
Fifth and Monument Streets, Alton, Illinois

Lovejoy, the brother of Owen Lovejoy, arrived in the Midwest from New England in 1833 and began to publish the *Observor*, an abolitionist newspaper, in St. Louis. Forced out of the slave state, he began to publish the *Alton Observor*, just cross the river, in 1836. Mobs wrecked his presses on two separate raids, throwing them into the Mississippi, and then killed him during a third raid in 1837. Remains of one of the ruined presses are on display in the lobby of the Telegraph Building, 111 East Broadway. *For further information: Alton Area Historical Society 618-462-5853.*

JUNCTION

Hickory Hill: Old Slave House
Route 13, Junction, Illinois
Open to the public

The home has a bizarre history. Built in 1834 by John Crenshaw, a grandson of a signer of the Declaration of Independence, it was used to detain runaway slaves who were captured by Crenshaw and his friends and then sold to southern slavers. Kidnapped slaves, and reportedly freedmen, were held in chains on the third floor, where a "breeding room" was reportedly maintained to mate male and female slaves.

QUINCY

Dr. Richard Eells House
322 Main Street, Quincy, Illinois
Open to the public

Runaways were told to find Eells' house as soon as they arrived in Illinois. He hid, clothed, and fed the fugitives and then, working with a large network of underground colleagues in the area, sent them northeast toward Chicago on a carefully laid out route of safe houses. Eells, like others, was constantly watched by proslavery residents of the area and in 1842 was convicted of harboring a runaway and fined $400. An angry Eells refused to pay the fine and began a protracted, decade-long legal battle that went all the way to the U.S. Supreme Court, which ruled against him. *For further information: Historical Society of Quincy and Adams County 217-222-1835.*

Grau Mill
Spring and York Roads, Quincy, Illinois
Open to the public

Miller Grau was a German immigrant who started a new life in Illinois, which had one of the largest German populations in America. He ran a mill in Quincy and sheltered slaves in his farmhouse nearby. The mill and its grounds, with an Underground Railroad exhibit, are now a museum.

SPRINGFIELD

Abraham Lincoln Home
Jackson and Eighth Streets, Springfield, Illinois
Open to the public

The Lincoln home had no connection to the Underground Railroad, but any visit to Illinois' underground routes would be enhanced by a trip to the residence of the sixteenth President. Lincoln was a very careful politician who deplored slavery and privately wanted to abolish it. Despite the heated anti-slavery climate in the North in the 1850s, Lincoln believed, correctly, that a true radical who supported the immediate elimination of slavery could not be elected to high public office. Until the beginning of the Civil War, President Lincoln believed slavery could be retained where it existed, distasteful as it was, but could not be authorized in any new territories. Ironically, one of the keys to Lincoln's success in the 1860 Presidential election was his ability to distance himself from the growing number of fiery abolitionists. He was certain that close ties to the abolitionists in Illinois and elsewhere would cost him the moderate vote. Abraham Lincoln was elected President on November 6, 1860. The Civil War began on April 12, 1861 and on January 1, 1863, with his Emancipation Proclamation, Lincoln achieved his lifelong goal of ending slavery.

Zion Baptist Missionary Church
1601 East Laurel Street, Springfield, Illinois
Open to the public

The church was founded by former slave Thomas Houston, who fled to Springfield from Missouri. He used his home in Springfield as a station in the underground and organized secret raids back into Missouri to free his brother and his brother's family. The Houstons operated their underground station for years and went on to become one of the most prominent African-American families in the country. Houston fought for the Union Army during the Civil War. A descendant, Charles Houston, was a law professor at Howard University, who numbered among his students Thurgood Marshall, who later helped overturn segregation in the public schools as lead counsel in the *Brown vs. Board of Education* case in 1954. *For further information: Illinois State Historical Society 217-782-4836; Springfield Convention and Visitors' Center 217-525-7980.*

GALESBURG

Knox College, Galesburg, Illinois
Open to the public

The Knox College campus is well known as the site of one of the Lincoln-Douglas debates in 1858 and the college's main building is on the National Register of Historical Sites. The college also served as a major stop on the Illinois underground; professors and students frequently hid runaways who were traveling through the state to Chicago.

For further information on sites in the state: Illinois Historical Society 217-782-4836; Illinois Office of Tourism 217-785-6334.

Wisconsin

There were few underground depots in Wisconsin because the state was so far north; it was faster for slaves to get to Chicago or Canada from western areas. Several did move through Wisconsin, however, often sent there from stations in Iowa or Illinois when too many slavecatchers were spotted. Some of these fugitives were hurried from towns in Wisconsin to Chicago, where they lived in the free black community, or all the way to Detroit and then across the Detroit River into Canada.

* * *

Rescue in Milwaukee

Racine, Wisconsin, was one of several towns in the state where runaways felt comfortable. It had a black community and residents of the integrated town lived in general harmony. That was shattered on March 10, 1854, when deputy U.S. marshals, accompanied by slaveholder R. W. Garland, apprehended Garland's runaway, Joshua Glover, in a small farming community nearby. Glover fought back. In the fistfight, Glover was finally knocked to the ground, tied up, and put in a wagon. The marshals, fearful of trouble in Racine, where Glover was well liked, drove to Milwaukee as quickly as they could and planned to send him back south with Garland immediately after a formal hearing. Glover was put in a Milwaukee jail until a hearing could be scheduled.

The news of Glover's apprehension spread through the Racine area in hours and by nightfall a crowd of several hundred men and women, white and black, gathered in the town square. The crowd voted to pass a local ordinance to repeal the 1850 Fugitive Slave Act so they could travel to Milwaukee and somehow free Glover. More than one hundred of the protestors traveled by train to Milwaukee the next morning and were startled to find a crowd of more than 5,000 noisy protestors, black and white, already surrounding the jail, demanding Glover's release. The chief of police told the crowd to disperse but they would not and he called up the militia; the militia did not respond.

As soon as it was learned that the local militia was not coming, the leaders of the crowd pressed the police chief to free Glover, but he would not. Finally, late in the day, protestors found a large wooden pole and used it as a battering ram to break down the front door of the jail. As soon as the door shattered into splinters and collapsed, a wave of protestors stormed into the building and forced jailers to release the runaway. Glover was taken out the front door, cheered by the crowd, and then hurried to a wagon. The crowd roared its approval as two drivers spirited Glover out of Milwaukee and toward Chicago, where they planned to put him on a ship headed for Canada. The local police, confronted by the huge and unruly crowd outside the jail, were unable to pursue the fugitive and by the next day Glover was safely in Canada.

* * *

WAUKESHA

Goodnow Grave, Prairie Home Cemetery
Gosso Prairie Avenue, Waukesha, Illinois

Lyman Goodnow was reportedly the first underground leader in Wisconsin. In 1824, a 16-year-old slave girl named Caroline Quales, of St. Louis, fled after her mistress cut off her hair. She took a boat to Alton, hoping to find shelter there. The girl was pursued by slavecatchers and leaders of the Alton underground decided that since slavehunters might be suspicious of their usual routes, she was put on a stagecoach to Milwaukee, a safer route, where she arrived at an underground safe house. From there, she was put in the care of Lyman Goodnow, one of the first underground leaders in Wisconsin. He hid her for a few days and then transported her on the 600-mile trip to Detroit and then into Canada. *For further information: Waukesha County Historical Society 414-548-7186.*

JANESVILLE

Tallman Home
440 North Jackson Street, Janesville, Illinois
Private home

William Tallman ran an underground station in New York State in the 1840s and '50s. When he moved to Janesville in 1855, the wealthy businessman built one of the most elaborate underground stations in the country. The large brick mansion had twenty rooms, several entrances, and a "lookout" window in an eave on the roof. When runaways were spotted approaching the home, a bell was rung that alerted the servants. One then waved a lantern at a stained glass window, a signal, and fugitives entered the home through a basement door. Slaves lived in the servants' quarters until it was safe to travel. Runaways left through a secret door at the rear of a maid's closet, walked down some steps, and then left the building through a secret underground tunnel that took them to the banks of the nearby Milton River, where a waiting boat carried them downriver and out of town.

Tallman was a staunch Republican and in 1859 hosted a dinner party in his mansion for Abraham Lincoln, who was campaigning in the area for Republicans running for statewide offices. It is not known whether Lincoln was shown the secret passageways in the home or informed of Tallman's underground operations. *For further information: Rock County Historical Society 608-756-4509.*

MILTON

Milton Inn and Museum
440 North Jackson Street, Milton, Illinois
Open to the public

Joseph Goodrich built his Stage Coach Inn in Milton in 1844 to profit from travelers on the stage line and the growing Milton community, first established in 1839. He became part of the underground and during construction of the inn built a tunnel below the building and lawn that led to a log cabin about sixty yards away. Slaves were hidden in the basement of the inn, where Goodrich provided them with clothing and food before moving them on to another underground stop. It is unknown if slavecatchers ever discovered runaways at the inn. Milton's escape plan was simple if they did: slaves would move through a false door to the tunnel, and run the sixty yards to the cabin, where a rope dangled from the bottom of a trap door. Runaways would climb up the rope and into the cabin where they could hide or, if spotted there, flee. *For further information: Milton County Historical Association 608-868-7722.*

For further information on sites in the State: State Historical Society of Wisconsin 608-264-6535; Wisconsin Office of Tourism 608-266-7621.

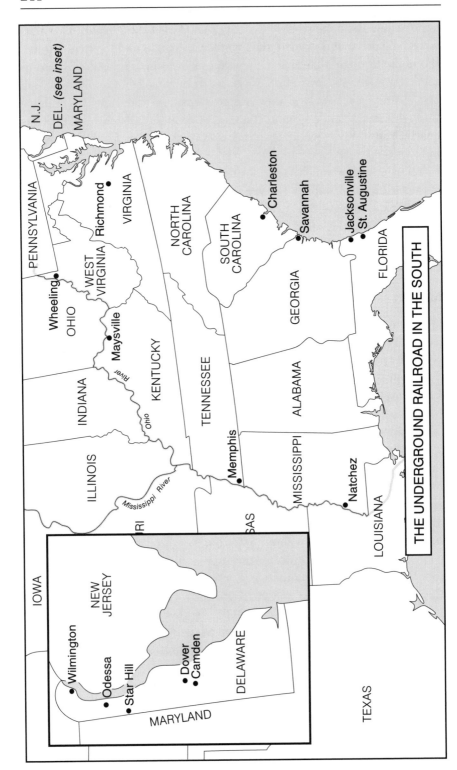

THE UNDERGROUND RAILROAD IN THE SOUTH

SOUTH

***

The Escape of Frederick Douglass

Frederick Douglass was nineteen when he organized a group of five
field hands into a team to escape from their plantation at St.
Michael's, on the eastern shore of Maryland, in 1836. They forged
passes which would permit them to travel as far as Baltimore, where
they planned to board trains and leave the slave state. They planned
to slip away from the fields at the end of the day, unseen, and
recover a supply of food and change of clothes hidden nearby. The
escape failed before it began because someone betrayed them. The
five were detained by their master and put in a nearby jail for
almost a week to teach them a lesson. Douglass did learn a lesson—
not to rely on others the next time he escaped.

The well-read slave, born in nearby Talbot County, was hired out
to another master in 1837, a shipyard administrator named Hugh
Auld, who put him to work as a caulker in the Baltimore shipyards.
Douglass worked there for more than a year, becoming an expert
caulker, and learned that his quickest route out of slavery was to go
alone, with real passes borrowed from someone, and in a believable
disguise. He could not slip away from the shipyard, either—he
needed to board a train that would get him out of the city quickly.

Douglass, then twenty-one, planned his escape for weeks and
decided to bolt for freedom in early September, 1838. He borrowed
money from his girlfriend and obtained actual U.S. navy sailors'
papers from a retired seaman he knew. He dressed up like a sailor,
in a bright red shirt, tarpaulin hat, and black cravat tie fastened
around his neck. He had learned the seaman's lingo at the shipyard
and used it while talking to people on the train, which he boarded
at the last minute. The moment of truth arrived when the
conductor checked his official residence papers, which according to

245

Frederick Douglass, a former slave, made it to the safety of New Bedford, Massachusetts, through the underground and then became one of the country's greatest anti-slavery orators. He was the editor of an abolitionist newspaper and harbored slaves in his Rochester, New York, newspaper office and nearby home. (Courtesy of the Frederick Douglass National Historic Site)

the law he had to do to prevent runaway slaves from boarding trains. Young Douglass did not have residence papers—only freed blacks carried them—but he bluffed and proudly told the conductor he was in the Navy and showed him his Navy papers, which had an impressive American eagle stamped boldly on them. "These papers will carry me around the world!" he bragged to the conductor and all who could hear him. The conductor, looking him over and determining that he seemed to act and dress like a sailor, shrugged and handed him back his papers. Douglass was on his way out of slavery.

The journey was not without danger. Several freed black men he knew from Baltimore walked past him in the train car but did not recognize him in the sailor's uniform. On a ferry that carried him across a bay in Delaware, he was recognized by another black acquaintance, who engaged him in a conversation that Douglass thought would result in his arrest. He finally left his friend and hid on the opposite side of the boat, well out of sight, until it docked. Then, at a train station close to Philadelphia, another train pulled up alongside the one Douglass rode and there, just a few feet away from Douglass' window, sat Captain Jack McGowan, his boss in the Baltimore shipyards just a few weeks before. McGowan, who was having trouble with his luggage, never looked out the window and never saw the escaping slave. Finally, just when Douglass believed he was safe, the door to the train car opened and a German blacksmith he knew from Maryland walked down the aisle. The man stopped and looked directly at Douglass and recognized him. He then moved his eyes towards the door of the car and moved on, never betraying him.

Douglass made it to New York by train a day later and lived there for several months before moving on to New Bedford, Massachusetts, after being warned by freed blacks in New York that he might be kidnapped by slavehunters. He worked as a day laborer in New Bedford for three years and in 1841 gave a heartfelt speech against slavery at a meeting on Nantucket Island attended by several leaders of the New England anti-slavery movement. They saw in him a forceful speaker, a former slave who could win many friends for the abolition movement, and enlisted him as a public orator. From 1841 to 1861, Douglass toured throughout northern states and even spent two years lecturing on the evils of slavery in Great Britain. He lived in Rochester for several years and his home became a busy station on the Underground Railroad, harboring up to a dozen fugitives at a time.

The former slave wrote his autobiography, served as editor of the *North Star*, an abolitionist newspaper, and advised President Lincoln on the enlistment of black troops during the Civil War. He served in a legation to Santo Domingo after the war and for a time was ambassador to Haiti, in addition to holding a number of government jobs. He died in 1895. More than any other former slave or black freedman and woman of the nineteenth century, Frederick Douglass came to be seen by historians and leaders of civil rights crusades as a true champion of the anti-slavery movement.

* * *

Delaware

The underground avenue of escape in one of the nation's smallest states was a rather simple, single, north and south route. Runaways entered the state from the eastern shore area of the Chesapeake Bay in Maryland and found refuge in a number of towns. Fugitives entering the southern part of Delaware found a stop at Camden first. Underground leaders there hurried them northward to stops at Odessa, Dover, Middleton, New Castle, and then to Wilmington, the terminus, and from there to Philadelphia. Others fled Maryland and went into Delaware at Willow Grove, then to Wilmington. Underground operators in Delaware had to be careful because although most of the blacks in the state were free, there were still nearly 2,000 slaves and their owners enjoyed substantial legal and political influence.

* * *

Thomas Garrett: Underground Wizard

The home of Garrett, one of the most passionate abolitionists in the
country and one of its most successful Underground Railroad
leaders, no longer stands. A small plaque in Peter Spencer Plaza, at
French Street and Ninth Streets in Wilmington, and a statue that
honors Garrett and Harriet Tubman is all that is left of the legacy of
one of the most efficient and daring leaders of the underground in
America in the 1840s and 1850s.

Garrett was born in Philadelphia in 1789 and moved to
Wilmington in 1822, where he immediately established an
Underground Railroad operation. There, in the middle of a slave
state, his work enabled approximately 2,700 fugitives to escape to
the North over a period of 38 years.

Garrett, a Quaker, became involved in the anti-slavery movement
at eighteen when he helped prevent slavecatchers from kidnapping a
woman who worked as a freed black for his family in Philadelphia.
His fervor increased over the years. By the mid-1830s, Garrett was
the head of a small but effective underground system in Delaware
that operated with the help of whites and blacks from Wilmington's
large free black community and continually functioned in the
shadows of the state's slave plantations. Along with John and Ezekial
Hunn, Garrett organized a network of people who harbored fugitives
from Maryland and Delaware. Most wound up in Wilmington with
Garrett, who then personally took them to Philadelphia over routes
that would carry them to Canada. Garrett's operation was efficient. If
he was unable to transport slaves by night, he furnished them with
gardening tools and instructed them to casually make their way to
his home in broad daylight, pretending to be freedmen working as
laborers on nearby farms. Garrett's house was a frequent stop for
slave rescuer Harriet Tubman, who also used underground homes in
Camden, Dover, Smyrna, and New Castle.

The outgoing Garrett, who bragged about his underground
activities, was a constant thorn in the side of Delaware slaveowners,
who continually sought ways to punish him. In 1848 they
succeeded. It was in that year that Garrett was asked to intercede
for a slave family caught by a local sheriff. Garrett, working with a
lawyer, managed to have the man and woman and four children
freed when they convinced the sheriff that the slaves' rather

Thomas Garrett of Wilmington, Delaware, was forced to sell his home and plunge into bankruptcy to pay a huge fine for harboring runaways sent to him by the Underground Railroad. He told the judge who fined him, "Send me more." (Courtesy of the Historical Society of Delaware)

confusing papers proved they were free. Garrett then transported them from Wilmington to Philadelphia.

He was later arrested and charged with illegally harboring and transporting slaves and brought to trial. Garrett was found guilty and fined $5,400, his life savings, ruining him. Slaveowners smugly predicted that his bankruptcy meant the end of the underground in Delaware.

Garrett was not upset by the fine or bankruptcy. He defiantly told the judge: "Thou has left me a dollar, but I wish to say to thee, and all in this courtroom, that if anyone knows of a fugitive who wants a shelter and a friend, send him to Thomas Garrett."

Garrett's trial received substantial publicity throughout the North and wealthy abolitionists came to his assistance, helping him rebuild his business and, at the same time, rebuild his underground operation, which flourished until 1861.

* * *

WILMINGTON

Mother African Union Protestant Church
Peter Spencer Plaza, French and Ninth Street, Wilmington, Delaware
Open to the public

Peter Spencer was one of many black pastors of African-American churches in free black communities who secretly worked on the Underground Railroad. Even though Delaware was technically a slave state, a large freed black community flourished in Wilmington and offered protection for runaways, who could be concealed at local homes for a few days without raising suspicion. Spencer led an organization within his congregation that hid blacks and also brought them food and clothing. Some slaves also hid in small rooms within the church. The church, built in 1813, was a way station for hundreds of fugitives over the years. *For further information: Historical Society of Delaware 302-655-7161; Wilmington Convention and Visitors Center 302-652-4088.*

SMYRNA

Clearfield Farm, historical marker on grounds of Delaware State Prison
Paddock Road, Smyrna, Delaware
Private

The farm of Daniel Corbet, cleared in 1755, is one of the oldest in the state. A farmhouse was built in the middle of the property in 1840 and expanded over the years. The farm was in a rural area of Delaware before the war and its remoteness enabled Corbet to offer runaways safety. The farmer, always worried about slavecatchers, turned his home into a rabbit warren of secret hallways, rooms, and closets to hide slaves: a high roof concealed a hidden attic over a bedroom; a hidden entrance behind a living room fireplace was built that led to an eight-foot-by-ten-foot secret cellar; and a false panel, designed to look like an actual one, would open to large closets where runaways could hide. *For further information: Duck Creek Historical Society 302-653-8844.*

DOVER

John Dickinson Plantation
Delaware on Kitts Hummock Road, Dover, Delaware
Open to the Public

The plantation never played a role in the operation of the Underground Railroad in the state, but is worth a visit for its historic value. John Dickinson, one of the wealthiest men in colonial America, was the author of the "Letters From a Pennsylvania Farmer," a series of newspaper columns published throughout the colonies in the 1770s which, along with the writings of Thomas Paine, helped mobilize Americans against the British Crown and bring about the American Revolution. Dickinson, whose closest friends were Quakers, came to loathe slavery as he grew older and in 1777 freed all of the slaves on his plantation along the St. Jones River. He attended the

U.S. Constitutional Convention in 1787 as a Delaware delegate. The plantation includes the family manor house and a re-created slave cabin and gardens. Tours are offered.

Woodburn Mansion
151 Kings Highway, Dover, Delaware
Private home

Woodburn Mansion is the official home of the governor of Delaware. It was built in 1793 and owned by several wealthy businessmen over the years. In the mid-nineteenth century Henry Cowgill, a Quaker, lived there and turned it into one of the largest underground stops in America. Cowgill and his family hid some slaves in the rooms of the mansion and harbored others in a nearby barn. Runaways who stayed with the Cowgills were treated as members of the family and even participated in parties. One party drew the attention of a gang of local slavecatchers who, learning escaped slaves were dancing in the Cowgill ballroom, raided the mansion. The Cowgills fought them off and quickly spirited the runaways north. *For further information: Dover Convention and Visitors Center 302-734-1736; Delaware Division of Historical Affairs 302-736-5314.*

CAMDEN

Wild Cat Manor and Great Geneva
River Road, Camden, Delaware
Open to the public once a year on "Dover Day"

John Hunn, who worked with Thomas Garrett in running the underground in the state, lived on these two large farms, owned by his family since the early 1700s. The farms and homes were frequently used depots on the railroad and a favorite resting place of Harriet Tubman on her rescue missions into Maryland. Hunn built a secret hideaway for slaves behind a revolving wall in his kitchen that was loaded with canned goods. It was never uncovered.

STAR HILL

Star Hill African Methodist Episcopal Church
Route 13 and Country Road, Star Hill, Delaware
Open to the public

The Star Hill A.M.E. church was one of many African-American churches that served the several free black communities in Delaware. Runaways were hidden within the church itself or in the homes of nearby underground operators. It is another example of the deep involvement of black churches and ministers in the anti-slavery movement. These ministers ran grave risks because their churches were in the middle of a slave state.

ODESSA

Appoquinimink Friends Meetinghouse
Route 13 and Main Street, Odessa, Delaware
Open to the Public

The tiny, red brick Quaker meetinghouse was built in 1793, the year the first Fugitive Slave Act was passed. The Quakers began to exert substantial religious and economic influence in the greater Philadelphia region at that time and were bold enough to build meetinghouses throughout the area, which also harbored runaway slaves. The Appoquinimink Congregation constructed a loft in the twenty-foot-square building to hide slaves for a night or two until underground operators could move them along the railroad to Philadelphia and then to Canada. It was a frequent stop for slaves fleeing Maryland and another stop for Harriet Tubman on her trips in and out of Maryland for rescues.

For further information on sites in the state: Historical Society of Delaware 302-655-7161; Delaware Office of Tourism 302-739-4271.

Washington, D.C.

There were no formal underground routes in the nation's capital. Individual citizens or ministers opened their doors to fugitives, who knew through word of mouth where they would find a friendly welcome. Churches frequently housed runaways for a night or two until they could flee the city. Although the halls of Congress were filled with the sounds of frequent debates about slavery, from the arguments concerning the Missouri Compromise in 1820 until the outbreak of the Civil War, slavery was not only legal in Washington, but flourished. Some of the country's most prosperous open air slave markets were located in the nation's capital, one within a block of the White House. Southern senators and congressmen championed slavery in the District of Columbia in order to flex their political muscle. Their view was that if slavery was ever abolished in the nation's capital it could not survive anywhere else. These men brought enormous pressure on city prosecutors and police to apprehend fugitives. Slavery was so entrenched in Washington that when Congressman Abraham Lincoln tried to introduce a bill to abolish slavery there in 1848, he was forced to abandon the idea by fellow congressmen who told him it had no chance of passing.

Despite this vigilance, the underground thrived in Washington and its conductors, different men and women over the years, often managed to send runaways from the city, or from nearby Virginia, north, sometimes in groups as large as sixteen and often in broad daylight. The small core of underground leaders organized a network of people who could aid in escapes, such as ministers who could hide slaves in their churches and livery stable operators who could provide horses and wagons.

One of the underground leaders was the Reverend Charles Torrey, a minister from Providence, Rhode Island, who gave up the pulpit to become a Washington correspondent for a group of abolitionist newspapers in 1838. He reported on a slaveholders' convention in Annapolis, Maryland, in 1842 and was arrested on charges of abolitionism for his stories. Acquitted after a well-publicized trial, Torrey returned to Washington and along with Thomas Smallwood, became an organizer of its underground.

Torrey was quite bold, often sending as many as a dozen slaves out of the city together in wagons he rented. Torrey once bought a wagon, hid fifteen slaves in it tucked under several layers of canvas, and personally drove them to Troy, New York, over 400 miles away. He also made secret trips in Virginia to rescue slaves and their families. He was caught on one trip in 1843 and sentenced to six years in prison. He proudly admitted his guilt: "If I am a guilty man, I am a very guilty one," he bragged, and said he had freed over 400 slaves in four years of work in the underground. Torrey died in prison in 1846.

Metropolitan A.M.E. Church
1518 M Street NW, Washington, D.C.
Open to the public

The imposing red brick church was not a station on the railroad, but became a notable site in African-American heritage in 1895 when the funeral of Frederick Douglass was held there, attended by approximately 2,500 people. The nearby Union Wesley Church, no longer standing, was rumored to have served as an underground station.

Douglass's final home in Washington, D.C., is open to the public as a museum. (Courtesy of the Frederick Douglass National Historic Site)

Cedar Hill, Frederick Douglass Home
1411 W St. SE, Washington, D.C.
Open to the public

Like the Metropolitan A.M.E. church, this home of Frederick Douglass never served as an underground stop. Douglass moved there in 1877 after his controversial marriage to a white woman, Helen Pitts, who asked that the home be preserved as a memorial. The house, which sits on nine acres, is maintained by the National Park Service.

Mt. Zion United African Methodist Episcopal Church
1334 29th St. SW, Washington, D.C.
Open to the public

The leaders of the Mt. Zion Church, one of the oldest African-American churches in the capital, were cautious. Unwilling to risk the capture of runaways who might be caught hiding in any of the church's rooms, they devised one of the cleverest hideouts of all. Mt. Zion had a large above-ground family burial vault in its cemetery. Ministers hid the slightly nervous slaves inside the vault, where no one ever bothered to look for them.

District of Columbia Wharf
Potomac River, Washington, D.C.
Open to the public

* * *

The Voyage of the *Pearl*

The capital wharf, like seaport harbors in Richmond, Savannah, and Charleston, served as a naval station for the underground. Runaways were hurried late at night aboard northbound ships run by friendly captains and hidden for the duration of the voyage. This practice began in the 1830s but came to a jarring halt on the evening of April 18, 1848.

Captain Daniel Drayton had spirited fugitives north on his schooner, the *Pearl*, for more than a year without attracting suspicion. He was approached by a Washington underground leader with a grand scheme. On the night of April 18 a huge torchlight parade, sponsored by the federal government, was planned for the city to celebrate the new French Republic. Residents would be at the parade and pay little attention to their slaves. At a pre-arranged time, seventy-six slaves fled their homes and quietly made their way to the wharf, where they boarded the *Pearl*. Drayton set sail immediately and made it to Cornfield Harbor, at the mouth of the Potomac and nearly 150 miles from Washington, before a storm forced him to drop anchor.

Within hours of his departure, a black coachman who helped several slaves board the *Pearl* told authorities of the escape and the government sent an armed ship after the schooner, forcing it to surrender at Cornfield. The return of the ship was greeted by a crowd of several thousand proslavery people, some of whom stormed the offices of the *National Era*, a local abolitionist newspaper, and threatened to shut it down (they did not). All seventy-six slaves were jailed and then returned to their owners. Drayton and two mates on the ship were arrested and jailed. They were all found guilty of aiding fugitives and fined over $10,000 each, an exhorbitant sum in that era. Unable to pay their fines, the men remained in prison.

The *Pearl* incident, taking place in Washington, caused a whole new round of denunciations of abolitionists and Washington city officials by southern legislators, who saw it as a perfect example of the lawlessness that threatened to topple the slave system. It was one of the main reasons why southern legislators lobbied so hard for the Fugitive Slave Act in 1850. President Millard Fillmore finally pardoned Drayton and his men in 1852, after they spent four years in prison.

* * *

For further information: Washington, D.C. Convention and Visitors Center 202-789-7000; Historical Society of Washington, D.C. 202-285-2068.

Maryland

Underground leaders in northern states believed that more slaves escaped from Maryland than any other southern slave state. The temptation to flee was great for several reasons: Maryland, a geographically narrow state, bordered on free Pennsylvania, and in the lower counties of Pennsylvania, such as Lancaster, York, and Adams, anti-slavery societies were in existence as early as the 1830s, their members eager to help any runaways; the eastern shore of Maryland, on the eastern side of the Chesapeake Bay, was riddled with small rivers where runaways in boats, or on foot, could escape with ample cover; and Baltimore, a large port and rail center, offered opportunities for escape via boats or trains. The port of Annapolis also offered a chance for escape on northbound ships.

Slaves began fleeing Maryland's plantations early. In 1837 alone, the Baltimore jailer reported that nearly 300 blacks had been arrested as either runaway slaves or suspected runaways without any papers. Even in the late 1850s, with the Fugitive Slave Act in effect, Baltimore police were reporting nearly sixty runaways a year. The unreported runaways, slaves who made it to freedom undetected, numbered in the thousands.

There was no organized underground in Maryland, but there were anti-slavery sympathizers in Baltimore, which had an anti-slavery society, and some small towns, particularly on the eastern shore, whose residents aided fugitives. Several church leaders also worked with the underground.

BALTIMORE

The Orchard Street Church
512 Orchard Street, Baltimore, Maryland
Open to the public as a museum

The present church, built in 1882, stands on the site of two former structures, believed to have been built in 1840 by the freed black congregation of the church. After the Civil War, freed blacks in Baltimore said that the church had harbored a number of fugitives from nearby plantations. Construction crews working on the church in the 1970s uncovered an underground tunnel believed to have been used by the church's railroad leaders in the pre-war era. Nearby, but no longer standing, was the home of freed black leader William Watkins, an influential abolitionist and member of the church, who hid runaways.

President Street Station
President and Fleet Streets, Washington, D.C.
Open to the public

The train station gained fame in 1861 when Abraham Lincoln arrived there secretly on his way to Washington in order to avoid assassination rumored to take place at another Baltimore train station. It was one of the city's most active, and often used by underground leaders to move slaves in and out of the town. Many slaves posing as freedmen, often with forged papers, used President Street Station because they could easily be overlooked amid the large crowds that used it daily. Slaves boldly posing as freedmen often talked their way past train personnel at the station. One of the boldest was Frederick Douglass, who ran away from his Maryland plantation and, dressed as a sailor, traveled by train into and then out of the station. Several slaves had themselves mailed in boxes or crates out of the station by underground leaders. *For further information: Maryland Historical Society 410-385-2105; Baltimore Visitors and Convention Center 410-659-7300.*

SHARPSBURG

Kennedy Farm, headquarters of John Brown
2604 Chestnut Grove Road, Sharpsburg, Maryland
Open to the public

Fiery abolitionist leader John Brown and his men hid out at the Kennedy Farm, just a few miles across the Potomac River from Harper's Ferry, before their fabled attack on the federal arsenal there on October 16, 1859. Brown and his men were secretive, although Brown did ride a few miles to meet with Frederick Douglass before the raid to inform him of his plans, hoping that Douglass would then lead a massive slave revolt, which did not happen. Brown's daughter and daughter-in-law were with him at the farm. Several dozen men, and a runaway slave, were part of his small army. Their attack on the arsenal at Harper's Ferry was one of the sparks that ignited the Civil War in 1861.

* * *

Runaways: Harriet Shephard

Harriet Shephard was the mother of five small children and lived on a plantation in Chestertown, Maryland. She had little education, no money, and no connections in the Underground Railroad. Unwilling to permit her children to grow up as slaves but fearful of capture and punishment, she decided that the easiest way for someone in her meager circumstances to escape was to do it in such a bold manner that no one would suspect she was a fugitive. On November 1, 1855, Harriet and her five children, plus five other adults, were ready to flee. Harriet rose early and walked to the barn where her master, one of the wealthiest men in Maryland, kept his buggies, wagons, and two of the most expensive enclosed traveling carriages in the South. The slaves hooked up two teams of the master's best horses to the carriages and rode slowly off their plantation.

They drove through much of Maryland and then Delaware, finally arriving at Wilmington. The adults and five children, hidden behind the doors and shades of the fine carriages, aroused no suspicion. Planters, overseers, and townspeople whom they passed naturally assumed the carriages carried some of the richest people in the state, driven by two slave servants. It was a perfect cover and it worked. All eleven were told by area blacks to locate Thomas Garrett, the underground leader in Wilmington, who soon moved the entire group to Philadelphia, leaving their carriages behind.

* * *

For further information on sites in the state: Maryland Historical Society 410-385-2105; Maryland Office of Tourism 410-767-3400.

Virginia

There are no known underground sites in Virginia, one of the most economically prosperous and politically powerful of the slave states before the Civil War. Slaves seeking freedom in Virginia often bribed sea captains $50 or more to sail as stowaways on their ships bound for New York, Boston, and Philadelphia, often using slaves who worked at the wharf in Richmond as intermediaries. Others made it out of Virginia to Maryland and then Pennsylvania on foot or by stealing horses or wagons from their plantations. There is an historical marker to commemorate the Nat Turner rebellion, but little more to commemorate the thousands of Virginia slaves who fled their plantations.

RICHMOND

Shockoe Slip Wharf Area, Richmond, Virginia
Open to the public

The Shockoe Slip historic district is close to the James River docks where slaves would slip aboard cargo ships bound for northern ports. Today the district is a lovely restored historic area filled with restaurants, nightclubs, and antique shops. Civil War history in the state's capital is chronicled in the Museum of the Confederacy near the state capital building. Monument Avenue, one of the city's loveliest streets, contains dozens of handsome monuments to heroes of the Civil War, anchored in well manicured parks. *For further information: Virginia Historical Society 804-342-9677; Richmond Convention and Visitors Center 804-782-2777.*

COURTLAND

Nat Turner Historic District
Route 35, Courtland, Virginia
Open to the public

Slave Nat Turner organized a rebellion in 1831 whose goal was to liberate all the slaves in Virginia. He and thirty-one armed followers raided several plantations in the Courtland area, killing fifty-one whites. All of the slaves were eventually caught; Nat Turner was hanged. The Southampton County Historical Society erected a monument near the highway concerning the insurrection.

* * *

Runaways: Robert Thomas

Robert Thomas, as a slave at a plantation just outside Richmond, was upset when he learned on Christmas Eve, 1858, that his wife and their four children were going to be sold to an owner in another state as punishment for her resistance to her owner's sexual advances. After his family was taken away, he sneaked into a barn, stole a horse and, in a driving rainstorm, rode north, determined to escape. Robert plunged into the Potomac River on his horse and the two made it to the other side despite wind and rain, and rode until morning. The horse was too tired to continue, so Thomas left him tied to a tree in Maryland. The escaping slave carried a small daguerreotype photo of his wife and snippets of hair from her and each of their children in his pocket. He continued his flight, walking two long days and nights north to Harrisburg, Pennsylvania. There, he asked several black men for assistance and eventually found shelter in the home of the underground leader. He was put on a train and arrived in Philadelphia a day later, where in a large but completely quiet room he showed the members of the Vigilance Committee his wife's photo and the locks of hair from his children, whom he feared he would never see again. He did not.

* * *

For further information on sites in the state: Virginia Historical Society 804-342-9677; Virginia Office of Tourism 804-786-2051.

West Virginia

West Virginia was the western part of the state of Virginia until 1863, when anti-slavery forces there put enough pressure on the Lincoln Administration to admit the area as a brand-new, free state and part of the Union. Pre-war feelings about slavery in West Virginia were very mixed and most of the farmers in the hilly area did not own slaves. Most slaves trying to flee

Virginia scurried north to Washington, D.C. and Maryland and then into Pennsylvania, a short route, but some took a much longer route northwest, following the Appalachian Trail into what is now West Virginia. The trail passed several small towns and Wheeling, one of the few large towns in the area. Several farmers who lived around Wheeling reportedly harbored fugitives who, rested and fed, moved on toward Ohio. Crossing the state line was relatively easy. The Ohio River in the Wheeling area is narrow, sometimes less than fifty yards, and both the West Virginia and Ohio banks, although steep, are covered with thick forests to afford maximum protection for runaways.

Wheeling is the only real site on the underground, although Charles Town was involved in underground history through John Brown. Local historians believe that several homes in the northwestern part of the state, near the Ohio River, might have served as underground stations. Popular river crossings there were near the Ohio towns of Ironton, Burlington, Proctorville, and Poke Patch.

HARPER'S FERRY

Harper's Ferry National Historic Park, Harper's Ferry, West Virginia
Open to the public

The name of tiny Harper's Ferry, a nondescript town on the Potomac seventy miles from Washington, D.C., was burned into history in October, 1859, when abolitionist John Brown and his band of twenty-one men, black and white, seized the federal munitions arsenal there in what Brown believed would be a political act strong enough to cause hundreds of thousands of slaves in the South to rebel. He was wrong. An army unit led by Colonel Robert E. Lee attacked Brown and his men, killing or capturing all, to end the seizure. Brown was hanged. Today the arsenal area is part of the Harper's Ferry National Historic Park. There are a number of small buildings in the park and a museum dedicated to the history of the large African-American population in the town just before and after the Civil War. *For further information: Harper's Ferry National Historic Association 304-535-6881.*

CHARLES TOWN

Jefferson County Museum, Courthouse, Old Jail Site
200 E. Washington Street, Charles Town, West Virginia
Open to the public Monday–Friday, 10–6 (closed December–April)

The county seat was the scene of John Brown's trial and execution. He was held in the old jail, now the post office, after his capture and until his hanging. He was arraigned and tried in the courthouse across the street and sentenced to death as hundreds of U.S. Army soldiers and batteries of cannons surrounded the building to prevent any rumored rescues. Surrounded by 1,500 troops commanded by Lee, he was hanged in a large yard, which is now the intersection of Samuel Street and Beckwith Alley. The wagon that carried him to his hanging is on exhibit in the Jefferson County Museum. *For further information: West Virginia Historical Society 304-348-2277; Jefferson County Historical Society 304-876-6712.*

WHEELING

Wheeling House Hotel
North Wheeling Historic District
Main and Tenth Streets, Wheeling, West Virginia
Closed

The proprietor of the hotel, a member of the underground, had to be very cautious in his work because of the proslavery forces in town; a slave auction block stood just a block away from the front doors of the hotel. The hotel owner may have housed some runaways in the vast confines of the old building, now closed, but it is more likely, according to some northerners who knew him, that he sent fugitives to the homes of nearby farmers with anti-slavery sentiments.

For further information on sites in the state: West Virginia Historical Society 304-348-2277; West Virginia Office of Tourism 304-558-2286.

North Carolina

There was no organized underground in North Carolina because it was a slave state, but there were some small pockets of slavery resistance where slaves knew they could gain help for a flight north, such as some farmers in the far western reaches of the state, several small Quaker communities, and anti-slavery seamen who sneaked runaways aboard ships at the port city of Wilmington.

The western area of North Carolina, a mountainous section of the state, was not particularly good for cultivating tobacco or other crops normally grown on slave plantations. This area was populated by men and women with small farms who did not support slavery like the farmers in the Durham/Raleigh area did, where tobacco production was very profitable. These farmers aided runaways who could make it that far. One pocket of anti-slavery feeling was the Mount Jefferson area, in Ashe County, nicknamed "nigger mountain" by slaveowners because so many runaways were harbored there before being sent northward. Two small Quaker communities thrived in High Point and Goldsboro where the Friends aided runaways in any manner they could. Anti-slavery captains and sailors in Wilmington, like seamen in many ports, hid fugitives on their ships and let them disembark when they reached northern ports. The number of underground stations in the state was small. They were apparently effective, however, because over the years North Carolina newspapers were filled with hundreds of ads seeking runaway slaves.

GUILFORD

Guilford College Historic District and Mendenhall Plantation
603 W. Main Street, Guilford, North Carolina
Open to the public

The first and best organized underground depot in the state was at the home of Vestal Coffin. The Quaker farmer, a member of a large family, began aiding fugitives as early as 1819. He harbored runaways in his home and, at night, he and relatives used their farm's teams of horses and wagons to drive them to other homes or out of the state. The Coffins were well known for their work in the underground by slaves in the area. A common practice for slaves was to run away and live in the woods for several days and nights until they could reach the Coffin home. They waited until no one was around and then quietly approached the home, knocking on a rear door (probably with some signal) to gain entry.

Vestal Coffin maintained his railroad, undetected, until the outbreak of the Civil War, assisting hundreds of runaways. His cousin Levi, who lived there as a young man, helped him run the depot, often driving wagons full of hidden slaves out of the state. Levi moved to Indiana in 1826, where he opened up his own underground station in Newport (now Fountain City). The Coffin home is now part of the Guilford College Historic District.

For further information on sites in the state: Federation of North Carolina Historical Societies 919-733-7305; North Carolina Office of Tourism 919-733-4171.

South Carolina

Because South Carolina was a deep south state, there was never any formal underground railroad to spirit slaves north. It was geographically difficult to move runaways through the state, to North Carolina, then Virginia, then to the northern states. It was politically and legally difficult, too, since South Carolina had the highest black/white ratio in the country and slaveowners dominated the political system and were more fearful of escapes than owners in other states. Owners sponsored patrols through the state's counties, and overseers usually had a team of bloodhounds to chase fugitives. The only major escape routes were via sea routes from Charleston or through the swamps of the coastal lowlands, through the forests to Georgia and then Florida, where slaves in earlier years were often assimilated by the Seminole Indian tribes in the area.

CHARLESTON

Charleston Battery, Charleston, South Carolina
Open to the public

The dock area of Charleston, one of the nation's busiest seaports before the Civil War, was a very busy area where runaways, if careful enough and with help from seamen, could sneak aboard and hide on vessels bound for northern ports. Slaves in the area came to know, through word of mouth, which sailors could get them on a ship (often for a price) and protect them. The plantations surrounding Charleston were some of the largest in the South and owners were strict in their surveillance of slaves. Many slaves lived in Charleston as house slaves and the city had a large slave market near the docks. Local police were constantly watching for suspicious African Americans.

Denmark Vesey House
52 Bull Street, Charleston, South Carolina
Private home

Vesey, a black freedman who had visited Haiti following the slave revolt there, secretly organized several hundred slaves in the Charleston area and planned a mass riot in 1822 that would gain all of them their freedom, even though it might have resulted in the deaths of many white owners and overseers. The rebellion failed when a house slave heard about it and informed on Vesey and his lieutenants. The leaders were arrested and after a highly publicized trial, thirty-six slaves and freedmen were hanged on the same gallows. The failed revolt terrified slaveowners throughout the state and they dramatically increased discipline and security on their plantations while adding new restrictions to slave life, making South Carolina one of the harshest states for slaves. *For further information: South Carolina Historical Society 803-723-3225; South Carolina Office of Tourism 803-734-0119.*

St. Helena Island

Penn Center, Beaufort, South Carolina
Open to the public

Penn Center is the former Penn School, one of the first schools for freed slaves established by the Union Army when it began to occupy areas of southern states during the Civil War. The school, built in a large grove of oak trees dripping with soft, green spanish moss, was established in 1862 following the Union Army assault on nearby Hilton Head Island. Two Quakers, Laura Towne and Ellen Murray, moved to St. Helena to run the school as administrators, joined by a teacher, Charlotte Forten, of Philadelphia, whose parents worked on the Pennsylvania Underground Railroad. The school was the first in a string of schools in the area established during the war. Many were later run by the Freedmen's Bureau, organized after the war to aid newly freed slaves.

The school prospered for nearly 100 years and educated thousands of black children throughout the Beaufort and the low country area. Today, it serves as a community center and museum of local history. It is worth a visit for the history of schooling for freed slaves during and after the Civil War and for its exhibits on the occupation of the Hilton Head/Beaufort area during the war.

Freed slaves who worked on the plantations of the low country islands were geographically separated from the mainland. Many remained on the island, living alone in small cabins or in tiny communities. They became known as the "gullah people," sporting their own, unusual dialect, which was a combination of African and Caribbean accents. Penn Center is a good source for the study of the gullah population of South Carolina and other low country areas. *For further information: Historic Beaufort Foundation 803-524-6334.*

For further information on sites in the state: South Carolina Historical Society 803-723-3225; South Carolina Office of Tourism 803-734-0138.

Georgia

Slavery was outlawed in Georgia until the early 1800s, when the booming cotton business convinced Georgians to change their minds. There was no organized underground in the slave state and most fugitives tried to find safe houses in Savannah, a river port where they might meet captains who would hide them on their ships and take them north. Others fled through woods and swamps to Florida. Despite the absence of an efficient underground, there were many runaways throughout the state. It was such a problem to slaveowners that many forced captured runaways to wear metal helmets with reindeer antlers and bells on their heads to prevent another escape.

SAVANNAH

First African Baptist Church
23 Montgomery Street on Franklin Square, Savannah, Georgia
Open to the public

The church has a place in religious as well as racial history. It was first organized on the Brompton Plantation, outside Savannah, in the middle of the eighteenth century when evangelical preachers of the First Great Awakening formed baptist congregations among the slave populations. When the present-day church was built in 1859, it was carefully constructed with four-foot-wide underground tunnels beneath it, with diamond shaped holes cut into the walls for ventilation, in order to harbor runaway slaves.

For further information on sites in the state: Georgia Historical Society 912-944-2128; Georgia Office of Tourism 404-656-3590.

Florida

The thick forests and swamps of Florida were a safe haven for thousands of runaways from Georgia in the late eighteenth and early nineteenth century. Many traveled through the northern part of the state and then eastward, to the coast, and the Spanish community of St. Augustine. Others hid out in the forests of northern Florida and lived with the Seminole Indians, who co-mingled and intermarried with the runaways over the years. Safety within the Indian nation improved considerably when the Seminole leader, Chief Osceola, married a runaway slave.

The Seminoles became a target of the U.S. Army in 1817 following reported Seminole raids on communities in Georgia and Alabama. General Andrew Jackson led an army into Florida that defeated the Seminoles in the first of what became known as the Seminole Wars of 1817–1818. A second, and final, Seminole war took place between 1836 and 1842 after the Seminoles refused to honor an 1832 treaty that required them to vacate Florida and orders from then President Jackson to turn over all their runaway slaves, said to be 20 percent of the Seminole nation, to their former owners. The Indians were crushed and forced to move to Arkansas, traveling what became known as the "trail of tears." Some northern politicians complained that the real purpose of the war, declared by Jackson, a slaveowner, was not to remove the Indians but to capture fugitive slaves. The war dragged on for seven years during which time hundreds of Indians, runaways, and U.S. soldiers were killed.

SUMATRA

Fort Gadsden State Park
Route 65, Florida
Open to the public

This is the only underground site in the state. The British occupied Fort Gadsden for several years but were forced to evacuate it in 1816, following the War of 1812. The abandoned fort was promptly taken over by the Seminole Indians and the hundreds of runaways who lived with them. It provided good protection for the Indians against any attacks and for runaways fearful of capture by slavehunters. The African Americans in the tribe called Gadsden "Fort Negro." The Indian and slave defenders were no match for the U.S. Army, however, and the fort was destroyed in an assault in 1817 in the first Seminole War. Over 300 Indians and runaways, plus some women and children, were killed in the battle. The ruins left at the park include earthworks and trenches.

For further information on sites in the state: Florida Historical Society 904-488-1484; Florida Office of Tourism 888-735-2872.

Kentucky

The only underground railroad line in Kentucky was a direct route out of the state. Runaways managed to get to the Ohio River, bordering the northern part of the state, and paid friendly boatmen to cross it. Some clever slaves, after years of building up trust by taking their owners' produce to markets in cities such as Cincinnati, simply fled one day. Others, such as Eliza Harris, walked across the Ohio when it was frozen, moving from one huge sheet of ice to another. Even though Kentucky did not join the Confederacy when the Civil War began, remaining loyal to the Union, many of its residents joined southern forces on their own and the state remained strongly proslavery. Any resident aiding fugitives was punished severely. There were few underground stations anywhere in the state.

WASHINGTON

Old Slave Market & Paxton Inn
Old Main Street, Washington, Kentucky
Open to the public

The slave market in Washington was similar to those in Covington, Lexington, and other southern communities. Harriet Beecher Stowe, visiting the town in 1833, witnessed a slave auction on the slave block in the middle of the town square and was sickened by it (the slave block still stands today). She used it for her slave auction scenes in *Uncle Tom's Cabin*. Underground activity in Kentucky was extremely dangerous, but a lawyer, James Paxton, bravely harbored runaways in the cellar of his downtown building. Paxton, related to the family of Chief Justice John Marshall through marriage, later moved to Ohio when other lawyers in the state began to suspect him of aiding slaves.

MAYSVILLE

National Underground Railroad Museum
115 E. Third Street, Maysville, Kentucky
Open to the public

This town is home to the oldest Underground Railroad museum in the country. The museum houses the country's most comprehensive collection of underground memorabilia, including slave sale broadsides and runaway diaries and letters. The museum has long been the recipient of various underground artifacts. All are tied together in different exhibits to help tell the story of the runaways and their protectors.

Harriet Beecher Stowe Slavery to Freedom Museum
2124 Main Street, Maysville, Kentucky
Open to the public

This relatively new museum houses a large collection of artifacts connected to the Underground Railroad plus a collection of memorabilia and some of the papers of Harriet Beecher Stowe, the author of *Uncle Tom's Cabin*, who lived in Cincinnati for several years and traveled through the Maysville area to witness slave auctions. Much of her material on plantation life for the novel was gathered in these trips. Along with the National Underground Railroad Museum, it is a popular stop for tourists and schoolchildren each year. *For further information: National Museum 606-564-6986; Stowe Museum 606-759-4860.*

For further information on sites in the state: Kentucky Historical Society 502-564-3016; Kentucky Office of Tourism 502-564-4930.

Tennessee

There was no established underground network in Tennessee. Slaves seeking escape to northern states sometimes made their way through Kentucky and toward the Ohio River, but it was dangerous to travel through two slave states. A safer route for Tennessee slaves, and those in the northern counties of Mississippi, was to work their way through fields and forests toward Memphis, where a few abolitionists there harbored them and tried to get them passage on Mississippi steamers headed toward Ohio.

MEMPHIS

Hunt-Phelan Home
533 Beale Street, Memphis, Tennessee
Open to the public

The home was built by slaves for their owner in 1828. Just before the start of the Civil War it was rumored that some runaways hid here before trying to sneak aboard riverboats headed north. Memphis was a key port on the Mississippi and both Union and Confederate armies occupied it during the war. Confederate President Jefferson Davis held meetings in the Hunt-Phelan home, as did Confederate General Nathan Bedford Forrest. Later, when Union forces moved through Tennessee, General Ulysses Grant used the elegant home as his headquarters. It was in the home's library that Grant planned the historic campaign against Vicksburg. The home served as a Freedman's school for area black children when the war ended.

Burkle Estate
826 North Second Street, Memphis, Tennessee
Open to the public

German immigrant Jacob Burkle moved to Memphis in 1849 and began a successful business there. He remained in the city until the Civil War and used the small white, clapboard home as a safe house for the Underground Railroad, one of the few safe houses in southern states. Burkle hid slaves in his cellar and, using false papers, helped them board steamers. It is rumored that Burkle hid over 1,000 slaves in the twelve years he operated his safe house. *[Tours: Both sites are part of an African-American history tour of Memphis organized by Heritage Tours Inc. (901-527-3427)]*

For further information on sites in the state: Tennessee Historical Society 615-741-8939; Tennessee Office of Tourism 615-741-2159.

CANADA

In the same year that the United States passed the first Fugitive Slave Act, 1793, the legislature of Upper Canada (now Ontario Province) outlawed slavery. Slavery ended in Quebec Province via court decisions in 1800 and in the rest of the country in 1833. Runaway slaves, aware of Canada's laws, began appearing just after the turn of the century and by the 1830s started to arrive on a regular basis, sometimes a dozen or more at a time. The largest immigration began in 1851, after the passage of the second Fugitive Slave Act in America, and continued until the start of the Civil War. Although fugitives who moved to Canada did face racial discrimination there (sections of the country still had "black" and "white" drinking fountains in the 1940s), they were at least free.

Canada was not utopia, though. Slaves who migrated there led marginal lives, working as farmers and laborers, and struggled to survive economically. In 1857, a devastating depression swept through Canada, as it did the United States, and the many former slaves in its provinces suffered along with the Canadians.

In 1860, about two percent of Canada's population, about 50,000 people, were runaway slaves. By then, they had established successful black communities in various cities with much assistance from the Refugee Home Society in Ontario Province, created by Henry Bibb to aid arriving slaves. Black communities thrived in Canada starting in the 1830s and 1840s and by the mid-1850s black journalists such as Mary Ann Shadd were publishing abolitionist newspapers in the country. Other black refugees started black churches and schools. By 1850, many of the towns where fugitives settled had their own black doctors, lawyers, and schoolteachers. Following the Civil War, approximately half of the runaways returned to the United States to be reunited with their families, but the remaining 25,000 or more stayed in Canada.

There were four main entrances to Canada via the underground. The easternmost was along the boundary between Maine and New Brunswick Province. Runaways exited Maine and made their way to the town of St. John's. A second route was out of Vermont and across the St. Lawrence River to either Quebec or Montreal. A third, and heavily traveled road, was to Niagara Falls or across the Niagara River some twenty miles below it, near Buffalo. Runaways crossed a long suspension bridge over the Niagara River at the falls and then settled in the nearby Canadian towns of Niagara-on-the-Lake, St. Catharine's, Queenston, Niagara Falls, Fort Erie and, further north, Toronto. Those crossing at Fort Erie, near Buffalo, either traveled on steamers, ferries, and rowboats, or swam. The westernmost route was across the Detroit river at Detroit and into Ontario Province at Windsor. Fugitives crossing the river, usually by ferry, settled in the nearby communities of Fort Malden, Windsor, Sandwich, Dawn, Buxton, Chatham, Elgin, Dresden, and Amherstburg. Numerous towns on the southern shores of Ontario Province, from Fort Erie to Amherstburg, were debarkation points for runaways who crossed Lake Erie in boats from Cleveland, Lorain, Sandusky, and Toledo in Ohio and Erie, in Pennsylvania.

Western Ontario Province

AMHERSTBURG

North American Black Historical Museum
227 King Street, Amherstburg, Ontario
Open to the public

Many of the slaves fleeing the United States crossed the Detroit River at its narrowest point, at Detroit, and settled in nearby Amherstburg. The museum has a number of exhibits relating to the town's Underground Railroad and the history of the town's black community. Its archives contain numerous letters and diaries of early black leaders and rare copies of Canadian abolitionist newspapers that chronicled the lives of the black immigrants in the area. *For further information: 517-736-5433.*

WINDSOR

Sandwich Baptist Church
3652 Peter Street, Windsor, Ontario
Open to the public

Most of the slaves entered Canada at Windsor, directly across the Detroit River from Detroit; by 1850 over twenty-five percent of the community was black. The black community thrived there (Sandwich, now part of Windsor, was a separate community in the 1850s) in the pre-Civil War era and continues to do so today. The original church was a large log cabin built by the runaways so they could have their own house of worship. The present church was built in 1851, also by runaways. *For further information: 517-252-4917.*

PUCE

John Freeman Walls Historic Site
County Road 25, Puce, Ontario
Open to the public

The Walls site ("Where the Underground Railroad has its end" reads the welcome sign) is a dramatic experience for travelers tracing the route of the Underground Railroad. It has several restored buildings, including the home lived in by Walls, a slave who fled to Canada in 1846 with his Scotch-Irish wife. There is a trail that goes through a nearby wooded area on which visitors, through a speaker, can hear the sounds of the Underground Railroad, such as bloodhounds yelping and men shouting. It is a vivid recreation of a runaway's flight to freedom. *For further information: 519-258-6253.*

CHATHAM

First Baptist Church
135 King Street East, Chatham, Ontario
Open to the public during Sunday services

It was here in 1858 that abolitionist John Brown, with others, announced an outline for a new constitution for the United States, one without slavery. Brown did not visit Ontario often, but he had the support of leading Canadian anti-slavery leaders, black and white. *For further information: 519-352-9553.*

NORTH BUXTON

Buxton Historic Site and Museum
County Road 6, North Buxton, Ontario
Open to the public

The museum sits on the site of the Elgin Settlement, a black community started in 1849 that grew to 2,000 residents by the 1860s. The community thrived and by 1860 had its own newspaper, grist mill, factory, brickyard, blacksmith shop, hotel, and dry goods store. Many of its resident worked on the construction of the Cross-Canada Railway. The museum celebrates the history and heritage of the residents of Elgin. It includes an archive of old diaries, letters, and newspapers. The nearby Old School of Elgin, founded in 1861, has been restored and is open to the public. So is the settlement's cemetery, restored to its 1860's condition. The museum has a wide variety of activities and in February, Black History Month in Canada as well as the United States, it offers additional programs. *For further information: 519-352-4799.*

Dresden

Uncle Tom's Cabin Historic Site
County Road 40, Dresden, Ontario
Open to the public

Josiah Henson, born in 1789, was a slave in Kentucky who fled with his family to Dresden in 1830, entering Canada at Fort Erie, after walking all the way from Kentucky with his family, carrying his two toddlers in a knapsack. Once in Canada, he opened his home to runaways and helped them settle in the area. The story of his life in bondage was reportedly used by Harriet Beecher Stowe to create the character of "Uncle Tom" in *Uncle Tom's Cabin*. On Henson's gravestone is inscribed, simply, "Uncle Tom." The historic site, a popular tourist stop in Canada visited by 8,000 people a year, includes Henson's original, restored home and several other buildings including a church. *For further information: 519-683-2978.*

For further information on these sites in western Ontario, contact the Windsor, Essex County, and Pelee Island Convention & Visitors Bureau 519-255-6530 or 1-800-265-3633.

Eastern Ontario Province

Fort Erie

Bertie Hall (today the Mahoney Silver Jubilee Doll House Gallery)
857 Niagara Parkway, Fort Erie, Ontario
Open to the public

Bertie Hall was one of the first homes fugitives found in Canada when they crossed the Niagara River from the Buffalo area, about 20 miles beneath Niagara Falls. They had to remain hidden there because bold slavecatchers, defying Canadian law, often rode through the area looking for runaways. A tunnel was reportedly dug beneath the home to connect it to the river.

LITTLE AFRICA

This small riverfront community near Fort Erie provided shipyard jobs to many newly arrived African Americans. The runaways also worked in the lumber business (there were thick forests nearby). Non-existent today, the area is honored with an historic marker.

NIAGARA FALLS

British Methodist Church
5674 Peer Street, Niagara Falls, Ontario
Open to the public
The church was first built in 1836 as a church for the growing black community in Niagara Falls. It was moved to its present site in 1856 and became part of the new British Methodist sect. Runaways joined the church as soon as they arrived. It remains a pillar of the black community in the area today, containing the Norval Johnson Library, with books and archives chronicling the history of black Canadians.

QUEENSTON/NIAGARA-ON-THE-LAKE

Parliament Oak School
325 King Street, Niagara-on-the-Lake, Ontario
Open to the public
The school has no connection to the underground, but is an interesting tourist stop because a wall sculpture there commemorates the 1793 sign- ing of the anti-slavery law that opened up Canada to America's runaway slaves.

Queenston Public Library
Open to the public
The local library, a gothic revival building, was built in 1845 as the com- munity's Baptist church and had a large black membership.

ST. CATHARINE'S

Welland Canal Museum
Lock Three, St. Catharine's, Ontario
Open to the public

This rather odd location is home to one of Canada's best Underground Railroad exhibits. The curator decided to establish a permanent exhibit about the underground and the early history of blacks in the eastern Ontario area and called it "Follow the North Star." Thousands of tourists visit each year.

Anthony Burns Grave Site and Victoria Lawn Cemetery
Queenston Street, St. Catharine's, Ontario
Open to the public

Anthony Burns, the runaway slave captured and sent back to Virginia after his historic Fugitive Slave Act hearing in Boston in 1854, eventually bought his freedom with funds raised by New England abolitionists. He moved to St. Catharine's in 1860 and became the pastor of the Zion Baptist Church. He died in 1862 and was buried here. An historic plaque marks the grave of the man whose trial was one of the events that led to the Civil War.

Harriet Tubman Marker
92 Geneva Street, St. Catharine's, Ontario

Harriet Tubman, who lived in several communities during her lifetime, moved to St. Catharine's in 1851 and lived in a boardinghouse there throughout most of the 1850s. She became a leader of anti-slavery groups in Canada and frequently went back into the United States for anti-slavery meetings and speeches. She left St. Catharine's to join the Union Army when the Civil War began. A plaque on Geneva Street commemorates her years there.

Zion Baptist Church
25 Raymond Street, St. Catharine's, Ontario
Open to the public for Sunday services

The Baptist Church was founded in the area in 1833, but it was not until 1844 that the Zion Church was erected. Anthony Burns was perhaps the most famous minister at the church, which had a large black congregation, but there were others who worked with the black community in St. Catharine's. The church has served the community ever since.

BME Church; Salem Chapel
92 Geneva Street, St. Catharine's, Ontario
Open to the public

The church has always been a symbol of integration in Canada. The land for the first church was purchased by a group of former American slaves for five pounds sterling and a log cabin was built. By the end of the 1840s, the congregation was too large for the church but its members did not have enough money to build a new one. Hearing of their plight, the all-white congregation of the nearby St. Paul Street Methodist Church raised money in special collections and turned it over to their black neighbors. The present church was then built in 1851. It not only served as a house of worship for the black community, but was a social center and concert hall.

For further information on Eastern Ontario sites: Niagara Economic & Tourism Corporation 905-884-3626, or 1-800-263-2988.

BIBLIOGRAPHY

Baker, T. Lindsay, and Julie Baker, eds. *The WPA Oklahoma Slave Narratives.* Norman, Oklahoma: University of Oklahoma Press, 1996.

Blassingame, John. *The Slave Community: Plantation Life in the Antebellum South.* New York: Oxford University Press, 1979.

_____, ed. *Slave Testimony: Two Centuries of Letters, Speeches, Interviews, and Autobiographies.* Baton Rouge, Louisiana: Louisiana University Press, 1977.

Blockson, Charles. *The Hippocrene Guide to the Underground Railroad.* New York: Hippocrene Books, 1994.

_____. *The Underground Railroad.* New York: Prentice Hall, 1987.

Botkin, Benjamin A. *A Treasury of Mississippi River Folklore.* New York: Crown Publishers, 1955.

Brandt, Nat. *The Town That Started the Civil War.* Syracuse, New York: Syracuse University Press, 1990.

Breyfogle, William. *Make Free: The Study of the Underground Railroad.* New York: J.B. Lippincott Company, 1958.

Buckmaster, Henrietta. *Let My People Go: The Story of the Underground Railroad and the Growth of the Abolition Movement.* Columbia, South Carolina: University of South Carolina Press, 1992. Originally published by Harper & Brothers, 1941.

Campbell, Edward, Jr., and Kym Rice, eds. *Before Freedom Came: African American Life in the Antebellum South.* Richmond, Virginia: The Museum of the Confederacy and the University Press of Virginia, 1991.

Cantor, George. *Black Landmarks: A Traveler's Guide.* Detroit: Visible Ink Press, 1991.

Coffin, Levi. *Reminiscences.* Cincinnati: Western Tract Society, 1876.

Douglass, Frederick. *Life and Times of Frederick Douglass.* Reprint, New York: Collier Books, 1962. Originally printed in 1892.

Eakin, Susan. *Solomon Northrup's Twelve Years As a Slave, 1841–1853.* Bossier City, Louisiana: Everett Company, 1990.

Fields, Barbara. *Slavery and Freedom on the Middle Ground: Maryland During the Nineteenth Century.* New Haven, Connecticut: Yale University Press, 1985.

Filler, Louis. *The Crusade Against Slavery, 1830–1860.* New York: Harper and Row, 1960.

Folkerts, Jean, and Dwight Teeter. *Voices of a Nation: A History of Mass Media in the United States.* New York: Macmillan Publishing, 1994.

Foster, William. *The Negro People in American History.* New York: International Publisher, reprint, 1982.

Franklin, John Hope, and Alfred Moss Jr. *From Slavery to Freedom: A History of Negro Americans.* 6th ed. New York: McGraw-Hill, 1988.

Gara, Larry. *The Liberty Line: The Legend of the Underground Railroad.* Lexington, Kentucky: University of Kentucky Press, 1961.

Gutman, Herbert. *The Black Family in Slavery and Freedom, 1750–1925.* New York: Vintage Books, 1976.

Hamilton, Virginia. *Many Thousands Gone: African Americans from Slavery to Freedom.* New York: Alfred Knopf, 1993.

Haskins, James. *Get on Board: The Story of the Underground Railroad.* New York: Scholastic, 1993.

Hawkins, Hugh. *The Abolitionists: Immediatism and the Question of Means.* Boston: D.C. Heath and Company, 1964.

Meier, August, and Elliot Rudwick. *From Plantation to Ghetto.* 3rd ed. New York: Hill and Wang, 1976.

Mitchell, W. M. *Underground Railroad.* Westport, Connecticut: Greenwood Press, 1970.

Mordell, Albert. *Quaker Militant: John Greenleaf Whittier.* Port Washington: Kennikat Press, 1935.

Quarles, Benjamin. *Black Abolitionists.* New York: Oxford University Press, 1969.

Siebert, Wilbur. *The Underground Railroad From Slavery to Freedom.* New York: Russell & Russell, 1898.

_____. *Vermont's Anti-Slavery and Underground Railroad Record.* New York: Negro Universities Press, 1937.

Smead, Howard. *The Afro-Americans.* New York: Chelsea House Publishers, 1989.

Sterling, Dorothy. *Freedom Train: The Story of Harriet Tubman.* New York: Scholastic, 1954.

Still, William. *The Underground Railroad.* Chicago: Johnson Publishing, 1970. Reprint of an 1872 edition.

Strickland, Arvarh E., and Jerome Reich. *The Black Experience: From Slavery Through Reconstruction.* New York: Harcourt Brace Jovanovich, 1974.

Strother, Horatio. *The Underground Railroad in Connecticut.* Middletown, Connecticut: Wesleyan University Press, 1962.

Thompson, Vincent. *The Making of the Africa Diaspora in the Americas, 1441–1900.* New York: Longman Co., 1987.

Ward, Samuel Ringgold. *Autobiography of a Fugitive Negro.* New York: Arno Press and New York Times, 1968.

Winks, Robin. *The Blacks in Canada: A History.* New Haven, Connecticut: Yale University Press, 1971.

Yetman, Norman, ed. *Voices From Slavery.* New York: Holt, Rinehart & Winston, 1970.

INDEX

283